EMERSON
The Enraptured Yankee

R.W. Emerson.

A HITHERTO UNPUBLISHED PORTRAIT

EMERSON
THE ENRAPTURED YANKEE

BY
RÉGIS MICHAUD

TRANSLATED FROM THE FRENCH BY
GEORGE BOAS

~~~~~~~~

Life is an ecstasy.
—R. W. E.

~~~~~~~~

New York HARPER & BROTHERS *London*
· PUBLISHERS ·

~~~~~~~~~

To My American Wife
Who Watched and Fostered the Birth and Growth
of this Book.

To the Memory of Dr. Edward Emerson
and to the Citizens of Concord for Their Kind Hospitality.

To the American People
Whom I Learned to Know Better and Love
Through the Books of Their Great Seer.

~~~~~~~~~

CONTENTS

vii

CONTENTS

PART THREE

THE WORLD'S DESTINY

ILLUSTRATIONS

PREFACE

M. Michaud's life of Emerson is not, like so many biographies of the moment, a book prepared to answer a public mood or a problematical need. It has grown naturally and, I hasten to add at once, beautifully out of the love and preoccupation of many years. Coming in his youth to America, seeking in land and folk, in speech and book something conformable to his soul, M. Michaud found the object of his search in the moderate loveliness of the New England hills, in the sobriety and idealism of the New England folk and, above all, in him whom still today, not without a tender irony visible throughout his book, he calls Ralph Waldo.

Many years have gone since that early quest. Today Emerson is a part of Michaud's past, of his youth. But our youth projects into our later years; we may wholly change our attitude toward its idols; something of natural piety toward those idols remains. And this is perhaps the ideal relation between a biographer of Emerson and his subject: a disillusioned tenderness. For Emerson, so heroic and heartening in theory, so timid and chill, except on one historic occasion, in all else, might easily arouse in another kind of biographer an irritation which would lead to flagrant injustice. But M. Michaud has loved Ralph Waldo too long to be irritated by him and, not being an American, is not troubled to project the present into the past and to ask how different a thousand phenomena in our culture would have been, had the heroism of the New England sages not been so "inglorious."

I borrow this phrase "héroïsme sans gloire" from M. Michaud himself; I borrow from him another phrase descriptive of Emerson and far less easy to render into English: "colporteur de l'idéal." In such phrases there is a vast amount of quiet understanding not only of Emerson, but of a thousand daily things in American life which M. Michaud perceives with quiet exactitude but wholly without rancor. His love not being the fierce love of the disappointed American, he can hold the balance of criticism far more level and

PREFACE

paint a portrait in which the colors are distributed
with justice, exactness and grace. It is for all these
reasons that I find M. Michaud's life of Emerson the truest, deepest and most satisfactory of
recent biographies on American themes. M.
Michaud had, in the vulgar phrase, no axe to
grind; he did not desire polemically either to
smash or to erect an idol, to produce a deterrent
or persuasive example. His work is just, lucid,
vivid; his style adds to its natural grace and precision constant over and undertones that are drawn
from the prose and verse of Emerson and its
rhythms interpret by a quiet inner music all that
is best and most lovable in the New England
landscape and its sons.

LUDWIG LEWISOHN

Paris, March 2, 1930.

FOREWORD

This book is the result of several years of my life spent in intimacy with Ralph Waldo Emerson. I conceived the idea of it in the very house of the sage among his books and his notes, in the landscape and among the scenes familiar to him. Step by step I went over his reading and his walks. I questioned those who knew him. How shall I ever forget those delightful weeks under the beautiful elms of Concord, in the forests of maple and pine, on the banks of Walden? . . . How shall I forget the touching hospitality of the Emerson family? Years have passed. During the war I carried the Essays for three years in my knapsack in the little Nelson edition. Then I continued my researches in American libraries, and in order to know the sage better I made it my purpose to resuscitate those who had surrounded him, reading books, newspapers, magazines, letters, reading and rereading Carlyle and Thoreau. . . . Of the vast Emersonian literature I do not

FOREWORD

think I have missed anything important, while constantly and fervently returning to the Journal and the works of Emerson. For each line of my book I could, therefore, give references, and often I have put into a few pages entire volumes. . . .

I have neither embellished nor added anything. I have merely dramatized, trying to feel and to reproduce the movement, the very rhythm of Emerson's life, his search for unity, his worship of thought. Of romance, in the popular sense of the word, there is not a trace in the existence of Emerson. External events are nothing, he declared; the inner man is all. Yet he never ceased to assert the highly romantic character of existence. His life was a perpetual exercise of curiosity, a perpetual expectation, a perpetual admiration. The romance of life, according to him, was the meeting, the possible drawing together of the real and the ideal, of the universe lived and the universe thought in a vast spirit and a warm heart, meeting, approach, always uncertain, contingent, problematical, which, he believed, gave life its adventurous and poetic character. . . .

I relate the spiritual adventures of Emerson. This book is the history of a thought, of a man-

FOREWORD

thought whom nothing ever came to distract from his task, the worship of laws, meditations on the mysteries of the soul and of life. Beside Emerson I have shown his contemporaries, his friends, his country, the United States at the most critical, the most tragical turn of their history—1830–1865; transcendental New England, practical and matter-of-fact America. Emerson's problems were his country's problems: how to reconcile the one and the many, quality and quantity, culture, solitude and multitude, thought and action, individualism and democracy. Those were America's problems yesterday and they are today.

Is my portrait of this great representative American—one of the greatest—true to life? It is for the reader to say.

RÉGIS MICHAUD.

———————

PART ONE

En Route to the Ideal

———————

CHAPTER I

The New Mayflower

IN BOSTON, two steps from the house of Benjamin Franklin, on May 25, 1803 (one year before the coronation of Napoleon at Notre Dame), the blue eyes of a little boy opened to the light. May—the late and violent spring of America! Pink maple buds give place to pretty triangular leaves. The elm (*Ulmus americanus*) sways in the wind its harps and lyres. The bluebird, arriving with the snowflakes of the last blizzard, has begun to make its nest under the roof of the old shed. The American thrush tunes its flute in the cedars. The American red-breast, with its red waistcoat and claw-hammer coat, minutely examines the lawns with its bill. *Puer natus est nobis:* a little boy, with eyes the color of the sky, is born to us from the rough Puritan stock.

He is descended in a direct line from those

idealistic Pilgrims from beyond the sea who emigrated on the caravels of fortune to seek adventure and serve God in freedom. In the seventeenth century the dissenters of Great Britain took, as best they could, the road to the New World. In order to sing their hymns in peace, to give the Bible a personal meaning, to escape the impurities of the great Babylon, fleeing from the Stuarts and their simoniacal bishops, they placed between themselves and Europe 3,000 miles of ocean. On the rough shore that stretches from the Saint Lawrence to the sands of Long Island the redskin danced the scalp-dance before his wigwams. What of it? The Pilgrims hugged their Bibles to their hearts, and with their muskets on their shoulders, their buckled shoes, their ample cloaks, their sugar-loaf hats, their broad collars, they walked through the forest. In those days the fleurs-de-lys were floating over Quebec; the emissaries of the King of France were prowling along the Saint Lawrence, the Ohio, and the Mississippi. It was about the period when Richelieu was founding the Academy, when Corneille was producing "The Cid," when Descartes, a soldier of the Thirty Years War, was meditating upon his *Cogito Ergo Sum.* . . . At this time a fellow of Saint John's at Cambridge gave up his parish of Woodhill in Bedfordshire and went over to the New World to defend free thinking and conquer a kingdom for God. His name was Peter Bulkeley. Salute him: he was the ancestor and the founder of Concord, where his descendant, the blue-eyed child, Ralph Waldo Emerson, was to adore the Over-Soul. On the waves of the Atlantic the Puritan exile was thoroughly shaken. Predestination overshadowed his sleep with nightmares; but he believed in the promises of the Scriptures, and he was nourished on stoical treatises. He disembarked; he flourished his charter. He took possession of America *ad maiorem Dei gloriam.* He dedicated the New World to an exemplary sanctity which was to make it the envy of all the nations. It was summer; heat flooded everything. The forests blazed with color on all sides—maples, elms, sumacs. The odor of the sweet-ferns was intoxicating. The earth was soft and warm, and the redskin sharpened his arrows. *Vade retro Satanas!* Then suddenly the stillness of calm water. Musketaquid, River of the Meadows! I baptize you Concord, Peace, *in nomine Domini*, amen. Quick, an ax, thick planks, a blockhouse, a meeting-house, a town hall. Help yourself and Heaven will help you! What Peter Bulkeley, apostle of the Gospel, thus founded in his covenant was Concord, the town of Emerson; but it was also the United States of America emerging fully armed from the visions of the Old Testament.

And the genealogy of the Emersons began. *Thomas genuit Joseph qui genuit Edward qui genuit.* . . . There were six ancestors between the seventeenth and nineteenth centuries: Thomas, Joseph, Edward, Joseph II, William, William II. Among the women there were Elizabeths, Marys, Ruths, Phœbes, Rebeccas. It was a Rebecca, wife of Edward Emerson, who introduced the forename Waldo into the family, in honor of Pierre Valdo, or de Vaux, founder of the Vaudois, Provençal heretics of the twelfth century, of whom we are told that they were "remarkable for the purity of their habits." History adds that Francis I exterminated them, but it does not tell us if this was because of their irreproachable habits. Among all these ancestors

6

there were two laymen. All the others were clergymen. All were idealists, all lettered, all duly polished with Hebrew, Latin, and Greek, great lovers of controversy, fiery polemists, and past masters of the art of argument.

Oh, you bankers, trust-makers, stock-jobbers, petroleum kings, kings of steel, gold, copper, masters of the earth and the sea, look upon these idealists, founders of your America; look upon these lilies of the field who toiled not, neither did they spin. Architects of skyscrapers (always higher! always farther away!) and of gigantic bridges, you who have built railways to the Pacific, lovers of everything that is biggest, greatest, the best in the world, and you wild lovers of sports, and you jazzists and saxophonists, behold. These men had left all to follow the word of the Master. Their kingdom was not of this world. Liberty, prayer, poverty. They had not read either Carnegie's *Gospel of Wealth* or Roosevelt's *Strenuous Life*. They had chosen the better part, those truest treasures which are threatened neither by rust nor by thieves. Renunciation, prayer, poverty—this was the daily bread of the Emersons, from father to son. There was one of

7

them who every evening prayed that his descendants should remain poor. Another (ah, those Yankees, murmurs the devil's advocate, humorists even in charity!) gave to those as poor as himself his wife's only pair of shoes. These were not people in the style of Greuze. Their lachrymal glands were not hypertrophied, the women's especially. The daughter-in-law of Joseph Emerson left the dead body of her husband, still warm on his bed, to run to church. 1776! Fifes and drums, Washington, Lafayette, and Rochambeau. The Emersons took part in the celebrations of Independence. William I lived in the Old Manse at Concord, and, as luck would have it, a pitched battle was fought under his windows between the American minute-men and King George's Hessian grenadiers, six feet tall, with red coats, white leggings, a shako all brass like a skyscraper. Bang! bang! bang! (The shot heard round the world.) William I, military chaplain, died of fever in the army. This was the father of Ralph's father and of his terrible aunt, Mary Moody. A consistent idealist, Emerson himself was to demand, one day, the right to shoulder a gun for every honest self-respecting man.

The father of the worshiper of the Over-Soul was naturally also a clergyman. On an Indian-summer night, flooded with lingering warmth, serenity, beauty, abandon, mirage, when the fields of New England were full of goldenrod and when maple woods were more resplendent than the purple of kings, Ralph was conceived. His father was a comely, cheerful, very scholarly man, like the clergymen of the period. He loved books like those who love them well, to the point of sacrificing for them his last cent. He had musical tastes. His favorite instrument was the bass viol upon which he played solos. Divine Providence was forsakening him, and the Reverend William was obliged to repair with his violin to the pawn-shop. They had no bread in the house. Before becoming the pastor of the First Church in Boston, William Emerson, reverend though he was, had been very hard up. He had struggled with poverty in the American way, by trying all the trades, keeping a boarding-house, giving private lessons, working in the fields. In Boston, the Athens of New England, he cut a very fine figure.

He was handsome, eloquent, sociable, jovial,

distinguished, without any of the timidity that
was to paralyze his son. He was admired for his
flowery eloquence, the fashion of the day. Chaplain of the Senate of Massachusetts, Overseer of
Harvard, the Reverend Mr. Emerson was a fervent lover of belles-lettres: he founded reviews,
established libraries and athæneums. This excellent man, whom his son resembled, on the whole,
very little, save in his love of books, left Ralph an
orphan at the age of eight. A pity. If he had
lived, Ralph, in contact with him, would probably have lost his frigidity. He would have
yielded more to that sunny side of his nature,
which we see shining in his youth, then suddenly
extinguished later.

At the death of his father in 1811 the five little Emersons, all boys under ten, were left with
their mother in poverty. Nothing to drink, nothing to eat, no means of keeping warm—and God
knows that from November to May the Boston
winters are severe. Edward and Ralph had only
one overcoat for the two of them. Good Uncle
Ripley sent in from Concord a milch-cow, and it
was Ralph with his regal step who led it out to
pasture. (He already walked "as if the earth was

not good enough to carry him.") He who was one day to advise his readers to "hitch their wagon to a star" had for the moment hitched his fortune and that of his family to the tether of his cow. Like every other woman in the history of the Puritans, Mrs. Emerson was brave. The daughter of a sea-captain, who later became a prosperous merchant, she was gentle and energetic, devoted but not expansive, much more the friend than the mother of her children. Emerson's maternal grandmother had had her thirteenth child at the age of twenty-eight. People had not yet practised birth control, malthusianism, in America. In the midst of adversity nothing troubled the serenity and assurance of this saint, who, for that matter, was not forgotten by the charity of her friends. William, Ralph, Edward Bliss, Robert Bulkeley, Charles Chauncy, in order of seniority from ten to three years—this was the nestful confided to Providence. The childhood of these youngsters was hardly cheerful. It was austere but without tension, less by deliberate purpose than by the force of circumstances. The Emersons made a fine virtue of necessity. They had few amusements at home; they prayed much and they worked still

EMERSON

more. The Emersons were precocious. There
were excellent schools in Boston. At five or six
years of age they studied Latin and the humanities. In the case of Ralph mathematics was the
only stumbling-block. Transcendentalist in germ,
it was impossible to make him believe that one
and one were only two. For him they were a thousand. As he appears in his letters, Ralph at the
age of ten had already a clever pen, a firm good
sense, a positive spirit. He was an excellent little
boy—conscientious, docile, peaceful, quiet; on
rare occasions he indulged in a day of truancy
punished by a bit of dry bread. Frolics were possible only in the vacations at Concord, at Uncle
Ripley's. Then Ralph roamed the woods and went
fishing. In Boston their manner of living was severe. Ralph got up at daybreak, lit the fire, arranged the table for prayers, wakened his mother.
They breakfasted on a cup of chocolate and un-
buttered toast. When day appeared, Ralph began
his lessons and was off to school. (He had, it appears, some difficulty learning to write.) And thus
the day passed. The Bible at home, Virgil at
school, and the English classics learned by heart.
Returning home, he did his errands, brought in

12

the wood (and we must not forget the cow). They dined frugally, they sang hymns. They read the Bible together, a chapter of the good Rollin; sometimes they declaimed a fine piece from the *Anthology*. At eight o'clock everyone was in bed. On Sunday the discipline was slightly relaxed. There were visits from relatives, friends, and old parishioners, to whom they served what refreshments they could. There were no moving pictures for the children in those days. . . . Were there, indeed, any real children? But there were firemen, the irresistible American firemen, the soldiers who marched past on great days, and in 1812, at the time of the war with England, Ralph remembered having gone to dig trenches at the entrance to the port of Boston. At the age of nine! He must have been bluffing.

His literary talent was precocious. At twelve he was full of quotations. He wrote with a firm hand, and his verses cost him no trouble. Later they were to cost him more. Not to mention many quatrains on his vacation escapades and his heroic strophes on the War of 1812, he was the author of an epic poem *Fortus*—a "Poem of Chivalry, complete in one volume, with critical and explanatory notes, by Ralph Waldo Emerson, LL.D." It tells of a paladin flanked by two dragons annihilating legions of knights. The blank verse of Ralph Waldo flowed from him without effort; it had discipline, vigor, verve. This is how the author of the *Essays* amused himself at the age of twelve, in the same year as Waterloo. The Emersons were very literary. Ralph had already read and in part retained Shakespeare, Milton, Addison, Pope, and Young. In French he was very familiar with his *Télémaque* and the *Charles XII* of Voltaire. There was a physical defect in the family, a congenital infirmity, a misdirected force. The Emersons did not have very strong chests; in consequence, they were extremely nervous. Robert Bulkeley was weak-minded; Edward Bliss had an attack of insanity and died prematurely, Charles Chauncy likewise. William, the elder, was morbidly scrupulous and missed his vocation. As for Ralph Waldo, he complained early that "a mouse was gnawing at his chest," and he was to suffer during his whole life from his coldness, his hereditary apathy which he called ironically his "silliness." But what a charming group and what a fine harmony among the brothers, talented, ambitious, precocious, eloquent! Edward Bliss, sententious, profound, for whom people predicted a brilliant future as a lawyer; Charles Chauncy, scholar, pantheist, and poet, with a Greek head on Yankee shoulders; William, theologian and exegetist, whom his scruples were to lead one day to the door of Goethe at Weimar, and who, in spite of the opportunist counsels of the master, abandoned the pulpit for the bar. Ralph himself was to disarm a hostile destiny with a smile and conquer it by abandonment. In short, there was nothing stilted among the Emersons. Their religion was virile and active, mixed with fine and solid reading. No trace of bigotry. Ralph confessed very early his inattentiveness at church. He found endless amusement over those grave worshipers who flourished huge handkerchiefs and shook with their nasal thunder the vaults of the sanctuary. He would often bring with him the *Pensées* of Pascal, in place of a prayer-book.

Mrs. Emerson made stoics of her sons. The task of forming them into idealists fell to Aunt Mary Moody, Tnamurya, as Ralph Waldo called her familiarly. She was the daughter of the military chaplain of Ticonderoga, who died on the field of honor. She loved war; she spoke in praise of it and rebuked sharply the pacifism of the great Unitarian orator, the gentle Channing. She had a genius for objurgation and apostrophe; she burst into controversies with the ardor with which an attack is launched in war. A strange and almost terrifying woman, very different in any case from the peaceful old maids of whom New England has always made a specialty. She had consecrated her virginity to the education and elevation of the young Emersons. She led them with a high hand, always prophesying, always fulminating. Ralph Waldo called her "the Sibyl."

Always on the lookout, always importunate and greedy of distinction for her nephews, she would fling them terse and biting bits of advice: "Despise trifles," "Look high," "Do boldly what costs you the most." It was she who awakened Ralph Waldo from his lethargy, snatched him from contingencies, and made him a transcendentalist. "Ralph, look high above. Ralph, turn up your nose at glory, honor, money! Excelsior, excelsior!" "Come, get up, gallop!" She might have been lashing a circus horse. The young Emerson listened with open mouth; the seeress was irresistible. Tnamurya seemed as if disincarnated in that habitual solitude which haunted her and which she praised unceasingly to her nephew. She lived in a hermitage in the woods, in Elm Vale at the foot of Bear Mountain. From the height of her eyrie one discerned farther to the south the chain of the White Mountains. A pond, a little house, a Judas tree, a cold bare cell. Rising at dawn, the Sibyl attended to her housework, baked her bread, and then meditated on the Bible, Milton, Marcus Aurelius, and the Puritan books of sermons. Reading Herder and Byron, whose "Don Juan" she had made her nephews learn by heart, she mixed for herself a strange cocktail of Calvinism and Romanticism. She had a taste for the fantastic and lived habitually in the thought of death. She had arranged for herself a bed in the shape of a coffin. In the evening, when the young crescent moon squinted under the elms, one sometimes heard the gallop of a horse mounted by a strange cavalier. It was Tnamurya draped in a shroud playing at Valkyrie.

Any one but Ralph Waldo would have been

afraid, but his Yankee common sense, aided by his "silliness," his natural apathy saved him. He allowed himself to be scolded, lashed by the seeress. This was the price of exaltation. Aunt Mary knew the secrets of the inner life and the art of awakening the "still small voice" in the depths of the heart. Very sensitive to the picturesque and to the symbolism of words, she had the gift of images. Ralph inserted in his Journal numerous quotations from her letters, and when he became an author he put them in his books. When he read her she made him think of the passage of the wind over the mountain, of the swaying of flowers, of the flight of birds; and all this floated between waking and dreaming. Ralph wanted to be a poet, and he confided his ambitions to Tnamurya. But did he really know what poetry was? Ah, smite your heart, she answered him. It is there that are born and blossom the sweet immortal images like anemones in the green gardens of the sea. What need for professors of style and rhetoric! Language is born in us spontaneously. It was enough to live in the intimacy of nature to which Mary spoke familiarly and which she pitied as if it had a soul in pain. She anathe-

matized Time. She lived in pure duration, in
the eternal. Her pantheism did not exclude a very
lively and almost sardonic feeling for human
misery. But the optimist, Ralph, took from all
this only the poetry. Mary Moody died in 1863
at the age of eighty-eight, when Emerson had already produced his best work. She had borne him
for half a century in her womb; it was she who
had created him.

CHAPTER II

At Queen Mab's—Emerson Explores the Wide World

THE little boys of that time were precocious; Emerson entered the university at fourteen. Harvard was still, it is true, only a "college," an academy in the English style. There were twenty-four professors and about four hundred students. It was an aristocratic institution, a college for gentlemen; it was very strong in classical studies, excellent in the humanities. It prepared clergymen, lawyers, doctors, and professors. Greek, Latin, Hebrew, history, philosophy, and literature were the basis of instruction. The faculty included some very good scholars, skilled professors far above their pupils in age and learning—an important factor in "educating" them. There was George Ticknor, brilliant lecturer in romance languages; there was Edward Channing, the brother of the great Unitarian orator, a skilled

professor of rhetoric, who through books sought
man and formed character. Channing was not
satisfied with a superficial polish. He expected
his pupils to plumb to the depths the authors they
read and, as Montaigne said, to assimilate them,
to convert them into their blood and nourishment.
A very clear mind and the enemy of all mysticism, he had none the less started Ralph Waldo
on the road, and it was he who had given him the
habit of keeping a journal. Edward Everett,
professor of ancient literature, was a man of
very extensive knowledge. He had been a student at Göttingen; he had visited Goethe. He
was a learned Hellenist, but by no means desic-
cated by his learning. He felt for the ancients a
veritable enthusiasm. He was a hero-worshiper,
and it was he who fanned Ralph's nascent fervor
for "representative men." Everett was also a skill-
ful orator, both profane and sacred. Whenever he
spoke, the young Emerson followed him about
as the hunter follows his quarry. Besides the humanities, philosophy and what was called natural
theology occupied an important place in the Harvard programme. A citadel of Protestant liberalism, Harvard formed gentlemen and Christians.

It armed them for eventual controversies. Faith and learning walked hand in hand in the American colleges. But the men at Harvard were sensible. Theirs was a Christianity very much enlarged by the discussion of eighteenth century ideas and by the necessity of forming before everything practical men, men of action. No mysticism in their case. The champion of reason placed at the service of the faith was Locke, with his "Essay on Human Understanding"— a solid, cold, and calculated apology for the discursive reason which Ralph Waldo was one day to denounce and to which he was to oppose the revelations of a warm intuition. In order to infuse a little flame into this glacier Harvard summoned to its aid the Scottish philosophers, Dugald Stewart and Reid, theorists of the moral sense, at bottom almost as cold as Locke. In the direct defense of the faith Harvard deferred to the professional apologists. They were very dry for the most part, to judge by the one among them who was in authority at the seminaries— that William Paley whose "natural theology" naïvely mobilized the natural sciences in the support of theodicy. Paley proved God with the aid

of anatomical plates and by the marvels of the
Eustachian tube or the elephant's trunk. If nothing designated him to set Ralph Waldo on the
road to the Over-Soul, at least he could give him
the idea of associating the knowledge of man with
that of nature and of studying the analogies, the
"compensations" (the word is in the good Paley),
between the two orders. Nobody was less disposed
than our student in any case to accept the divine
through rational demonstration. At anything that
was dry or purely rational science, Ralph Waldo
Emerson scarcely nibbled, and mathematics he
frankly declared he hated.

But the methods of Harvard were already those
of the American universities of today. And in
them youth is very active, very sociable, its *esprit
de corps* very much developed. The American
democracy has an unquenchable thirst for eloquence. The practice of public speaking was held
in high honor in Harvard. There were debates,
oratorical jousts, public competitions. Every com-
mencement had its class orators, its poets. The
clubs, the literary societies were numerous, and
Ralph Waldo played his part. Who knows better
than the American student how to make his extra-

curricular existence colorful, anticipating the life
he will lead once he is out in the world? It was
outside of his courses that Ralph Waldo's vocation outlined itself. Gentleman among gentlemen,
his life was hard. Dame Poverty had escorted
him to the university. The band of Emersons was
in need, but this did not prevent it from sending
Ralph and two of his brothers to college. One
need not be ashamed of poverty in America. Parents, friends, were on the watch. Ralph had
scholarships, and he put in practice the American
motto, "Heaven helps those that help themselves," that self-reliance upon which he was to
compose a beautiful essay. The president of Harvard had taken him directly into his service. It
was he who transmitted orders, assigned duties
and punishments. This did not make him popular,
but his great personal integrity made people for-
give him all, and he had his lodgings for nothing.
He gave lessons; he waited on his fellow students
at table. What did it matter? Had he not already
led the family cow to pasture? Idealist in germ,
he had his feet on the earth and his head in the
clouds; and he loved his mother so much, he was
proud of buying her a shawl or paying her bills

with his savings. There were lazy fellows, do-nothings, at Harvard as everywhere. Ralph made up for their use little essays which he sold them, although he was not very proud of them.

He did not work them over too carefully, fearing that the professor would recognize his style, and he confessed that they were not worth the fifty cents he got for them. . . . Thus, thanks to stoicism and transcendentalism, Ralph Waldo made his way and put into practice the counsels of Tnamurya: "Do what costs you most," "Aim high," "Laugh at trifles!" He was not, moreover, the young savage one might expect. His comrades knew he had a fine pen in prose or in verse. When they needed some *carmina burana*, a drinking song, or a satiric couplet, they applied to the future author of the *Essays*, who needed no urging. Many of these improvisations turned out very well. Ralph's friends founded a club with a sonorous name, the Club of the Pythologians. He was the secretary. The Pythologians had meetings on fixed dates; they specialized in public readings and the discussion of essays on topical, historical, or moral themes. Every one chose his own subject. "What best assures the happiness of man, marriage or celibacy?" "Which is the stronger passion, love or ambition?" "Is it better to live in the city or in the country?" Ralph Waldo had treated the two latter subjects, in what way we are not told; but from what we know of him and from what we shall presently see, there is no doubt that he took the side of ambition against love. As for the life of the country or the city, the author of *Society and Solitude* must have discriminated carefully and entirely in favor of isolation and sauntering in the fields and along the beaches, the taste for which was very strong in him. But youth is youth. The students of 1820 loved to amuse themselves like those of today, but Harvard ruled them with an iron hand. There was a fine of ten dollars for every one who went to the theater. They were obliged to create their own amusements, and there were, from time to time, explosions of collective insubordination. The university authorities had expelled a few headstrong young men. The whole Sophomore class took sides with them and left the university. Ralph Waldo very wisely went home to allow the storm to pass.

They sang among themselves; they drank. America at that time was still wet, and Ralph, who was to decree one day that the only nectar worthy of the poet was pure water in a wooden cup, for the moment did not disdain libations. He confessed to having formed a taste for the corner grocer's malaga wine, but he added—oh, irony! —that the more he drank the sadder the wine made him. He preferred to intoxicate himself with eloquence. . . .

Freshman, Sophomore, Junior, Senior, the four college years were quickly over. In reality, Ralph Waldo had lived all this time a subterranean life. Those who saw this lanky, shy, and taciturn boy passing under the elms of Cambridge never suspected the electricity which he bore in him. Ralph Waldo shone very little in his courses: his mind wandered, he was slow in his work, he was even reprimanded—for his mind was elsewhere. In the evening, when the lamps were lighted behind the narrow panes of the windows or when daybreak reddened the old brick walls of the college, Ralph made an excursion into fairyland. He had his books, but he had especially his dreams, his castles in Spain which he constructed with great strokes of his pen on the thick schoolboy's copy-books. He wrote a journal which he grandiosely entitled his "Wide Worlds," worlds of the imagination that half opened before him their dazzling halls, their groves gladdened by the song of birds—

> Là, tout n'est qu'ordre et beauté,
> Luxe, calme, et volupté. [1]

Mab who threw peas at the nose of Sylvestre Bonnard, Gloriana her companion, the elves, the gnomes, the sylphs, the spirits of Earth, Water and Fire, hastened to the rendezvous with King Arthur and the ancient paladins. Like little Alice, Ralph explored Wonderland. He courted the White Queens who came down to him on a ray of moonlight. He began a romance entitled *The Magician*. In the land of marvels were born the daily notes from which the *Essays* emerged. Ralph moved in the super-real and transcendent. He daydreamed, practiced automatic writing and speech, drew mermen, consulted the *sortes*

---

[1] I have not the temerity to attempt a translation of these lines from Baudelaire myself. My colleague, Mr. Piaget Shanks, permits me to quote his own approximation to them:
> "Land of peace and luxury,
> Pleasure, beauty, symmetry."—Tr.

virgilianæ. He believed in omens, magical
charms, involuntary influences. This nearly did
him an ill turn. One day in class he received the
electric shock of two enigmatic blue eyes that
haunted him and penetrated to his very heart. It
had happened; he was captured, he was smitten.
The only time he loved was in dream, but he took
his dream seriously. He desired, he suffered, he
implored, but the blue eyes remained indifferent
and cold.

O cruel Alexis, why are you deaf to my songs?
Alexis, it appeared, was hardly worth the trouble.
Suddenly the enchantment fell; Ralph Waldo
returned to his senses. The magical spell had
lasted two years, during which the two persons
concerned had not exchanged more than ten
words. Let us not forget this incident; it shows
us the power of Emerson's imagination at work
and the fires that smouldered in him under the
embers.

World of the imagination, world of the heart!
—Ralph Waldo adventured equally far into the
world of books. Ah, what to him were Dugald
Stewart, Reid, Paley, and Locke, cold reasoners,
moralists without fervor! He had all Shakespeare

29

at his fingertips; he imitated him, knew him by heart. He had in Latin his Plato, in whose works (a superb folio of Basel, 1561) he lovingly wrote his name—an old acquaintance whom he had already devoured, almost a child, wrapped up in his blanket in the garret. There was Montaigne, an early and durable friendship, Montaigne from whom he borrowed quotations on friendship destined for the cruel Alexis of Harvard, who inspired his discourse on Socrates, and thanks to whom he took the part not of an actor but a spectator in the affairs of this world. Shakespeare, Plato, Montaigne: the three central figures of his *Representative Men*, were found. Add to them Milton, who without exaggeration had turned his head, on whom he had been nourished, and whose memory excited his precocious ambitions, Milton who spoke with the enthusiasm of a prophet, who reasoned with the precision of a philosopher, and lived with the purity of a saint. Ralph Waldo at the age of twenty complained of not having conquered the world. It would be difficult to understand so much juvenile pride if it were not the direct offspring of that sonnet in which the poet of *Paradise Lost*, scarcely master of himself, hurls his anathemas at pitiless Time and reproaches it with having made nothing great of him. At Harvard Ralph Waldo devoured books: history, philosophy, poetry, oratory. He burned to rewrite the *Essays* of Bacon. He meditated on those of Hume. In French he had read Joinville, Montesquieu, Chateaubriand, Corneille, Descartes, Racine. And now we see him discovering Wordsworth and Byron. He had not altogether wasted his time. He doted on poetry and eloquence; he knew the chief passages of twenty good authors by heart. He had scribbled many and many a page. He tried his hand at prose and at verse. He managed, with a marked predilection for the oratorical, a clear, firm, sententious, and classic style. In 1821 he was eighteen years old. And now he was a bachelor of arts. At his graduation he ranked only thirtieth out of fifty-nine, but he had been class poet, and two of his essays, one on Socrates and the other on the evolution of morals, had been given prizes, essays that contained more words than thought—simple rhetorical exercises in which Ralph Waldo orientated himself toward his favorite themes. One day these common places garlanded in rhetoric

31

would grow light within, revealing infinite horizons of thought. For the moment, Ralph Waldo was especially sensitive to the charm of words and the cadence of fine periods. His dream was to become a professor of eloquence and poetry.

CHAPTER III

A Superman in a Girl's Boarding-School

His solitary reveries at Harvard had given rein in Ralph Waldo to vague but ardent ambitions. He wished to be talked about. He wished to be an orator, a poet; but he was poor, and this obliged him first to earn his living. His older brother William managed a school in Boston for young ladies, and he took Ralph as an assistant. Poor, timid, awkward, frozen Ralph, in a classroom full of pretty young girls. They did not leave him indifferent. He even confessed that he admired them in secret. With his blue eyes, the transcendental carriage of his head, his angelic smile, his faraway dreamy air, he made an impression on women. Later, going out from his lectures, one of them confessed that on hearing him one felt that one could never sin again. Contain yourself, Ralph; remember the cruel Alexis of

33

Harvard and the fascination of blue eyes. These
young ladies of Boston were very fortunate; except for his shyness, Ralph was an excellent in-
structor. He was a living anthology. He read very
well. He had a deep and impressive note in his
voice. He steeped his pupils in poetry. His ambition as much as his natural coldness protected him.
At twenty Ralph scarcely dreamt of flirting. He
was in love with glory. Since his childhood, the
names of great men had rung in his ears. He had
read too much Milton, Shakespeare, Byron, and
Chateaubriand. All this had gone to his head and
intoxicated him. He envied the Channings, the
Everetts, the Daniel Websters, who swayed
crowds with the sound of their voices. He would
like to see the world crowd to the foot of his pulpit. He dreamt of the superman who died in
chains on a faraway island the year he left Harvard and who had overthrown the universe. He
too would have cried gladly like all roman-
ticists: "Be Bonaparte or nothing!" Then the
wings fell from him. His dreams were nothing
but dreams. Neither physically nor mentally did
he feel himself at the level of his ambitions. He
had taken French leave of the fairies, the White

Queens, cavalierly, ironically. They might well avenge themselves. See him devoured by scruples, doubts, fancies without issue. His "Wide Worlds," his Journal, became a receptacle for dolorous confidences, an arena in which the apathetic Ralph Waldo tried to knock out the ambitious Ralph Waldo. Ah, how much he needed a professor of humility! To be a hero, a saint, or a poet: he was ambitious of all this at the age of nineteen. He envied his more fortunate comrades, who excelled him and aimed less loftily than he.

Journal, 13 May, 1822. 19 years old. "In twelve days I shall be nineteen years old; which I count a miserable thing. Has any other educated person lived so many years (How old is he then?) and lost so many days? I do not say acquired so little, for by an ease of thought and a certain looseness of mind I have perhaps been the subject of as many ideas as many of mine age. But mine approaching maturity is attended with a goading sense of emptiness and wasted capacity; with the conviction that vanity has been content to admire the little circle of natural accomplishments, and has travelled again and again the narrow round, instead of adding sedulously the gems of knowl-

edge to their number. Too tired and too indolent
to travel up the mountain path which leads to
good learning, to wisdom and to fame, I must be
satisfied with beholding with an envious eye the
laborious journey and final success of my fellows,
remaining stationary myself, until my inferiors
and juniors have reached and outgone me. And
how long is this to last? How long shall I hold
the little acclivity which four or six years ago I
flattered myself was enviable, but which has become contemptible now? It is a child's place, and
if I hold it longer, I may quite well resume the
bauble and the rattle, grow old with a baby's red
jockey on my head and a picture-book in my hand,
instead of Plato and Newton."

And yet his child's imagination made an idol
of glory. He aspired to the highest honors, he
"dared to contend for fame with those who are
hallowed by time and the approbation of ages!"
The heavenly Muses have made of him "the
organ of remarkable sentiments and feelings" far
above his habitual train. Shall he renounce the
ambition "to belong to that family of giant minds
which live on earth many ages and rule the world
when their bones are slumbering, no matter

36

whether under a pyramid or a primrose"? The
Bostonians, they say, have a talent for hyperbole,
and Ralph Waldo truly doubted nothing. He had
arrived at encephalitis and megalomania.

How far he still is from the transcendental
fatalism of his later years and from the silent and
submissive adoration of the Fates! As for the
history of his heart:

"A blank, my lord. I have not the kind affections of a pigeon. Ungenerous and selfish, cau-
tious and cold, I yet wish to be romantic; have not
sufficient feeling to speak a natural, hearty welcome to a friend or stranger, and yet send abroad
wishes and fancies of a friendship with a man I
never knew. There is not in the whole wide Universe of God (my relations to Himself I do not
understand) one being to whom I am attached
with warm and entire devotion. . . . not a being
to whom I have joined fate for weal or woe, not
one whose interests I have nearly and dearly at
heart; . . . and this I say at the most susceptible
age of man. Perhaps at the distance of a score of
years, if I then inhabit this world, or still more,
if I do not, these will appear frightful confes-

sions; they may or they may not, . . . it is a true picture of a barren and desolate soul."

The following year he was harping on the same string. *Journal: March , 1823. 19 years old*: "After two moons I shall have fulfilled twenty years. Amid the fleeting generations of the human race and in the abyss of years I lift my solitary voice unheeded and unknown, and complain unto inexorable Time:—'Stop, Destroyer, overwhelmer, stop one brief moment this uncontrollable career.' Fool! you implore the deaf torrent to relax the speed of its cataract. . . . How many thousands before have cast up to Time the same look of fear and sorrow when they have contemplated the terrible flight of Time. But this infinite Extinguisher or Changer of being continues his supreme agency without exception or interval." Ah, if Ralph Waldo could resemble those sublime spirits, those martyrs who take up the cross of renunciation and consecrate their days and nights to meditation, to study and prayer, blessed by earth and heaven! "God, in the watches of the starry night, fed their imaginations with secret influences of divinity, and swelled their conceptions with showers of healing water from the fountains of Paradise." But to reach this stage it is not enough to flirt with the Fairies, to stupefy oneself with the fumes of wine, even if it is only the innocent malaga of the Cambridge grocer; it is not enough to evoke Dame Memory and her enchantress daughters. One must, like Milton, by whom Ralph was completely dazzled, deserve the dispensations of the eternal spirit.

Ralph reproved himself, mortified himself, fighting his sin. He was indolent, lazy. Courage, audacity, confidence! Let him hasten to accomplish his designs, to realize his ambitions. The work is long, time is short, the opportunity fleeting. Mortification, humility. The soul is a fertile but delicate soil that must be cultivated carefully.

The following year Ralph Waldo once more examined his conscience. It was the year of his coming-of-age. He was still oppressed with uncertainty. He had not chosen his vocation; his natural apathy had assumed the upper hand. He regretted once more the time lost with Queen Mab. Law, medicine, theology—he scarcely knew what to choose. The truth he sought was not in the sciences or even in the philosophies. Metaphysics brought order but no increase to knowledge. It taught nothing that Ralph Waldo did not already know. Ethics was a science external to men. All it did was to distinguish the general from the particular. Neither one nor the other went very deeply into the study of our nature and our destinies. So there were doubts upon doubts. Ralph Waldo dismissed alike the rationalists and the mystics, philosophers and Christians. Science bewildered him. His contact with the transformism of Lamarck disconcerted his idealism by showing him an ascending series of animals rising up to man. How could the latter assume the right to believe himself superior to his fellows of the stable and the pasture? Ralph Waldo was perplexed; the horizon was dark, the flame flickered in his soul. Was his soul dead or sleeping?

God be thanked for Tnamurya; the Sibyl was on the watch. To her Ralph confided his doubts, and with her impetuosity and her habitual sarcasms she came to the rescue. At bottom, it was indeed she who was responsible for the inner crisis of pride that was disturbing her nephew. It was she who had turned his head and unchained those ambitions which now terrified him. "Ralph, aim high! Ralph, turn up your nose at trifles! Excel-

sior, excelsior!" He had followed these counsels
to the letter. She rebuked him sharply. Better late
than never. How badly Ralph had understood
her! The distinction which she coveted for him
was of the supernatural order, and he spoke only
of applause and crowns of laurel! She wished for
him the glory of Plato and Augustine, and it was
the pagans Cæsar and Cicero whom he extolled!
There he was, caught in a trap of sonorous phrases
and earthly passions, he a child so well born, so
carefully brought up! He wanted glory and
power; well, let him deserve them through contemplation, solitude, and work. It was thus one
became a Byron, a Wordsworth. Ralph Waldo
wished to be a poet: let him descend then into the
depths of his heart. The images, the sweet immortal images are within us. . . . Renunciation,
silence, abnegation. Ralph was not deaf to
the appeal. It seemed to come to him from the
truest, the deepest part of himself. If doubt tormented him, he knew also the assurances of the
inner tribunal; he had had its revelations, he
heard its voices. He, too, in the watches of the
starry nights consecrated to prayer, to meditation,
to study, he, too, had been visited by the heavenly

41

Muses. He had had the experience of "certain high intellectual exercises of which our best and loftiest contemplations afford some faint symbol." The spiritual kingdoms opened before him. In the strongest of his doubts he returned with love to his "Wide Worlds," that universe of his soul which he had begun to explore. He was not yet sure of himself. He remained the first to be surprised by the abyss which he discovered, but he was on the way. He knew the joys of thought, the beatitude of intellect at the height of its employment. Splendors of nature, ravishments of the spirit—these were his domain, the scene of his exaltations. "The air is fanned by innumerable wings, the green woods are vocal with the song of the insect and the bird; the beasts of the field fill all the lands untenanted by man, and beneath the sod the mole and the worm take their pleasure. All this vast mass of animated matter is moving and basking under the broad orb of the sun,—is drinking in the sweetness of the air, is feeding on the fruits of nature,—is pleased with life, and loth to lose it." "It is a great flood which encircles the universe and is poured out in unnumbered channels to feed the fountains of life and the wants of Creation, but everywhere runs back again and is swallowed up in its eternal source. That source is God."

But what are the marvels of the cosmos in comparison with those of the spirit, tormented by an insatiable need to vary and project outside itself its thoughts, "combining and separating, comparing and judging, remembering and inventing all things"? There are those states of pleasure of which Emerson had already become conscious, the pleasures of power and perception. The spirit "is a ticket of admission to another world of ineffable grandeur—to unknown orders of things which are as *real* as they are stupendous." These thoughts ravish us with their greatness and their novelty. They liberate our spiritual energy. They suggest each other, give birth to each other, "and thus draw the mind on in a path which it perceives is interminable, and is of interminable joy. . . ." Save the happiness it finds in self-possession, there is nothing comparable to that intuitive consciousness which thought derives from itself.

To every one his Sinai, his oak of Dodona. The inner evidence is henceforth the only one that

Emerson accepts in the quest for truth. He is the first to be alarmed at his pride, but the call of the spirit that tempts him is irresistible. There are still vacant seats at the Table of the Gods, and the reserves of genius are inexhaustible. "And shall those hearts which have throbbed to the secret urgency of the spirit (perchance it was the same spirit that urges all existence) shall they faint in the outset? Onward, onward, the Sun is already high over your head. . . . The windows of heaven are opened, and they whose faces are as the day, Seraphim and Cherubim, beckon to the children of Man and bid him, 'Be bold.' "

Launched on this royal road, Emerson does not stop on the way. If God is in man, who knows whether man might not be God? "For God is within him, God about him, he is a part of God himself." Discarding time and space, he discovers before him nothing but "an antiquity that is without beginning and a futurity that is without end." He celebrates the hours in which the thinking mind "is the recipient of uncommon and awful thought," those instants "when somewhat larger draughts of the Spiritual Universe are let in upon the soul." Then the soul "breathes eloquent

ejaculations to God and would cease to be the
plaything of petty events and would become a
portion of that world in which it has sojourned."
Alas! the spirit relapses in the company of other
antipathetic spirits. "Good manners," the pro-
prieties, "freeze the tongue that should drop
heaven's wisdom to dumbness." Why must the
eye, struck by the glory of paradise, be levelled to
the earth?

Such were the secret thoughts of the timid lad
who was conducting young ladies' classes in
Boston. These thoughts were not all his own. He
exulted in the fire of Milton, the mystics, the
poets whom he devoured. Out of these inner discoveries, indeed before all else he intended to
make literature in prose and in verse. He had
never blackened so much paper. He roamed over
the outskirts of Boston; he sauntered along the
banks of the Concord, which his imagination
peopled with gold fish and swans. He dedicated
an ode to the blackbird, celebrated the Temple of
Nature, praised misanthropy, bade the world
farewell. He who just now had complained of
being ignored, trampled under foot, as his aunt
Mary Moody had counseled him, "the pride of

Greece and Rome." He saluted his native hills;
he stretched himself out under the pines to see
the evening star rising. . . . All this was only
a literary exercise. Ralph Waldo did not seem to
suspect that these very uneven essays were not to
give him the glory he sought, but that he would
find it at the end of those secret paths of the soul
which he had already begun to explore. Yes, let
him bid farewell to the world. Good-by, proud
world! God was to meet him in the bush; he
could not say more. Meanwhile, the future was
still very uncertain. Emerson left his young ladies'
seminary. He was very proud; he had earned
from two to three thousand dollars—a good wind-
fall for his family.

CHAPTER IV

Plato, Calvin, or Channing?

IN FEBRUARY, 1825, an unexpected event, Emerson announced his decision to enter the school of Theology at Cambridge. How had the idea come to him? Let us try to understand him. At first he followed the line of least resistance. All his past and that of his family urged him toward the pastorate. He was following in the steps of his ancestors. As a clergyman, he could assure bread for the Emerson household, and, for a stripling thirsting for eloquence, this was the career open to talent. Ralph Waldo doubtless gives us the impression of an odd divinity student. Theology meant nothing to him, and he abhorred Calvinism. He called dogmas the "measles and mumps of the soul." Before this natural optimism and the strange mental apathy in which he gloried, the gravest problems evaporated. Good

47

and evil, free will, predestination—what mattered such things to him! He felt God in the
depths of his heart, and all nature proved His existence to him. A fervent rationalist, he referred
everything to inner evidence. He had no need
of the church. On the very eve of taking the step,
he sharpened his finest pen and addressed his beloved Plato an audacious, paradoxical, hardly
Christian letter. It was his Prayer on the Acrop-
olis. He compared Calvin of Geneva to Plato of
Athens and gave the palm to the latter. He lamented the thought that the pillars of the Porch
were broken and the Groves of the Academy
felled to the ground. He regretted that God had
chosen Hebrew and not Greek to speak to men.
He asked pardon of Plato for addressing him in a
barbarous idiom. Save for a naïve reserve touching the superiority of the constitution of the
United States, and in spite of oratorical precautions, everything was in Plato's favor in Emerson's letter, everything was for paganism against
Christianity. Ralph Waldo placed the sublime
speculations of the pagan Plato on the same level
with Revelation. He declared reason anterior and
in every case indispensable to faith. He made

ironical reflections on the assumed moral and social superiority of Christianity, and he ended by throwing Calvinism into the discard. A strange letter, strange theology, still stranger divinity student. It was true that the Unitarians were extremely liberal.

Protestantism had known many variations. Bossuet, if he had traveled in America, would have remarked upon innumerable and very curious ones. But there was no stranger hybrid about 1825 than the Unitarianism of Boston. The time of mystical crusades was past. The Puritan theocracy was dissolved; it went contrary to the spirit of colonization. Calvinism was not a religion for pioneers. It was too pessimistic. Its hegemony had not withstood the necessities of conquest and expansion. It preached renunciation of the good things of this world, held the human will as corrupt, denied free will, established in heaven an inexorable Jehovah while leaving here below man disabled with his feet in the fetters of the devil. Like puritan society it rested on the anti-democratic system of castes—in this world the saints and the laity, in the other the elect and the damned. Go then and colonize: clear fields, build, fight the redskin and the elements, uncertain of a just reward and with the laugh of the Evil One at your heels. Then the age of the Enlightenment had arrived. Dogmas had melted away under the light of reason. Deism in the United States was already a foregone conclusion. Free will and reason were on an equality. The Puritan theocracy itself was founded on the supremacy of the individual conscience in revolt against the mass, the indulgences, and the decretals of the established Church. In America, more than elsewhere, it was necessary for man to be free, and, in order to be free, reasonable. Neither mistaken reason nor mistaken will would have annexed a continent. Calvinism had chosen the wrong road, and liberalism had disputed its conquests. It was all the worse when the revolutionists unexpectedly appeared with their constitutions and their charters made by the hands of men to govern laically their fellow creatures. The day when the Constitution of the United States decreed that the end of government was to guarantee the happiness of citizens in this world, Calvinism was a lost cause. The American Revolution was made in opposition to all its postulates, divine rights, and predestinations. What a distance from the Christian institution to the Declaration of the Rights of Man and the Citizen! All American Christianity had been involved in the adventure. It had laicized itself. If any country was poorly made to damn men in spite of themselves and refuse them the full usage of free will, it was indeed the United States.

Unitarianism had profited by everything that Calvinism had lost. Unitarianism was hardly a sect, hardly a church; it was a synod of gentlemen. It was born in the eighteenth century of a wager that consisted—given the exigencies of the world and the "progress of enlightenment"—in allowing the supernatural as small a part as possible in religion without eliminating it completely. On the most embarrassing points it had removed the venom from dogma. It placed confidence in reason, rehabilitated liberty, and missed no opportunity to humanize the divine. It was through respect for the inner light that it juggled away the Holy Ghost, through deference to human personality that it claimed for all men the rank of sons of God. Very free in the individual interpretation of the Scriptures, but friendly to decorum,

the Unitarians asked the faithful only to cover
their dissidences in a respectful silence, by means
of which all heresies, all schisms were possible,
even allowable, so long as they made no noise.
In public worship Unitarianism, limited in
imagination and constrained by respectability, retained only a minimum of ritual. The communion and public prayer had caused many
Unitarians before Emerson to revolt. Everything
was reduced to preaching, which was monop-
olized by scholarly and eloquent clergymen.
Calvin humiliated human nature; Unitarianism
did it too much honor. The one allowed grace too
much; the other suppressed the supernatural almost entirely and offered nothing in its place. A
cold, sensible, indulgent, practical religion, it reduced dogma to ethics and to a laicized ethics.
With its baggage little encumbered by observances and rites, its optimism, its minimum of
mysticism, its decorum, nothing was more practical, more American than the Christianity of
Boston. At the moment when Emerson dedicated
himself to it, Unitarianism still cut a good figure,
but it was secretly undermined. Hitherto it had
never been anything but a compromise between

an inhuman religion and a superficial philosophy, and now it was anæmic and disarmed precisely when its adversaries were falling upon it. It believed it had taken shelter with Locke and his "Essay on Human Understanding," but this refuge was falling into ruins under the blows dealt it by Kant, reinforced by science, history, and exegesis. If only Unitarianism had been able to renew itself inwardly; but the pale gleams of Lockean rationalism gave even less warmth than light. Unitarianism knew nothing but reason; it had nothing to offer the soul. The wave of romanticism came to sweep it away like a straw.

One man, however, was trying to breathe into the dying faith a new life. This was Channing. Renan has been very indulgent to the great Unitarian preacher when he reproached him for haggling with the supernatural. Channing did not haggle with it; he suppressed it by surrounding it with garlands of beautiful phrases. He had been the great laicizer of Christianity in the United States; he had tried to substitute for it a vague spiritualism in the manner of Cousin, a spiritualism with which most of his compatriots are still content. He was born in the Calvinist

53

nightmare. He had been one of those children
gorged with Puritan sermons; before he was ten
years old he had already read his Bible eighteen
times and been terrorized in the catechism by such
questions as the following: "Why has God created
out of nothing everything that exists?—For
himself.—What do you personally deserve?—
Eternal damnation in hell.—If you go to hell,
how long will you remain there?—Forever, as
long as God exists." Unfortunately for Calvin, little Channing had common sense and
he was a born observer. One day, coming back
from the meeting-house where they had duly
damned him in advance, he heard his father
joyously whistling as he walked back from church
with him. "Come," he said to himself, "my father
is damned, and my father is whistling!" This
seemed to him surprising and contradictory, and
henceforth he refused all faith to Calvin. But
he swung too far in the other direction, and, the
better to avenge himself, he opened his doors wide
to the Utopians. He had Fénelon, Rousseau, and
the Ideologists in his blood, and he had padded
his optimism with all the romantic mists accumulated by the de Staëls, the Wordsworths, the

Coleridges, the Fichtes, and the Cousins. With all
this he claimed to be enlarging spirituality, but
in so confused a fog Christianity lost all
consistency.

After having thrown overboard the somber and
inhuman Calvinist theology, Channing set to
work to filter religion, and in order to adapt it
better to the needs of the century, to the optimistic
ardors of young America, he sweetened it to the
point of insipidity. In his sermons he juggled
with the verities of the faith, as Cousin had done
with philosophic systems. Masking poverty of
logic under harmonious periods, he piled up
antinomies. Was he a Christian or a pantheist?
Was his Christ a man or a God? Was he speaking
of the Church or the phalanstery, of religion or
philanthropy? His optimism was inexhaustible.
His sermons were a geyser of comforting and
unproved ejaculations. He was sickeningly good.
With him there was nothing but co-opera-
tion, love, kindness, gratitude, inspiration; everything was good, beautiful, perfect, supreme,
infinite. The universe was divine, nature was
good, man was sacred and all men brothers.
Channing eulogized work, trade, industry, trade

unions, gas, railroads, progress. The future of the United States of America roused his enthusiasm. As he laicized dogma, so he laicized the Christian virtues. For him the theological virtues, asceticism and perfection, did not exist; there were only altruism, munificence, civic virtue, honesty in business. He replaced the calendar of the saints by that of the great inventors. He anathematized Napoleon and all military men. With his cult of superlatives and hyperboles, we are tempted to see in him merely the Babbitt of the Christian pulpit.

But this would be unjust, for Channing had some very noble aspects. He spoke well, too well; public oratory had often been fatal for him. It masked reality for him and made him take words for truth. For the sake of the many profound intuitions appearing here and there in his sermons we must pardon his chimeras. In his famous panegyrics on Fénelon and Milton he went very deeply into the understanding of the inner life. He gave an immanent definition to religion that was well calculated to please Emerson. Religion was "the soul itself rising towards its creator." Emerson recognized in him the gift of exciting the moral imagination. What a pity that his transcendentalism was so verbal and that his social zeal, his religion of progress had led him to squander true mysticism and fervor in an order of things purely external and with which they were not concerned. Ralph Waldo greatly admired Channing. He took notes on his sermons, and many pages of his *Journal*, the most declamatory, the most flowery, echo Channing a mile off. The great Unitarian seems to have been aware of Ralph Waldo's sudden calling. By example and advice he must have shown him that the pastorate was the best means of realizing his dreams, and it was he who recommended to him the Faculty of Theology at Cambridge. Tnamurya was not satisfied. She distrusted the liberalism of Harvard. She would have wished for her nephew the more orthodox seminary of Andover. But how condemn people from the height of a pulpit when tuberculosis threatens you, as was unhappily the case with Ralph Waldo at the moment when he began his theological studies?

CHAPTER V

*The Mouse in His Chest—Under the Palms of
Florida—Licentia Prædicandi—A
Representative Man*

THE cells of Divinity Hall were cold, but less
cold than the atavistic dough of which the
Emersons were kneaded and from which many
of them suffered. Ralph Waldo was between life
and death. Trouble with his eyes, pains in the
hip, pulmonary inflammations. The mouse was
gnawing at his chest. Sad beginnings for the
apostolate. For good or ill and to satisfy his conscience, he attended his courses at intervals, did
his reading, took notes, and outlined sermons for
which he had little taste. Tnamurya was always
his confidante. She continued to chide him, but
he outstripped her with his transcendentalism
and dizzied her with his ideas. Some are saddened by the truth; others turn pale and weep
over problems. He serenely discarded them and

left them to the reckoning of the Eternal. First
of all there was the problem of Evidence. Apologetics mobilized the natural, moral, and historical
sciences in order to prove the verities of the faith.
For what purpose? The inner evidence alone concerned him. For him faith and reason were one
and the same illumination. The voice of the soul
was the voice of God. If divine order is found in
nature, some intelligence must first have placed
it there. The mind is self-sufficient. The problem
of God goes back to that of thought. Final causes
lead less surely to Him than the study of great
souls, of Socrates, Plato, Milton, Thomas à
Kempis, grand incarnations of the universal soul
at its apogee. It was in them that Emerson delighted with a fine eclecticism that confused
pagans and Christians alike.

Touching the problem of evil—the obsession
of the Puritan theologians and the center, for
more than a century, of thorny controversies—the
natural optimism of Emerson inspired in him a
reassuring theory which he called "compensation." This was the system of balance. Good and
evil, virtue and vice, happiness and unhappiness
balanced one another. Everything was deter-

mined, but by an inner and moral determinism. Every act was completed by its contrary and carried in itself its retribution. Actions and rewards or punishments evoked and balanced each other. Judgment took place automatically, *hic et nunc*, in the very nature of the delinquent. Responsibilities are not superadded nor posterior to action; they form part of it. Equilibrium and the moral order are thus spontaneously, inevitably assured. One might as well say that evil does not exist, that it is inseparable from its contrary, but what then becomes in this system of the intervention of God, the fall and the redemption? Every one of us is the artisan of his destiny. Everything is balanced, equalized, harmonized. If we cannot foresee and calculate, it is enough at least to have faith and trust the future. The moral laws apply themselves.

The problem of scepticism no longer disturbs the transcendental optimism of Emerson, the student of theology. He considers doubt as a natural and necessary spiritual stage, indeed the very condition of spiritual progress. It is not in vain that he has read with Montaigne. He is not with the sceptics; he is rather above them, in an observatory, a serene firmament into which he pulls everything after him. What to him are Hume, Gibbon, Voltaire, the school of Tübingen, Eichhorn, De Wette, and Schleiermacher? To each his heaven, his sphere, his personal truth. To believe too much is dangerous and leads to atheism. The true sceptic doubts not from lack of faith, but from excess of it. Contradictions, logic, controversies, arguments pro and con—he pays no heed to all these things. The spirit moves freely; it carries itself whither it will; it blows where it listeth. Its mobility does not alter the divine decrees, the great universal laws. In his letters to Tnamurya, Ralph Waldo delivers himself over to the sport of subtle speculations without issue. He can give himself the pleasure of the joyful wisdom because he has faith in the inner oracle, the demon, the still small voice that accompanies it.

Seeing him so unconstrained and sure in doubt, one recalls in spite of oneself the painful crises of conscience of a Chateaubriand, a Jouffroy, a Renan, in their search for truth. "I wept and I believed!" What childishness! Why weep? Is it not natural to believe? "How dogmas come to an end," pondered Jouffroy. What does it matter if dogmas come to an end' if the soul remains? To dispute the authenticity of the gospels, the date, the composition, in order to know whether Christianity is true or false is so much time lost. What does it matter, if Christianity like morality is salutary and eternal; and what have Hebrew, Greek, and Aramaic to do with all this? The sceptics may be right, and Christianity be no less indispensable. False historically, it may remain true morally and socially; and, as Voltaire said of God, if it did not exist, it would doubtless be necessary to invent it. But even when upheld by universal consent and confirmed by historians and philosophers, it is enough that Ralph Waldo Emerson deny it for religion to be false, or *vice versa*. Try to answer that, once plunged in the midst of immanence.

Again we say, a strange divinity student, but one whose serene laxity could make *ad libitum* a heretic or a pillar of the church. You dispute; you bring up arguments, syllogisms. He answers you that thought is spontaneous by nature, capricious, miraculous, unforeseeable, changing. The spirit bloweth where it listeth. The soul acts by sharp mutations, sudden impulses.

"Thought shoots up like maize . . . it spawns like fish." Go and seize the intangible. You quote the testimonies of history, but how connect with the past a sovereign spirit that denies time and space and affirms its perpetual creation? The problem of the soul and body disturbs you. The antinomy, spirit-matter, arrests you. Emerson himself dissociates the soul from the body, thought from act. He denies that they have anything in common. How vain all this is when one can plunge into the marvels of the soul and freely explore the supernatural. Ah, renounce then your arguments and your proofs, and, before speaking of the soul, know it. Fugitive, mysterious, changing, instinctive, it escapes the philosophers' calculations and analysis. Its law is an all-powerful necessity. Why exaggerate to ourselves the importance of our actions? Nothing matters but the center whence they emanate. Abandon, rest, expectation, ecstasy. Let us envy the delights of quietism; let us imitate the silence of the Quaker. Emerson claims to prove the reality of the divine by the very instability of our states of soul. Life is "droll," he declares. "The only humor proper to it seems quiet astonishment." "Others laugh, weep, sell or proselyte. I admire." An admiration closely resembling the joyful wisdom of Nietzsche. "Be the theories as they may, it suits my humor to sit and speculate, a civil philosopher, mild and composed in the presence of little and majestic minds; without contempt of reptiles, and, as the stoics say, without being afraid of the gods."

And it was this fine indifference which in 1826 won for Ralph Waldo the approbation of the Unitarian Synod and the *licentia prædicandi*! He delivered his first sermon the same year that he confided to his *Journal* those blasphemous and Renan-like designs. Yes, truly the Unitarians of Boston were indulgent. But what will the parishioners make of this pastor who tumbled down from the Empyrean, and how will he dare to direct souls, the souls of others?

Emerson was not destined to enter upon his life work so soon: the mouse in his chest did not permit it. His condition grew more serious. He had no animation or ardor. He compared himself to Sisyphus tragically pushing his rock. In the autumn of 1826 his condition grew still worse; but Providence was watching over its Benjamin, and good uncle Samuel Ripley of Concord (the same who had sent the Emersons the milch-cow in their destitution) gave Emerson traveling money. He set sail for the South. Let us wish for this journey a happier end than that of his younger brother Edward who died in Porto Rico.

So we see Ralph Waldo en route for Florida, *via* Charleston, eight days at sea. It was the first time he had set foot on a boat. He was never to make a brilliant globe-trotter; he did not believe in traveling. His philosophy and his natural apathy forbade it. Why seek oneself without? An atom held the infinite in miniature. "The soul contained the whole universe." One finds at a distance nothing but what one has just left behind. Florida, the Gulf of Mexico, palms, orange trees, lemons, negroes, blue sky, ancient Spanish citadels, Latin bell-towers—what do they matter? The landscape did not interest him save when it harmonized with his thoughts. Give him the skies of the North, changing and variegated, the snow, the aurora borealis, the simple and familiar places. How trivial was travel. Seasickness seemed to him an insult to his respectability. It was an involuntary intoxication. The music of the sea

was very monotonous but he loved the clouds
and the wind. Reaching Charleston, he shiv-
ered and hastened to St. Augustine. The shore
was perfumed, the sea aflame; the boat came to
anchor under the Spanish bastions. Emerson
rented a room in the old town. He felt about him
a past of grandeur that bewildered him because
it was not Puritan. He sought in the sand for
traces of the conquistadors. He roamed about the
narrow little streets—closed doors, barred windows. This was the first time he had seen ruins.
He deciphered the inscriptions. From the postern
of the old Spanish fort he copied one and translated it:

"Don Ferdinand VI, being King of Spain, and
the Field Marshall Don Alonzo Fernandez
de Heredia, being governor and Captain-
general of this place of St. Augustine in
Florida . . ."

Emerson and Heredia, transcendentalism and
Parnassus, the soul and the senses—a complete
contrast. Respectability, morality, and hygiene:
even in the Parthenon and before the Bay of Naples, an Anglo-Saxon never forgets these unless he
is a Byron or a Shelley. Certain reflections of

Emerson recall Mark Twain's "Innocents Abroad." He notes in his *Journal*:

"St. Augustine is the oldest town of Europeans in North America; 1564; full of ruins,—chimneyless houses, lazy people; horsekeeping intolerably dear, and bad milk from swamp grass, because all the hay comes from the north. 40 (?) miles from here is nevertheless the richest crop of grass growing untouched. Why? Because there is no scythe in St. Augustine, and if there were, no man who knows how to use one."

Ah, these Latins! Quick, American business men, central heating, dairies, model breeding-studs, agricultural machines. And we thought Ralph Waldo was above trifles! But he is homesick, he has the "blues," he regrets his native hills, he is bored, he does not play billiards. His only distraction is to stroll along the beach swinging his cane and playing hockey with a lemon.

But he was going to meet his first superman in the flesh at St. Augustine in the person of Achille Murat, nephew of Napoleon and son of Joachim, King of Naples, who had been shot by his subjects. Caroline Bonaparte had taken refuge with

her son in Austria, and since his majority Achille
had come to rejoin in the United States old
King Joseph, his uncle. He had Americanized
himself with the promptness and fervor of a modern immigrant. No one had pronounced the *civis
sum Americanus* with more pride than this imperial scion. Planter, lawyer, explorer, soldier,
even postmaster in the pay of Uncle Sam, the life
of this ex-royal Prince of the Two Sicilies had
teemed with adventures. The love of liberty
which had brought him to America recalled him
to Europe a few years after his meeting with
Emerson, but the Holy Alliance having canceled
his commission as colonel of the Belgian lancers,
he came back to fire a shot against the Seminole
Indians. He married a granddaughter of Washington and died at Tallahassee in 1847, late
enough to have been able to read the *Essays* of
Emerson. A fervent admirer of American democracy, he wrote on it—even before Tocqueville's
work—a book entitled, *A Moral and Political
Sketch of the United States of North America.*
This is a satirical tableau, but well intentioned, in
which Murat lavished perspicacious notes on the
Yankees and their civilization. Jacobin and atheist

though he was, Murat gave among other things many compliments to the Unitarians. He praised their brief, simple, reasonable dogmas, their pure and elegant worship, "stripped of every kind of ceremony and superstition." He congratulated them for addressing themselves only to reason. He saluted in Channing "a veritable Plato."

How Murat discovered at St. Augustine the presence of the young Unitarian minister from Boston, history does not tell us; but, from Emerson's confession, we know that it was love at first sight. He notes this important event in his *Journal*. He had encountered for the first time what he had believed until then purely imaginary, "a consistent atheist, an intrepid doubter," whose soul was as noble and whose virtue as sublime as that of a Sadducee. He confessed that he could not help "honoring and loving" this unbeliever. When, at the end of the summer, Ralph Waldo was going home, he found Murat on the boat that was making the nine-day passage to Charleston. During all this time the two friends "talked incessantly," and the subject of their conversation was the religious question. Little

inclined as Emerson was to controversy, it was
difficult this time for him to escape. He was
obliged to defend his position as a minister, and
how could he remain gaping? But he must have
passed a difficult moment. Murat had gone
squarely to the charge and spared nothing to scandalize Emerson. In order to defend Christianity,
the latter fell back upon the argument of relativity. He praised with more or less conviction,
although probably not without eloquence, the
moral and social superiority of that Christian institution which he had himself attacked in his bold
letter to Plato. The two disputants parted with an
amicable *status quo*, but they had promised each
other to resume the discussion by correspondence.
In the autumn of 1827 Murat kept his word and
kept it with a perfect candor. He confessed quite
unceremoniously to Ralph Waldo that on many
important points he was no longer so sure of himself. "Your system," he avowed, "has acquired as
much in proberbility (sic) as mine has lost in
certainty, both seem to me now nearly equally
proberable (sic). I have accordingly only one test
left—that of expediency." But he did not hold to
this pragmatic distinction, which resembles

closely the famous criterion of William James ("that which is the truest for us is that which we find the best"). Murat shifted the ground of the argument and enlarged it considerably. Before discussing the greater or less amount of truth in Christianity, he wished to know what truth was, and he promised to send his correspondent a "monography" of his own on the subject.

We do not know whether the "consistent atheist," the "intrepid doubter," and the worshipper of the mysterious compensations ever met again in the flesh, but Emerson never forgot Murat. Soon, in the course of a grave moral upset—the only one he underwent in his life—he too was to discard relativity and go straight to the truth. He praised the heroic manners of his Florida friend. He classed him among the best of men, those who have ministered to his highest wants, simple men "whose charm to him is wonderful," like the Vagabond in Wordsworth's "Excursion," those men who are in themselves the argument for the spiritual world. "Nothing is impossible since such communion has already been." "Whilst we hear them speak, how frivolous are the distinctions of fortune! and the voice of fame is as unaffecting

as the tinkle of the passing sleigh-bell." In short, a little humility: let us render thanks to the atheist, Murat.

Ralph slowly traveled northward again, preaching, musing, lamenting his sins, always oscillating between warm and cold, fervor and desolation:

"The night is fine; the stars shed down their severe influences upon me, and I feel a joy in my solitude that the merriment of vulgar society can never communicate. There is a pleasure in the thought that the particular tone of my mind at the moment may be new in the universe; that the emotions of this hour may be peculiar and unexampled in the whole eternity of moral being. [See the pride that overtakes him.] I lead a new life. I occupy new ground in the world of spirits, untenanted before. I commence a career of thought and action which is expanding before me into a distant and dazzling infinity. Strange thoughts start up like angels in my way and beckon me onward. I doubt not I tread on the highway that leads to the Divinity."

But Ralph Waldo was too quickly canonizing

himself, and *acedia* made him expiate his sins
against the Holy Ghost.

Here he is again lamenting, alone, unknown,
weak, and still ill. He compares himself with
the paladin whose courser paws the ground with
impatience but who does not know whither he is
about to dash. What if he were going to renew
the exploits of Don Quixote? To console himself
Ralph read Walter Scott; he rambled through
the woods of Concord where his Uncle Ripley
had welcomed him. He dreamed in the Old
Manse whose phantoms Nathaniel Hawthorne
was soon to evoke. He amused himself botanizing.
Will he be a poet or a scholar? (But is he not
already a minister?)

CHAPTER VI

Ellen

O N HIS return from Florida Emerson was not cured. His view of life was dark. Like all candidates for the pastorate, he preached by invitation from the churches. He declined several pulpits; he was awaiting his hour and what fortune should bring him. He made a provision of sermons which he wished never to preach. His eyes were in bad condition, and preaching was forbidden him; but he fell back upon meditation and thought and listened to the "still small voice." When the weather was good, he left his cell in Divinity Hall, whither he had returned, and rambled about the fields. He was twenty-five years old—a tall thin young man with blue eyes, an abundant mane of chestnut hair, an oval face framed in budding whiskers, and the romantic air of a smiling Chateaubriand. He bore a name that was known among the Boston aristocracy. He was cold and a little stiff, but he spoke well and people sought after him. Under this calm and serene air bubbled measureless ambitions, supported by the tenacious pride of the idealist. Twenty-five years old, the springtide of life, and the man of ice prided himself upon never having loved. So he informs the imaginary readers of his *Journal*. He is a celibate, he has never been a lover. This defiance of Eros was going to bring on the vengeance of the little god, for with his blue eyes, his cello-like voice, his benignity, his air of thoughtless seduction, he had everything to please women. Those who knew him compared him to Apollo Musagetes, his brow crowned with ivy and garlands about his lyre. In September, 1827, Ralph Waldo met his Eloa. She was seventeen years old; her name was Ellen. She was beautiful and frail as a picture from a keepsake, with a riotous head of thick curls, great hungry eyes, a pretty nose, impeccable throat and neck, a perfect bosom, a wasplike waist. Seventeen years old! They had met, had parted, re-met, and were finally united. What was he going to do with this lily, he who

reproached himself for his coldness and his lack
of cordiality? Let us not expect romantic effusions
from him. He is too apathetic to feel passion,
but on the other hand let us not consider him
a fleshless idealist. He liked women, admired
them through a veil of idealism like the rosy mist
which he pretended they diffused and with which
they colored everything about them. Remote, un-
real, ethereal, dispensers of illusion, they were a
living poem, the sweetest of all music. To them
belonged society, conversation, flowers, dances,
colors, beautiful forms. Harmonious architecture
and landscapes were their natural frame. Muses
and Sibyls, they inspired by their presence. Their
spontaneity, their instinct put our slow wisdom to
shame. Impulsive, they betrayed themselves even
in their dolls. Eyes opened, tongues loosened in
contact with them. Man became a child and trod
on fields of flowers. Through them chalices over-
flowed with joy, wine, roses whose perfume sweet-
ens the house. Women were poets who believed in
their poetry. Sadi, Hafiz, and Firdousi have
praised them, as is becoming, in the Persian Lilla
irradiating the joy of life. The whole universe

flowed toward them, and the poets were right in adorning them with everything that is most beautiful in the world. Alas! Delicate, tender, and sensitive, they were for that very reason vulnerable and tragic. Their life was a long sorrow.

How attach to ourselves these beings who brush past us and tempt us? Ellen's lover was very sceptical about love and still more so about marriage. As soon as love was caught it took flight, fugitive, impersonal, transcendent, illusory—so spoke Emerson, as a fervent Platonist faithful to the doctrine of reminiscence. Souls seek each other in the body, pass and ascend, without ever attaching themselves. Before everything, love should be free; it should enfranchise itself by dint of gifts, and, having given all, it should remain faithful to itself. Attraction and repulsion: on the human plane everything is completed and paired. The union of the sexes forms part of the universal compensations, but what institution is so coarse as marriage! And how astonishing that the poets should have covered with flowers chains so hard to carry! Marriage is a snare, a beneficial illusion, the Pandora's box from which good and evil escape. Those involved in it would be only too glad to extricate themselves, and those who have not entered it long for it. Socrates, approved by Panurge, humorously declared that whether one take a woman or not, there is regret in either case. In the spiritual world marriage is impossible. There is no equality between the subject and the object. In love, conscience and perception are not synonyms of possession. Between Him and Her there is always an abyss, that which separates the portrait from the original. Two human beings in love are related as are two spheres which cannot meet save at a single point. The longer love lasts, the more the points which have no contact attract each other and tend to destroy the total harmony. How could love be satisfied with the chimney-corner and the nuptial chamber? In the supernatural world marriage is useless. Our souls are hermaphrodite, the sexes interchangeable. Thus thinks Emerson, quoting Plato, Milton, and Swedenborg. But there is one point beyond a doubt ——

All the world loves a lover.

And Ralph Waldo loved Ellen. He seemed to have loved no one but her. The fiancée of seventeen, found so early, lost so soon, was no stranger to this disillusioned Platonism, this poetic scepticism. Eros and Psyche met. Eros had a mouse in his chest, and Psyche was dying of consumption. Ralph Waldo was perfect. He took his little betrothed on drives through the calm landscapes of New England. When she, in her turn, traveled South, he wrote her pretty letters in prose and in verse. He sent her poetical bouquets in which he compared her to the faraway voice of the nightingale. As messengers he sent breezes and delegations of flowers to invite her to return. He asked her for an amulet that would bring her before him, red when Ellen loved him, pale and blue when she forgot him. A tragic presentiment obsessed him. He was afraid that Eros and Psyche, like Romeo and Juliet, would be united only in death. And Psyche replied, also in the language of the gods. On her love, of which she dreamed as of a cloudless peace, a day without night, a world without sin, Ellen improvised unpretentious but pathetic verses. She compared herself to the violet that dies unknown in the great woods. Poor violet! Betrothed in September, 1828, she was married in September, 1829. In January, 1831,

EMERSON

making a last prayer to sincerity, Ellen died a heroic death. The following year Emerson opened Ellen's coffin to shut up there the only sentimental episode of his existence of which history has preserved the memory.

CHAPTER VII

*The Second Church—"Young Man, You Do
Not Know Your Business"—A Man
Against the Sky*

IN MARCH, 1829, Emerson had been appointed
assistant, then full pastor, of the Second
Church in Boston. He was married; he was
getting better; he was in possession of a pulpit
where he could make himelf heard. He shouted
victory, but modestly, without taking his eye off
Nemesis. The burden of the pastorate was to be
very heavy for his shoulders. Twenty-six years
old and a director of souls when, like him, one is
independent and detached! Children to baptize
and instruct, the sick and the dying to visit, the
dead to bury, the poor, money-offerings, etc.,
tasks very fastidious for an idealist—with what
heart would he consecrate himself to the func-
tions of his charge? There was no difficulty as
concerned the preaching. With his natural gifts

and the years of reflection back of him, his words attracted people, and those who heard him compared him to a heavenly messenger. Without abandoning entirely the traditional and classic forms of eloquence, he brought down the truth from heaven to earth; he preached from the very bottom of his heart and from heart to heart; he surrounded himself with familiar topical examples. He was a preacher for whom the external world existed. He had not yet found his oracular manner, his style wavered and remained declamatory, his prose was poetical, full of images, cadenced; but already he was preaching the substance of the *Essays*, the divine presence in the soul, self-reliance, the compensations. He was pleasing, touching, and people flocked to his sermons.

On the practical side things went less well. He had little heart for his duties. The sick bored him, the dead repelled him. His timidity and his transcendentalism embarrassed him at the death-bed. He who lived in the spirit could only ill conceive how one might mobilize heaven and earth to help a human being to die. He scarcely believed in death. There were criticisms, murmurings, such as those of that old soldier who made him come to his death-bed and found him awkward, hesitant in handling his spiritual arms. He grew angry: "Young man, you do not know your business; you had better go back to your home." People murmured around him that he was not made for a minister. Unitarianism was not very exigent in the observance of rites. It had reduced them to their simplest expression, preserved nothing in the way of ceremony but the communion and public prayer. But even this was too much for Emerson and wounded his deepest convictions. He believed in the Spirit, not in signs. Every materialization of an idea seemed to him blasphemy against the supernatural. He was quite willing to pray, but all alone. By what right did a man arrogate to himself the power to present to God by proxy his fellow beings, and how could a man who respected himself betray aloud his secrets with the Eternal?

"There is no being in the universe whose integrity is so precious to you as that of your soul."

"Does not every consciousness contain its own evidence?"

"Internal evidence outweighs all other to the inner man."

"All wisdom, all genius is reception."

"To think is to receive; to reflect is to receive truth immediately from God without any medium."

What need then is there of a church, and what is Emerson doing in the pastorate? Every church conspires against the solitude of the soul; the faithful is never alone with his God. There is a hierarchy of divine persons, the sacraments, prayer, the Scriptures, the rites. Emerson refused to pray. What use to appeal to God who never leaves us, who is the life in life, the soul in the soul, Emmanuel?

> God dwells in thee.
> It is no metaphor nor parable. . . .
> Give up to thy soul ——
> Let it have its way ——
> It is, I tell thee, God himself. . . .
> Therefore be great,
> Not proud,—too great to be proud. . . .
> In thee resides
> The Spirit that lives in all. . . .
> Thou art the *law*,
> The rest is straw. . . .

There is nothing else but God. . . .
That which is in me lives in the whole.

Imagine this pantheistic and Spinoza-like
prayer uttered aloud in a meeting-house without
the vaults falling in upon the blasphemer! And
yet this was indeed the prayer that Emerson re-
cited inwardly, thanks to the "respectful silence"
which the Unitarians recommended.

The Unitarians observed the rite of the Lord's
Supper. This was the only aspect of the sacrament
that they had kept, and they held it as a divine
institution. Emerson bluntly refused it. He carried to the point of a phobia his horror of acts
and rites, that instinctive fear which the Anglo-
Saxon and the Puritan experiences at the thought
of making a fool of himself in public. Everything
he did not feel to be evident he refused to accept
as true, and this was the case with the communion. So he suggested to his parishioners that they
dispense with it. He would not preside at the rite,
save it be under the form of a pious memorial
and without the use of bread and wine. Upon
which there was friction and schism between
Emerson and the wardens of the Second Church

of Boston. A committee assembled to examine the pastor's proposal and rejected it. It was for Emerson now to submit or be dismissed. The moment was serious. Unitarianism was a great and large mansion. Was he going to hide his light under a bushel and sacrifice his brilliant future to scruples? With him scruples were a mania; he was obstinate and proud. His social sense awoke. Was he going to cope with a whole church? He remembered his conversations with Murat. He had found in a philosophic work (the *Phædo* of Moses Mendelssohn) the argument of relativity. "All that which, being admitted as true, would procure the human race a real advantage or a feeble consolation, acquires by that alone a high degree of probability." He scolded himself, he reproved himself. If the immemorial rite of the communion was a consolation and a comfort for Christians, did Emerson have the right to sacrifice the general interest to his personal convictions? He had not received the *monography* on truth which Murat had promised him, but the problem that arrested him was indeed the same question. *Quid est veritas?*

To make a decision Emerson retired to the

White Mountains. It is June, 1832. Absolute solitude. It is cold on the peaks. Clouds cover the
summits, woods shut off the horizon; in his
empty cottage Emerson has for companion only
a peacock (the bird of Juno, symbol of vanity
and pride). How is he going to solve the "mortal
problem"? He summons to him his intercessors,
those who desire above everything the truth:
Goethe, George Fox, Swedenborg, Montaigne,
Washington. "To be genuine—Goethe was
wholly so, George Fox was . . . Swedenborg
was, George Washington was." "The sublime of
morals seems ever to be of this kind, frail man
intimating this defiance of the universe and gathering himself into his shell." Ah, how good this
crisis is for him, how it deepens and toughens
him, he so optimistic, so easy-going hitherto.
Now or never is the moment to be heroic. He has
no more time to muse. Emerson descends to the
Inn of Suffering. Ellen is dead; he is alone. One
would say that there was no more reason to beat
about the bush. He will embrace the truth, cost
what it may, as he has found it on the heights.

"I should like to know if anyone ever went up
on a mountain so high as that he overlooked right

and wrong and saw them confounded, saw their streams mix, that justice did not mean anything to his mind."

"Wisdom is insight, ignorance outward sight."

"Let a man set down his foot and say, 'this or that thing I can't and won't do,' and stand it out."

Would you not think you were listening to Nietzsche on the heights of Sils Maria?

Doubts summon doubts. All his accumulated distrust of official Christianity was crystallized about these strivings of conscience. Everything that was personally good in him revolted against "official goodness." It seems to him that "it is the best part of the man that revolts most against his being a minister. His good revolts from official goodness." He declared the profession "antiquated." It seemed to him that a Socratic paganism was better "than an effete Christianity," and that an afflux of scepticism, even of atheism, was necessary to vivify religion. . . . Come, Ralph Waldo, descend from the mountain; it is time to confess that you have no vocation, that you never had one; bravely make your sacrifice. Farewell to pulpit glory. You will never be either a Channing or an Everett, but you will have the still

88

small voice and its oracles. You will not be a preacher, but a poet, philosopher, and theosophist. Who can complain of that?

In September, 1832, he had made up his mind. Emerson risked all on all. He would speak the truth, nothing but the truth—and before sending in his resignation he preached his sermon on the Lord's Supper. He had never been so dogmatic, so trenchant, so uncompromising. His battle was quickly fought and won although it was himself he sacrificed, his ambitions, his future, if not his entire livelihood. His sermon, outright, concise, abrupt, centered upon two points: (1) Christ did not institute the Lord's Supper as a ritual for all time. True Christianity is moral, it has nothing to do with symbols and rites. Symbols and rites are good for pagans, Jews, and Orientals, but not for Boston gentlemen. People make too much ado over the person of Christ. There is only one God who lives in our souls, only one right, duty. (2) Even if it were proved, moreover, which is not certain, that Christ instituted the Lord's Supper, the fact that Ralph Waldo Emerson refused to accept it sufficed to make it useless. And off he went. In reality, he had left long before; he had long ceased to adhere with his heart to Unitarianism or to any church:

"I suppose it is not wise, not being natural, to belong to any religious party. In the Bible you are not directed to be a Unitarian, or a Calvinist or an Episcopalian. Now if a man is wise, he will not only not profess himself to be a Unitarian, but he will say to himself, I am not a member of that or of any party."

"As fast as any man becomes great, that is, thinks, he becomes a new party."

"A sect or party is an elegant incognito devised to save a man from the vexation of thinking."

Emerson had thrown down the gauntlet. He had left the Church; God remained to him. In a brief pantheistic poem he celebrated the presence of Emmanuel in himself. He shook off the yoke of all human opinions. He bade farewell to priests, books, and the world.

> I will not live out of me.
> I will not see with others' eyes;
> My good is good, my evil ill.
> . . . I will be
> Light-hearted as a bird and live with God.
> I find him in the bottom of my heart,

I hear continually his voice therein, . . .
From God it came. It is the Deity.

Ralph Waldo at thirty. In the face of his broken career, he considered sadly the exploits at his age of Alexander, Scipio, and Hannibal. He was most dejected and anxious when, in the winter of 1832, he set sail for Sicily, placing a whole ocean between the past and himself. Perhaps he would find his ideal in Europe.

CHAPTER VIII

*In Europe—The Land of the Gods—A
Disillusioned Traveler—Paris, the City
Beautiful—Parrots and Birds of Paradise*

A^{T THAT} time a long month was necessary for
a sailing vessel to make the trip between
America and Europe. One set out on a boat of
three or four hundred tons and arrived at one's
destination by the grace of God, bruised from
having suffered all the agonies of seasickness.
Emerson embarked on Christmas, 1832, on a little brig, the *Jasper*, bound for Malta. (O *Ile de
France*, O *Leviathan*!) There were five passen-
gers on board. Poor Ralph Waldo! Seasickness,
lack of comfort, and close quarters on board, the
promiscuities of the cabin explain to us his disillusioned philosophy of travel. Storms from the
moment of departure. The little vessel rolled,
pitched, snorted, played pranks. For thirty days
Ralph Waldo was condemned to undergo the con-

tact of people who counted their warts and rubbed
their gums. What punishment for an idealist! At
dawn, when the weather permits, he goes and
meditates "under the lee of the spencer-sheet."
His gaze loses itself in the heights; with his eyes
he follows the clouds which the west wind carries
toward Europe. He reads Milton and Goldoni,
but he has no sea legs; he is in a very bad humor,
and this takes away all his courage. No distractions on board. A sea-gull, a porpoise, the frolics
of the wind on the water, with the great monotonous murmur of the sea, which makes him
think of that of the soul. Ah, if a sea-shell could
amplify the mysterious inner voices! Wind,
moonlight dimmed with showers. What is a boat?
A prison with the chance of being drowned.
"What is a passenger? He is a much-enduring
man who bends under the load of his leisure."
The wind drums on the sails, those spots of white-
ness up there, like angels that carry the *Jasper*
among the clouds. The sea foams, boils, thunders,
whistles. In the damp *caboose* the enraptured
voyager has laid aside his Milton. He dreams,
chin in hand. What are the caprices of the waves
in comparison with the fluctuations of the human

heart? Emerson has not completely lost either his good temper or his sense of humor. He retains enough to tease his fellow travelers.

> What is it to sail
> Upon the calm blue sea,
> To ride as a cloud
> Over the purple floor
> With golden mists for company?
> And Day and Night are drest
> Ever in their jocund vest,
> And the water is warm to the hands,
> And far below you see motes of light
> By day and streams of fire by night . . .

He assures them that a sea voyage is the best preparation for the voyage of life. At last he is on the quays of Malta. But what on earth is he going to do there? It is no romantic nostalgia that has driven him to the Old World. The passionate pilgrims of Henry James, Daisy Miller, and Milly Theale will come later, with the *Innocents* of Mark Twain. Sicily, Naples, Rome, Florence, Venice—what has he come to seek on these shores where the traces of Byron, Shelley, and Goethe are still fresh, where Lamartine and Musset are still to come? Solitudes of the lagoon, gardens of Rome, beaches of Sorrento and Baia,

to others passions unleashed among divine landscapes, harmonious regrets cast to the centuries'
echoes, beautiful sins wreathed with lyricism,
temples, statues of the gods, groves, fountains,
feasts of the soul and the senses. Emerson is deaf
and blind to all this. As in Florida he regrets his
native hills, the ponds lost in the maple woods,
the white cottages on the lawns, the Common, the
Unitarian spire of Concord, the Musketaquid.
. . . An idealist, he suffers from a paradoxical
infirmity, the infirmity of the "already seen." A
man who has read too much Plato sees everywhere nothing but the shadows of the cave, weak
symbols of the divine ideas in his soul. *Il più nel
uno!* All in each! Everything is in everything,
and what is the use of risking seasickness in order
to find at the end of the world what one has left
at home? Scarcely on shore, he was disappointed.
If he had come to Sicily, it was to please his older
brother William, the scholar, the former student
at Göttingen. After a brief stay at Malta, where
he visited the tomb of Commander Villiers de
l'Isle Adam, his guide book in hand, he "did"
Sicily. And now, despite the poignant memories
of the crossing, we see him chartering a brigan-

tine to transport him to Syracuse, *Il Santissimo
Ecce Homo*, a crew of fourteen men, fourteen
blackguards, the captain included, who jeer at
the Yankee, envy him his dollars, curse, fight,
gulp down wine while eating salt fish and raw
onions—O Transcendentalism! At the landing
place, Quarantine and the Customs. Ah, yes,
voyages are useless and an outrage to the respectability of the Boston gentleman.

Emerson "does" Sicily like a conscientious
Cook's tourist. From his room in Syracuse he perceives the temple of Jupiter, Ætna, and the tomb
of Archimedes. He goes to drink at the fountain
of Arethusa; he eats the honey of Hymettus and
quail from the island of Ortygia. He has passed
without accident between Scylla and Charybdis.
The Sirens did not want him. What would they
have done with him? He sails on the Anapus,
gathers wild flowers at the fountain of Cyane. He
notes, he reports; but he has failed to pray the
gods and no shade has risen in his path. Ralph
Waldo, we love your transcendentalism, but a
single prayer to divine beauty, such as was made
once by Sylvestre Bonnard before the Temple of
Agrigentum, would not have killed you. You

were more of a pagan and more of a poet when you wrote to Plato that letter which he never received. At Palermo a strange adventure took place. Emerson let himself be picked up by a mysterious lady who carried him off in a barouche, whom he escorted to her house, who closed the door in his face and left him to pay the cabman. He came back all chilled in a rainstorm. (Is this from Sterne or Casanova?) The beggars and the guides spoiled Naples for him. The little street Arabs escorted him to Virgil's tomb, shouting at the top of their lungs, *C'e un mariolo!* He's a cheat! His ears and nostrils were offended. The rain hid from him the most beautiful sky in the world. He "did" Baia, Pozzuoli, still escorted by hangers-on. Lake Lucrino seemed to him less picturesque than the ponds in Concord woods. He saw Herculaneum as nothing but a fine workshop of destruction. En route for Rome!

Will the Eternal City awaken his enthusiasm? It scarcely seems so. Modern Rome is a desert; as for the other, the real Rome, every man worthy of the name bears it in his heart. Monuments and statues are powerless to evoke it; one must have a great soul. Emerson knows Rome by heart; he has *already seen it;* but everything which reveals the human genius and character, human morality, makes him vibrate in sympathy. He is interested, like Montaigne, only in what bears the form of human conditions; and he will never forget his walk among the Antiques, among the sovereign portrait busts of those who were the "first born of the world." He reads Byron at Tivoli; he evokes Childe Harold before the Dying Gladiator. His Puritanism was offended by the ceremony of the Palms in the Sistine, but he thrilled as he heard the "Miserere." The splendors of Saint Peter's overwhelmed him.

At Florence he went to the Opera and laughed at the ballets, which seemed ridiculous to him. He came from the country where legs were called "limbs," lest modesty be offended, but his flesh trembled before the tomb of Michelangelo, and he went to Santa Croce to pay his respects to Machiavelli and Galileo. The idea of "representative men" haunted him; art he conceived as part of nature, as an organic creation, and natural scenery was just as good in his eyes. After having paid a visit to the author of the *Imaginary Conversations*, Landor, of whom he sketches a malicious portrait, he set out for Venice. Romantic travelers, veil your faces before this blasphemer. Emerson compares Venice with New York. He calls it "a city for beavers," a prison, and passes on. Farewell to Italy. Through Lombardy and Switzerland he makes his way toward Paris, hastening to encounter at last his superman, beyond, on the desolate hills of Scotland. At Geneva he evokes Mme. de Staël and Rousseau. The profession of faith of the Savoyard Vicar in *Émile* and the chapters from *Germany* on the religion of the infinite have turned his head, as they have turned the heads of all young America. At Lausanne he piously picked some linden and acacia leaves in Gibbon's garden. From Geneva to Paris the road passed through Ferney. Emerson paid a visit to Voltaire, but it was not his fault—he pretended to have been dragged there by friends. On Thursday, June 20, at noon he entered Paris, the Paris of the Bourgeois Revolution. "France, France!" An end to postilions and arrogant Italian innkeepers. Here every one was full of hospitality. Behold him in *la belle ville*. He is all admiration. Of France hitherto he had known very little. He knew French and had even taught it to young ladies. He knew the great French authors; he was suckled on Montaigne and was not ignorant of the French philosophers. Since the wave of romanticism had broken across the ocean, French thought had crossed the water. The French and American revolutions had gone hand in hand and on the same principles. The American Fathers were full of the French ideologists. Toward 1820 Jacobinism had given place to Romanticism. Kant had dethroned Locke; Cousin, Helvétius, and Condillac. French spiritualism extended its influence beyond the sea. The practical spirit of the Yankees found what it wanted in the filterings and dosings which French philosophers had given German metaphysics. The beautiful, the good, and the true flattered their taste for utopias, and they were greedy for ideas seasoned with eloquence. Hence the success of Cousin and Jouffroy among them. The "spontaneous reason" and the "reflective reason" seemed to them clearer and more attractive than the *Vernunft* and the *Verstandt*, followed by the platoon of Categories at a goose-step. Emerson did not swear by the word of any master, but he had plundered many of the French:

historians of philosophy, like Gérando, ger-
manophiles and Kantians like Barchou de Pen-
hoën and Charles de Villiers, Orientalists like
Burnouf. The Catholic romanticism of Monta-
lembert and Lacordaire had no great echo in
America, but the Philanthropists were quite the
rage. Saint-Simon, Auguste Comte, and Fourier
have dotted the United States with phalansteries.
Emerson just now is preparing his *De Rerum
Natura*, and he is curious about science. Lamarck
and Geoffroy Saint-Hilaire started him out.
He went to the lectures of Thénard and Gay-
Lussac at the Sorbonne and to a meeting of the
Academy of Sciences where he saw Biot, Arago,
and other eminent men of the time all cramped in
their enormous cravats, their necks imprisoned in
starch, pensive, long-haired, romantic.

Ralph Waldo stopped at the Hotel de Mont-
morency on the Boulevard Montmartre. He
crossed the Pont Neuf and saluted King Henry,
who still held the tricolor which the Republic of
1830 had stuck in his hands. He went to the
Louvre, sauntered along the boulevards, was
amused by the harangues of the hawkers. At the
Théâtre Français he heard Talma and Mars in

Casimir Delavigne's *Les Enfants d'Edouard*.
Mars impressed him as a princess. The Sorbonne,
the theatre, the Academy, he missed nothing. He
even "did" the illustrious tombs at Père La
Chaise, where he espied the inscription on the
grave of an admirer of his dear Montaigne. He
was present at a great banquet in honor of
Lafayette and shook hands with the hero. (Lafayette, I am here!) The climax of his stay in
Paris was his visit to the Jardin des Plantes. Since
he had been meditating on his treatise on *Nature*,
zoology interested him more than the fine arts.
Science had begun by disturbing him; it seemed
to him to have little tenderness for idealists. It
was all very well to wish to make everything divine, but still one must ask permission of the different kingdoms of nature. The spirit soars aloft,
but matter bars the road. What place does Emerson reserve in his synthesis for the monkey, the
tiger, and the cockatoo? How shall we conceive
the universe without contradiction? It was to reply to these questions that he went to the Jardin
du Roi. Watch him before the parrots' cage, his
great nose resembling theirs. The artistic marvels
of Italy did not succeed in moving him, but here

his heart leaps with excitement. What marvelous raiment; what fabulous beauty! Their odd medley of colors makes him think of certain pictures of Raphael. He stopped dumfounded before the humming birds, those infinitesimal creatures of the air—crimson, emerald, silver, flame-colored, birds with epaulettes, birds like peacocks, birds of paradise, magnificent flies, glorious little mites of birds. And the black swans, the white peacocks, the ibises, the toucans, the red flamingoes, the vultures. With what does all this harmonize? Butterflies, shellfish, birds, fish, insects, serpents —who amuses himself at such a game? Who is deceived here? If only beasts appeared like beasts, but they ape man and act the angel. Emerson reflected on these occult affinities, these velleities of centipede, crocodile, carp, eagle, and fox, which stir obscurely in our depths. He was troubled, here in the midst of Paris, before these mysterious cages. It was high time to oppose Plotinus and Swedenborg to Lamarck. Meanwhile he continued his journey. He was going to see Coleridge, Wordsworth, and Carlyle.

Teufelsdroeckh, or Meeting the Infinite

EMERSON merely passed through London. He was impatient to meet his superman. Coleridge was quite close by, at Highgate, Wordsworth on the banks of his lakes, Carlyle in his Scottish eyrie. Emerson began with Coleridge. It was not to the poet of the *"Ancient Mariner"* that he was paying a visit, but to the author of *The Friend*, the *Biographia Literaria*, and the *Aids to Reflection*. For ten or fifteen years Coleridge had been making a great impression in America. He was, with Carlyle, the inspirer, the prophet of the new times. Carlyle was a thunderbolt, Wordsworth an Æolian harp, Coleridge a Babel. In his head were jumbled together the mystics and the philosophers; he united Kant to Swedenborg and built his system on fogs thicker than the "pea soup" of London. In smoky books,

104

without method and without structure, he heaped up marvelous intuitions and the wildest nonsense of the imagination. This poet was the most pedantic of men. He piled together definitions, aphorisms, corollaries, glosses. His logic reeled and tottered. He bristled with German metaphysics. Against Locke he let loose Kant. From the mathematicians, from those who split hairs into four, who take the world to pieces like a clock and give it God as a clock-maker, from those "mechanico-corpuscular" philosophers who excited the bile of Carlyle, he rescued apologetics. He refused to base the supernatural on nature. In order to prove that religion was true, he showed that it was human. He based his apologetics on a new classification of the faculties of the mind which he borrowed from Kant. *Verstandt—Vernunft, Understanding—Reason,* the judgment and the intuitive reason, upon these two opposed planes he placed nature and grace, and for us to rise from one to the other he skillfully caused religion to intervene. Impossible, according to him, to be a philosopher without being a Kantian or a Kantian without being a Christian and an Anglican. The new generations recognized themselves in this opposition of reason and the heart. Emerson knew well the bad habits and the follies of Coleridge, but he had profited greatly from his famous *distinguo*. He was anxious to see the man; he saw him—a stout little old fellow, all dressed in black, who toddled along on his walking-stick and tapped on his snuff box. A pinch, then another pinch. The black suit was all sprinkled with snuff, but the blue eyes sparkled with dreams and malice. Impossible to get in a word. Coleridge, a fervent Anglican, charged down upon the Unitarians whom Emerson had just left, and plunged in his sword to the hilt. Should he read some verses to his American visitor? Emerson no longer knew where to begin, he who was all incarnate reserve and discretion. . . . Ah, how odd these great men were!

The same scene in Windermere with Wordsworth, whom Emerson went to interview. A man who knew Rousseau by heart, whose clothes were reddened by the flames of revolution, who had left the tatters of his heart on the thorns of forbidden loves, this man had grown peaceful, he had meditated, he had prayed. He had taken the son of the century, the vagabond Childe Harold,

by the throat and held him over the baptismal
font. He had remade his virginity on the edge of
calm waters, on hills where the silence was hardly
troubled by the tinkle of cow-bells. A whole century was threatening revolt; he uttered the joys
of leisure, contemplation, silence, humility, the
joys of humble peasant life. He had exorcised the
landscapes, spiritualized love. His poetry was a
prayer. O Saint Wordsworth, half pantheist, half
Anglican, how reposeful your wise verses, white,
so white, and monotonous like orphans in procession! Hitherto the supernatural was only accessible to the soul; Wordsworth rendered it tangible
to the senses. Like St. Francis, he spoke to the sun,
to the moon, to the birds, to the flowers; and the
sun, the moon, the birds, and the flowers replied
to him. His Providence resembled a brave horti-
culturer, a peaceful squire, who destroys the caterpillars on his roses and goes botanizing with blue
glasses and a tin box on his back. His odes are like
hymns, his long poems like pious tracts. Emerson
had not enjoyed the intimate charm of Wordsworth, whose transcendentalism was too earthy
for him. He reproached him with treating the
world like a child who breaks his toys to see

what is inside them, but he had carried him in his pockets on many walks and he had imitated him a great deal in his adolescent verses. And there he was at Rydal Mount, in one of the most beautiful and peaceful landscapes in the world. But how grotesque his Wordsworth was! He inveighed against Goethe. He scarcely saw his visitor. The sublime old man, even *he* made a fool of himself, made himself ridiculous standing up and declaiming his verses like a child on examination day. Human, all too human; it was high time to go and see Carlyle.

Here the bond had been formed long since, and the admiration was almost without reserve. He to whom Emerson was paying his visit was the Carlyle of Weissnichtwo, cloistered on the desolate moors of Dunscore, the Scottish Carlyle of the days before fame and dyspepsia, but whose roar the world had already heard. He had launched in the *Edinburgh Review* his famous iconoclastic essays and had engraved with vitriol and gall the portrait of man in *Sartor Resartus*. Be prudent, O benign Emerson; do not awaken the ire of Teufelsdroeckh. You have need of all your Yankee cunning to penetrate the den without danger. But Emerson is on his guard and he knows his man. Under the lightning and the thunder he has recognized an ideal like his own, with a force and an irony that he lacks. Carlyle is a volcano, but he too has "hitched his wagon to a star." With a stroke of his pen like the stroke of a hammer on an anvil, he forges sarcasms and truths that sizzle like red-hot iron in the tub. He strikes to the right, to the left, cutting and thrashing. He brandishes the club of Thor. What does he attack? Deceit, hypocrisy, cold calculation, the State, the Church, traditions, systems, everything that retards the advance of the soul struggling with matter. Emerson has read in the *Edinburgh Review* the "Characteristics" and the "Signs of the Times." He has meditated upon *Sartor Resartus*, a veritable breviary of transcendentalism which he is going to have published in the United States. Ah, certainly this is not his own way of thinking and writing, but the pilgrimage of Teufelsdroeckh, native of Weissnichtwo, interests him deeply. Carlyle has resuscitated Bunyan's Christian and led him by force of sarcasms toward the truth. The kingdom of appearances, the country of the Everlasting No—with what passion, what contagious savagery, what transcendent irony he drives him, and the age as well, toward the Everlasting Yea! O ye tailors, ye sceptics and hypocrites, off with your coats, and let the Truth make itself known! Ye pettifoggers, hold yourselves together, ye and your robes four times too big. Tartuffe, gather together your little cloak or beware! The lightning will flash forth and reveal you naked as worms.

Faith had disappeared from the world; spiritual energy had run dry. For want of good will, was it necessary to restore the stake and the guillotine? The infinite disregarded takes its revenge and calls itself Cromwell, Faust, Voltaire, or Robespierre. The Devil is preferable to Nothingness. Come, off with our masks and let us salute the day that is being born. The soul is eternally young and living. Before us opens Time without end. "Come, to work! To act is to know. What use remaining in one's chair planning, reasoning? Come, up! To work! Act, do something, and a new light will appear to you!" In the beginning was the Act. Such was Carlyle's *Marseillaise*. Shy as he was, Emerson had vibrated in unison. He came to Dunscore to see how this demon of a man was made.

He had crossed the Highlands in a continual downpour without a hat, a handkerchief knotted about his head, through the Trossachs and the lakes, over the uplands pink with heather. By Dumfries and Carlisle he reached Dunscore, a hole lost on the moors. Teufelsdroeckh lived there like a hermit, and Jane Carlyle kept the "sick giant" company. She was not yet the drudge of later years. They seemed a happy household, but Thomas was consumed with ambition. His body alone was in Scotland; from the height of his moors he looked toward London. He was thirty-eight years old—eight years older than Emerson —a big body, a great mop of hair, a bushy brow. He was full of life and humor, and he poured out anecdotes with a strong Scottish accent. He was without pity for his contemporaries, full of contempt for men of letters, and social iniquity drew from him heart-rending cries. He was all ejaculations and sarcasms. Emerson had fallen upon him from heaven. The Carlyles kept him for the night. The next day Thomas and Ralph Waldo

went for a walk on the moors whence they could
see the lake country in the distance. The irritated
giant calmed himself; he talked about God and
the immortality of the soul. With his finger he
pointed out to Emerson the spire of the humble
church of Dunscore, an homage rendered to the
soul by vanished generations. Come, all ideals are
not dead. . . . But suddenly piercing cries came
from the cottage. Thomas and Ralph were
snatched from their contemplation. It was St. An-
thony's pig which had escaped and which Carlyle brought back with great difficulty to the
house. Hear the laughter of Mephistopheles, and
let you lettered men of London carefully stop
your ears. "Ay, me!" But time was passing: all
human joy is brief. They talked about Goethe and
the German romantic literature, which Carlyle
fervently admired. Jane Carlyle showed her guest
the necklace which the author of *Faust* had sent
her. Emerson gave an attractive picture of America. Everything was in movement and ferment
over there; the young people hankering for the
ideal, waiting for a master. Why should not Carlyle come to the United States, take, for example,

the editorship of a great review, like the *Edinburgh Review*? If Carlyle wished, Emerson would gladly be his agent and find him a publisher in Boston. . . . "Ay, me! Ay, me!" All this was very tempting; Teufelsdroeckh was not rich. He would see, he would see. And Ralph Waldo left as he had come. Carlyle watched him disappearing like an angel over the hill. This time Emerson had not been disappointed. He had found his man; this was a friendship until death.

In September he waited for the boat at Liverpool. They showed him the first locomotives and predicted to him the crossing of the Atlantic by steam. The return was melancholy. The traveler summed things up. On the whole, Europe disappointed him. We see him returning toward America, desiring and calling her. He was going to preach a gospel; he was going to found a new religion. Meanwhile, his situation was hardly encouraging. He was alone once more, and he had burned his bridges behind him. What was he going to become? He was seized with discouragement; he would gladly have let himself slip to the bottom of the sea. But he had his Milton in his pocket, and he set to work again on his *Journal*. He prepared his *De Rerum Natura*, his little manual of pantheism. He thought of the Jardin des Plantes, of the humming-birds and the parrots. Land! land! Here he is in New York.

CHAPTER X

Fire in the Powder Magazine

A LL the youth of America was awaiting Emerson on the shore, bearing palms, the young
people, women especially, all longing to see the
man who had met Coleridge and Wordsworth and
who had spent the night at Carlyle's. The America of the 'Thirties did not seem gay to the young.
In politics its revolutions were finished. The great
Utopians were dead. The spirit of Franklin's
"Poor Richard," "a penny saved is a penny
earned," had taken the place of idealism. No more
adventures, no more great deeds. The great statesmen with broad views, the Washingtons, Hamil-
tons, Jeffersons, Paines, had been succeeded by
the Calhouns, Jacksons, Websters, practical men,
politicians, demagogues. Independence once declared and the peril of foreign intervention
averted, the United States had relapsed into ego-

ism, every one for himself, the North utilitarian, the distant West scarcely settled, in the South the canker of slavery. For thirty years, up to the War of Secession, there was no great cause, no appeal to generous emotions. The time of heroism was quite gone. Channing had set things going, and the young people had listened to him; but his idealism was very vague, and Puritan repression was still in force.

The *mal du siècle* in America seems paradoxical. Did not the young Americans have liberty and space? Did they not dwell in that New World of which the disillusioned of the Old World had dreamed so much? They had the whole future before them—a virgin land, an immense continent to conquer. No doubt; but they lacked inner liberty and self-confidence. Young America was timorous; at bottom, it remained Calvinist. Liberal as it was, Unitarianism was not a religion for youth. It distrusted enthusiasm, the emotions, mysticism; it was the product of cold reason. While all the world about them discussed banks, tariff duties, navigation acts, agrarian questions, the young Americans read Rousseau, Mme. de Staël, Kant, Herder, Coleridge, Wordsworth,

Chateaubriand, and Carlyle. They would happily abandon a life in which action was not associated with dream. The intellectual and moral life was dead, art non-existent, literature timid or second-hand. Washington Irving was a dilettante of the school of English writers. Whatever was great in the United States was in revolt. Fenimore Cooper was an exile in the interior; he turned his back on the world and buried himself in the primitive forest on the track of Leatherstocking. All of the others were engulfed in the sadness that continued to weigh even on the writers of the Golden Age. The most beautiful poem of Bryant, the veteran of American poetry, was a solemn hymn to Death. Edgar Allan Poe opened his imaginary palaces to Solitude and Silence. He took refuge on the Island of the Fairy and the domain of Arnheim to escape from the surrounding mediocrity and ugliness. He took for his companions sleep-walkers and ghosts: Ligeia, Morella, Annabel Lee. Later, to forget reality, Hawthorne and Melville descended into the depths of the fantastic and visionary. Belles-lettres had killed true literature. The people who wrote in prose and verse imitated the English

117

writers. Good judges no doubt declared that the Americans were more "intuitive," more "metaphysical," than the English, but added that they were all ashamed of themselves. They cut the American pine on the model of the English yew; they sang of Ilissus and the Mincius instead of the picturesque Indian rivers, the Susquehanna, the Aroostook, the Willimantic. They sacrificed the thrush and the bobolink to the lark and the nightingale, which does not exist in America. In the preface to *The Scarlet Letter*, Hawthorne excuses himself for romancing with provincial chronicles and falling back upon ghost stories, but there is no romance in America. The surrounding platitudes and philistinism, moreover, render life very hard for artists. The acrid and plentiful cabbage of mediocrity sprawls out and spreads its fleshy shadow over the beds of violets which it smothers.

Channing had denounced this famine. He pleaded eloquently in favor of the national literature, the literature of emotion. Nourished on Mme. de Staël, he refused to separate the destiny of literature from that of religion. The United States had no philosophers and thinkers worthy of it. A new type of humanity, of civilization, was developing in the United States. Literature must become inspired. Meanwhile, there was poverty of emotion, and the younger generations were in despair. People in America had never been so sad.

The youth of 1830, like the *enfants du siècle* in Europe, wanted to be all or nothing. They lamented the uselessness of existence. Repose weighed upon them. Everything they heard, everything they saw or did left them dissatisfied. The coal grates, the sofas, the table tops, the Oriental rugs—ah, how weary they were of these bourgeois trappings! They courted the autumn; they listened to the dead leaves singing their funeral song; their hearts responded to the rain that dripped on the damp soil. If only the autumn of their days would arrive; if only they might sleep for as many centuries as there were seconds, like Rip Van Winkle on the mountain, in order to find upon awakening a new world. They envied the Indian turning like a demon upon his victim and tossing his hair, dark as the crow's wing, while a virgin like Atala smiled at him with a smile pale as the moon. They dreamed of strange metamor-

phoses and abandoned themselves to the mysterious call of the wild, the attraction of the
elementary forces that brought them close to
primitive man. Oh, rise, storms so longed-for,
and bear these Renés of America to a faraway
isle where roses bloom, where the grass is soft and
the clouds of gold, the land of the song of Mignon: *Kennst du das Land*. . . .

People longed for magnificent palaces where
the setting sun tinged crimson the pictures and the
statues, while the sweet music of a lute resounded
and a snowstorm raged in at the windows. Anything rather than a so-called respectable life,
without a spark of true fire. Italy, Italy! land of
light and love, blue sky, burning sun! Ah, could
it but melt the ice stored up in their puritan
hearts! If only the Mayflower pilgrims had
brought with them into the wilderness the cave
of Father Aubry, the cross, incense, tapers, the
bell and holy water. Emerging from their tem-
pestuous moods Chactas and Atala would at last
have found rest. . . .

Such were the pathetic appeals of a disillusioned youth. The *mal du siècle* was grave. The
need of going abroad, of escape, went as far as

madness and suicide, especially among the women, such as that pagan and enigmatical Leila (introduced to the readers of the *Dial* by Margaret Fuller), with her equivocal virginity, an American Ophelia who ran through the woods half-naked, bathed at midnight in icy ponds, seduced and enticed the desires of men, and drove exaltation to the point of sadism and the taste for murder. How commonplace was America and how far away Europe! Joy, love, emotions, travel! It was high time for Emerson to return from Europe and preach to these children of the age in despair. To these dolorous brothers, it appears, he did not come back with full hands. He showed only an indifference bordering on contempt for the landscapes and the monuments of the Old World. In the midst of traveling he declaimed against travel and eulogized the common and ordinary. To historic sublimity he opposed homely sublimity and contentment with little, that very reality which most wounded the young. On his departure from Italy he had forbidden himself on principle to purchase the smallest *objet d'art*. He conducted himself, in short, like a Puritan.

No doubt; but he had his secret. He was going to give confidence to American youth by ways that were his alone. He was going to teach it the things that are and not those that seem to be and lead it with him to the peaks of the ideal, to those lofty mountains from which he had seen all things transformed. To human beings astray in the domain of circumstances he was going to reveal the cause of causes, the infinite, the supreme reality. He was going to snatch them away from idolatries, rules, narrow observances. Poor human beings who confound the ocean with its shores, the creator of the world with the world, force with its limits, Emerson is going to liberate in you the inner man, the man of the eternal sovereign voice who slumbers now. He is going to unloose spiritual energy. Property, government, religion, education, literature, let us boldly denounce everything that does not conform to the constitution of the spirit. The era of discoveries is not gone; like Columbus, let us steer to the West and discover new worlds. The universe is new; it has not yet been explored. Not a line has been written. In spite of all the poets there are in the world, our first genuine emotions in the woods and on the edge of the lake have not been sung. It is for us, who have been the first to feel it, to be its first poets. Let us remove the younger generation from calculation, from utilitarianism, and reveal to them the depths of intuition. Salvation is not in the Bible but in the humble docility of thought and heart, in self-abandonment to the great universe. The state, the school, the church, the factory, the charitable institutions, these are only mechanisms which a breath of the soul carries away. Let us revise the grandeur of our heroes. Nothing in history is permament or definitive. Society has only a secondary importance. It is the cuckoo who lays her eggs in the nest of other birds.

This was Emerson's thought in all its force, his secret thought which he confided only to his *Journal*, under cover of "respectful silence," but which finds its echo in his speeches. The problems that preoccupy young America he had experienced and suffered. The young would like to reconcile the ideal with the real and conceive the universe without contradictions. But had this not been Emerson's chief concern ever since he began to think? They hesitated between being and seeming and sought true liberty. But had not Emerson sacrificed everything to find it? The Americans wished to conquer the world; but did they know the world, and did they really know themselves? It is impossible to dispense with the culture of the Occident. But how be at once ancient and modern, European and American? To all these problems Emerson had a ready reply, a reply that was transcendental, but rich in everyday applications. He was no doctor either of letters or of science, but for years he had hoarded his reflections and questioned philosophers and scientists. A little innate science, moreover, is not displeasing to the "intuitive" Americans. He had lost his pulpit, but that was no objection. America was peopled with free institutions, universities, athenæums, lyceums, and the vogue of lectures had begun. Emerson would be a lecturer. He made his début at Boston on natural history, great men, English literature. He got through this very well, and the public flocked to hear him. He had found his medium. The *Essays*, the *Representative Men*, the *Conduct of Life* were there in

germ. He was fluent, eloquent, persuasive, a
scholar and poet; his force of conviction made up
for any coldness and stiltedness he may have had.
From a preacher he had become a philosopher and
moralist. His reign had begun.

CHAPTER XI

Sursum Corda!

IN HIS lectures Emerson seemed to be cheating the enthusiasm of the young. He tackled problems from within. It was not with oratory but with his habitual serenity that he preached the new gospel. His was not the forceful manner of Carlyle. He caught flies with honey. No lightning, no thunder. Instead of lashing and goading them, he made them think simply, familiarly. He admitted his audience to the very heart of his reflections. Hitherto the Americans had been fed on eloquence; once in the rôle of lay preacher, Emerson renounced his weakness, rhetoric. Nothing constrained him any longer, and the atmosphere of the lecture was no more that of the meeting-house. Of a sudden he had become a moralist. He neither fulminated nor declaimed; he persuaded by an oblique indirect path, by the path of intuition, through what he called the coincidence between the first and third thoughts. He made only remote allusions to the burning questions of the day. He established himself in the midst of transcendentalism; he arrived *via* the air, fell from the clouds with flashing glances into the soul, its intimate life, the analogies that bind together thought and the real world, into great men, into history—all this gravely, serenely, with a perfect indifference to the clamors of the times.

But from all this was born a great calm, a deep peace. Doubts melted away, souls knew how to conduct themselves. Hyperbolical as he might be, Emerson remained clear, practical, almost earthy. His metaphysics, as he said, had daily uses. This poet was a moralist. The young Americans wished to conquer the world, but what is the world? They have nothing but heroism in their heads, but what is a hero? In regard to nature and history Emerson preserves a sovereign independence. He admired it but he thought still more of converting it to his own use, of annexing it. This is the method of compensations. The world is the appanage of the soul, its satellite. Between man and the universe there is a pre-established harmony, an affinity, a correspondence—not final causes, for the Emersonian universe is self-sufficient and looks not beyond itself. Emerson set out to prove nothing; he explored the roadways of thought, the secrets of knowledge. Nature is the reverse of the soul; soul and nature are the two aspects of a single portrait. Thus he made the universe which is at our feet familiar and human, and he did the same thing for history. He humanized the hero. Properly speaking, there is no history; history is only biography. It is a school of exaltation. The great events of the past are for our use; history is made for us, in order that we may live it. It is our task, as we read it, to make ourselves Greek, Roman, king, martyr, or hangman, to fix these sublime images in the concrete reality of our experience.

Thus Emerson went along calmly, simply, never hurrying. From all this appeared a lofty and unique point of view, the famous *distinguo* of Coleridge, the opposition between dry reason and intuition. To soulless science Emerson opposed the revelations of the thinking heart, about which everything gravitates. And see how in hearing him his listeners understood and corrected themselves. They were seeking the beautiful and the good; they found the true still more precious. They formed a taste for the inner life. If in all this metaphysics there were something too remote, Emerson descended from the heights and translated it to them in familiar terms, for the idealist in him never lost hold of the practical Yankee.

The Americans, however, love set speeches, and they wished to have a direct contact with the man whom they already called their master. Emerson's reputation was increasing, especially in the universities and seminaries. Harvard did not forget its old pupil. In July, 1838, the Phi Beta Kappa society, foremost of those thousand and one university fraternities that swarm in America, invited Emerson to discourse on the American scholar. This address was a challenge and a personal confession. Too many books, too many libraries, too much meditation under the lamp; Emerson wanted men of action, living men. He addressed himself to those who guide the soul, the clergymen, professors, lawyers, and he signed for them a declaration of independence. American pride and optimism shone through his speech.

Books, nature, history, he subordinated all to man. He armed the scholar for the struggles of exist- ence, preached intellectual courage to him. He wished him a rough suffering existence like his own. Experience is the great professor. One must rely on himself. Why should one not rely on him- self? The soul is eternal, the world has hardly been created. Emerson welcomed the new times, he saluted with joy the revolutions which would open a new field to individual initiative, he cele- brated the majesty, the sovereignty of man, king of the universe. *De l'audace, encore de l'audace!* He turned toward America, he made her ashamed of her servility. Too long had she lent her ear to Europe. *Sursum corda!* Times had changed. American youth was disillusioned; let it regain confidence. Arise, boldness, courage, and the uni- verse is ours. But let us be ourselves. "We will walk on our own feet, we will work with our own hands, we will speak our own minds." Let America doubt not; the divine spirit is with her. She will be the first of nations.

The same self-confidence, the same imperial- ism was revealed a few months later in the speech on literary ethics delivered before the students of

Dartmouth, the picturesque New Hampshire college. The subject of this oration was again intellectual courage, but he had become more incisive, more earnest. He denounced again the intellectual timidity of his country. America had disappointed the hope of the world. He reproached her for her grace without grandeur, her self-effacement before Europe. He called her a "vase of fair outline, but empty." To fill the vase he promised the scholar the help of the whole universe, and he turned over to him nature and history. No great name should impose upon us; the great men transmit to us only what belongs to us. Charles V, Bayard, Scipio, Pericles are dead, but the world where they lived is the same. We must make the least of our days equal in prowess to theirs. To be great, let us give ourselves joyously to the universe, to the divine circulations, and take on the eternal youth of the world. If we remain faithful to ourselves, the universe will not fail us. Here Emerson grew excited, and with a brazenness altogether American he gave us what did not belong to him. "I give you the universe a virgin to-day." He compared the world to the American forest, open before the explorer. All was new, all young, history, philosophy, religion, politics. The soul was greater than the world.

Tartarinade, one would say, or bluff. How much farther along are the Americans! Just now Emerson compared them to empty vases, now he exhorts them to fill themselves from their own vacuity. The peroration of the Dartmouth address seems to contradict the exordium. After having warmed to a red heat the interest of his listeners, Emerson stops short. He has just cited Bonaparte to them as an example, and now he preaches to them the virtues of the average man, the "penny saved is a penny earned" of Franklin. Is this timidity, weakness, or prudence? It is rather, perhaps, the counsel of a high wisdom. Great flights do not suffice for Emerson. Others, in order to please, begin with austere counsels and end with fine transports; he follows the opposite method, lyricism first, morality afterward. He is a practical idealist.

CHAPTER XII

The Revolt of Uriel

A MONG many others this kindly man had unloosed two great scandals. In 1836 he published anonymously and under an azure cover a
little manual of pantheism entitled *Nature*. Under the common ægis of Lamarck and Plotinus,
this was a reply to his doubts in the Jardin des
Plantes, a *De Rerum Natura*, a poem in prose.
With his habitual serenity and without further
ado, he gave here the quintessence of his meditations and reading. The outer world embarrassed
him; it baffled his idealism. Emerson adroitly
juggled it away. His tactics toward the universe
might be called caressing. He began by adopting
the outer world and doing it the honor of believing it real. In a series of contemplations entitled
"Commodity," "Beauty," "Discipline," he declared that he embraced the universe. But he did

133

not remain faithful to it for long. In the chapter on language the outer world begins to evaporate. It is no longer anything but a dictionary of metaphors for the use of poets. And suddenly, disloyally, Emerson gives it the slip. Three final stages, where the lyricism ascends proportionally as we approach the dénouement, plunge us into the heart of pantheism, of mythology. The world is nothing more than a fiction of the mind. It is man who has created the sun, woman the moon. In the age of innocence the universe was the irradiation of our thoughts, but through our fault it has petrified on the surface. The universe crushes man, its inventor. Emerson does not consider this fall as definitive. In a final overflow of poetry he announces the eternal youth of the soul and of the universe. What the discursive reason has destroyed, let divine instinct reconstruct. Let the rejuvenated soul render to the world its primitive beauty and its unity. Let wisdom and love join hands and transfigure the ever youthful, the plastic universe.

There is recognizable beneath these beautiful myths a translation of the Christian dogma. It was Calvin set to music and transposed by Plato,

Plotinus, and Swedenborg. The theologians have
not been mistaken on the bearing of this Purana
and this new fashion of interpreting the dogma
of the fall and the redemption. Emerson juggles
away God as serenely as the world. For Jehovah
he boldly substitutes Prometheus. In the land of
the Puritans such audacity and poetry had never
been seen, but a whole generation of youth
thrilled at the voice of the Enchanter.

"Be bold, be bold, and ever more be bold!" Now
a still more formidable storm arose, and the scene
took place in the very heart of the holy of holies.
The chief problem that occupied young America
was the religious problem. Religion is always the
chief concern of the Americans; it is an obsession
with them. In vain had they enfranchised themselves from Calvinism; they had religion, mysticism, in their blood. Everything was changing
about them, everything had become modernized.
Science, history, exegesis had made gigantic
progress. It was necessary to adapt Christianity to
the needs of modern times, but nobody wished to
touch the essence of religion. The age of intuition, of introspection, of sentiment, of fervor, the
great revolution accomplished by Kant had over-

thrown all the disciplines. It was from the soul,
from the conscience that everything took its departure and to it that everything returned. They
wished no longer to be religious from without,
but from the very depths of the heart. The wave
of romantic immanence had carried all before it.
The seminaries, the universities, the Church were
full of heretics who had read Rousseau, Mme.
Guyon, Mme. de Staël, Herder, Cousin, Benjamin Constant, and the German critics. About
Channing, and less respectful than he to Christian
institutions, rough athletes arose. The élite clung
to cold Unitarianism, the crowds to the somber
theology of Calvin, but neither the one nor the
other still satisfied the bolder minds. Dogma was
cracking on all sides. Insufficient emphasis was
laid on free inquiry. What was the good of shak-
ing off the yoke of the Church only to subject
oneself to the Bible? What good was it to enlarge
Protestantism in order to preserve the externals
of ancient superstitions? The newcomers proclaimed that the church was too small for the
soul; man was greater than the Bible. Protestantism had broken with the Church to chain itself
to the Scriptures, Biblical criticism had repudiated

the Scriptures to return to the one and only Christ, but the modern soul denied all authority. It reduced Christianity to morality, and it declared the latter natural, human, instinctive.

Thus American Protestantism shed its skin for a new one; it reconciled itself with the age and retained from the religions of the past only that which flattered its aspirations. For a new people a new soul, a new religion. The Americans wanted a rational, active, optimistic Protestantism, and to modernize it they introduced into it all the Utopias, the Kantian Anglicanism of Coleridge, the Puritan pantheism of Carlyle, the spiritualism of Cousin, the religion of Humanity of the Phalansterians and Comte. On all sides they were groping and seeking, but everything came back to the problem of the soul and its fervor.

All these problems Emerson had solved in his heart in favor of the complete autonomy of conscience. Let us recall his doubts, his recantations, his revolts. He had reflected a great deal on the religious problem since he had left the pastorate and still more since his return from Europe. He had crossed the ocean to find a new

messiah, a new faith. He had come back disillusioned. The spiritual needs of America were not
those of the Old World. Criticism of Christian
institutions was familiar to him. From day to
day he had given himself to it, making no noise
over it, not letting it become known. He understood American Protestantism very well. He had
been a preacher and a pastor. His criticisms, as he
felt the influence of the times and of his own experience, grew more and more severe. In Christianity he saw a blind alley, an obstacle, an aspect
of the famous surface petrification which he was
denouncing. The needs and powers of the soul
are infinite, and Christianity is limited. It lives
by the letter and not by the spirit. What is the
Christian religion on the scale of the infinite?
Christianity claims to monopolize the divine, subject it to formulas, to rites. Between God and
ourselves it interposes the divine persons, ceremonies, the sermon, prayer. Of what use are
meeting-houses if God is present in our hearts?
The praying-desk, vestries, prayers, hymn tunes,
why mask the infinite for us in this way? Was
Jesus truly the perfect and divine type of man?
Emerson doubted it. Neither art nor science nor

nature interested him. Socrates, Shakespeare, Laplace were more complete than he. A prudent citizen and clever man, Emerson went to church every Sunday, and the ignorance of the ministers alarmed him. In order to believe in Christianity you would think it was necessary to doubt men. Christ announced our grandeur; the ministers talked only of the grandeur of Christ. There was no longer anything human in the Christian meeting-house. Emerson wished he were deaf and regretted that the collar of his overcoat was so narrow when the minister offered prayer. Glacial abstractions fell from the height of the pulpit. Religion was a hateful desert. The Church did not respect the soul of the faithful. It set actions on one side and responsibilities on the other. It was carnal and sensual.

The time was gone when he revealed to Murat the providential harmonies between Christianity and society. Doubtless there was a certain relationship between it and ourselves, but from the study of man one could deduce a still higher relationship.

The further he advanced on this path, the more Nietzschean Emerson became. To these criticisms he replied with fervent affirmations which we know already concerning the presence of God in us. Why set bounds to the shoreless ocean? Would not Jesus be more loved if he were worshiped less? Of what use are the Scriptures if God speaks to the depths of our hearts? What matter whether revelation is plenary or secondary if it is present and eternal within us? The heart of Christianity is the heart of all the philosophies, Stoic, Mohammedan, Buddhist; the soul of truth is everywhere. What is the use of chaining oneself to one Christ when there are a thousand?

Hitherto Emerson had kept his heresies to himself, but now the opportunity arose to spread them abroad. He had been dreaming for some time of addressing a manifesto to the American clergy. His heart was full of it, he could no longer restrain himself. The bomb was ready. On July 15, 1838, he attacked the Bastille. The theological students at Harvard had invited him to speak to them of the duties of clergyman and religion, and he yielded to their call.

This time it was to a clerical audience that he addressed himself, in the Unitarian chapel at Cambridge. There were two clear-cut camps in

the assembly: the young, all fire, all flame, and
the old, whose brows were wrinkled behind their
spectacles. The latter had not forgiven Emerson
for his little manual of pantheism, and ever since
the scandal of 1832 they had kept their eyes on
him. Emerson would be prudent, never fear; he
had the wisdom of the serpent and the innocence
of the dove. In his *Essays* he will follow the
ascending method, the andante at the beginning,
the allegro at the end; but today and once more
he would sacrifice æsthetics to prudence—first the
dive into the heart of immanence, the appeal to
emotions (so much the worse for the theologians
of the first rank!), then a slow, methodical,
adroit, and practical escape toward morality. The
moralist would reassure timorous or prejudiced
people whom the poet would horrify. A strange
homily, this pantheistic sermon in a Christian
meeting-house. Emerson discussed religion without uttering a word on the Scriptures, discussed
the divine without mentioning the name of God.
His sermon contained neither Biblical verses nor
prayer. It was a purely Kantian sermon. From
the start Emerson takes us to entirely new land;
he appeals to sentiment and the imagination;

he plunges his listeners into the midst of nature. He celebrates summer; he brings incense and flowers into the cold halls of the Protestant meeting. He evokes crystalline nights lit with stars. What then is this mysterious universe and what are we in its infinite bosom? The sublimity of the starry skies over our head is only a reflection of moral splendors. The infinite in our conscience responds to the infinite in the universe, the laws of the soul confirm those of nature. When a man says "I ought," the whole universe approves and runs to him. The sentiment of the sublime in nature and the soul is the true religious sentiment, innate and accessible to all men. Once upon the heights, Emerson turns to historic Christianity. Who would pretend to limit the infinite rights and privileges of the soul? People have made the divine the exclusive monopoly of certain individuals, certain epochs. What a mistake, and what an outrage to the right of the soul to dispose of itself. Let us take the person of Jesus. If he has merited the title of the "Son of God," it is through the unique fashion in which he has been able to exalt in himself the moral sense. His miracles were his wonderful virtues, his feelings, and his admirable habits, but history has made of him an Osiris and an Apollo. People limit the divine to Jesus; they impose upon the faithful the imitation of him who said to all men, "Be ye perfect even as your heavenly father is perfect." There is only one commandment: the loyalty that every one owes to himself and the worship of the God hidden in our hearts. Let us stir up great feelings in ourselves, and we shall become Christs. Religion is not a command from without; it is a growth in ourselves. Church folk who pretend to announce the truth, be ye first inspired, and may the subject of your sermons be the infinite grandeur of the human soul associated with the whole world. Sunsets and sunrises, wandering clouds, bird-songs and the scent of flowers, summon to you all the spectacles of nature. You who pretend to dictate to men their duty, be ye human yourselves, live, love, suffer, sympathize, and do not relegate religion to the museum of the curiosities of other days. You say that God *has spoken*, that He *has created*. Do not place the divine in the past, but in the present and actual. Say that God *creates* and that He *speaks*. The wisdom of

143

the soul defies all wisdom; the soul is higher than the universe. It is free and admits no master.

Whereupon the prudent and practical Emerson felt the need of lowering his tone, for fear of seeing the roof of the sanctuary cave in. As he had done in his discourse on the American scholar and his Dartmouth address, he stopped his flight short as if he were sorry for the insufficiencies of his audience. No, he would not ask them to found a new religion, but he wished them to breathe a new life into the old one, incorporating into it all beautiful sentiments. Religion, morality, science, love, beauty, all are one. . . .

Let us confess it, this finale is rather weak and disconcerting. One would say that Emerson did not have the courage of his convictions up to the end. He was much more courageous, much sharper in his intimate notes.

Or rather was he somewhat short of breath? In any case this caused a great storm. The young were thrilled; they had found the road to Damascus. Emerson made disciples, but the old guard did not disarm. Emerson had scandalized it. It was especially angry with him for having nourished and unloosed his heresy under shelter of its own broadmindedness. And immediately it made him feel it. Emerson had a horror of controversies; it was especially repugnant to him to break with his old masters and friends. But it was too late; he had thrown down the gauntlet to God; he had denied the church by substituting for it his own personal pride. As he had treated science in *Nature*, so he now relegated religion to the depths of the unconscious. The theologians were in arms; they denounced what they called "the latest form of infidelity." Emerson kept quiet. He had uttered what he felt to be the truth, *his* truth, and everything was said; but in his inner depths the storm was still raging. For the first time he had run against public opposition. Here he was, the silent and benign adorer of the Oversoul, criticized and calumniated in the newspapers and his name thrown to the crowd. . . . He found himself through his own principles disarmed before his opponents. Had he not preached the right to every one to what he believed his personal truth? He was caught in his own snare. For the first time the optimist Emerson found men evil. Sarcasms were born under his pen. What was the use of running with the hares and hunting with the

hounds? No one was grateful to him for the
damper he had put on his own lyricism. . . . His
career as a lecturer was badly compromised, and
what welcome could he prepare for his friend
Carlyle, whom he was expecting? He would be
obliged to give up the trip. Emerson was exasperated; he retired within himself. The angel
Uriel had doubted and revolted in Heaven itself.
The gods had veiled their faces but nothing
seemed changed in the firmament. Uriel was
silent. He retreated apparently in order, but revolt still rumbled in the depths of his heart and
the echo of his voice still troubled the celestial
spheres. The gods trembled on their thrones. A
new order was born with a new future. *Non
serviam!* Emerson became obstinate, but fleeing
from human malice he retired into the desert.

PART TWO

Saturnalia of Faith

CHAPTER I

Musketaquid

CONCORD was a charming desert—Concord, Peace. Emerson had already felt its charm. Upon his return from Europe in the autumn of 1834 he had taken refuge in the Old Manse, an ancient lonely cottage (to the north of the town) hung with moss, with a wild garden, pines, and willows, in a hollow by the river. The house unceremoniously turned its back to the street. It was a wooden cottage such as are common in America, with dark rooms, garrets full of cobwebs, hidden corners, dormers, shadows behind the square-paned windows. How often had Emerson as a boy come to dream there during his visits to good Dr. Ripley, his step-grandfather. It was in a room of the Old Manse that he had written *Nature* and it was through these windows that the charm of Concord had penetrated to him. One breathes it in his book.

The house was full of mysteries and memories. Nathaniel Hawthorne, who has immortalized it in one of his works, came there some time later to spend his honeymoon. If one may believe him the house was haunted. Rainy evenings when Hawthorne was reading and Sophia Hawthorne was sewing in the lamplight, they heard the rustle of a cloak. At night Sophia woke up with a start and swore that something had brushed her shoulder. There were two ghosts in the Old Manse, the minister who revisited his study perhaps to finish some sermon hastily thrown together, and the hired maid who was heard at midnight handling the dishes which she had badly washed while alive. In Concord they believed in dreams and Emerson himself was not indifferent to them. Did he not like to repeat that there was a sort of mirage in the atmosphere of the place?

Concord was a vast park, at once a museum and a garden. Its landscapes were full of history. Peter Bulkeley, the ancestor, the founder had well chosen the site. Fields, woods, hills, a slow winding river, so slow it scarcely knew itself the direction of its flow. Seventeen miles from Boston, the solitude was complete. The forest spread its branches everywhere, maple woods, pines, cedars, wastelands, dingles and sandpits, with bits of cool meadows by the water's edge and, in the clearings, ponds of which Walden was the pearl. Bordering the valley rocky crests and distant vistas upon the Wachusett and Mount Monadnock, Emerson's Platonic Idea of a mountain. Orchards, fallow fields, abandoned farms, old mills, apples on all sides and still more apples. Upon this woody soil, rocky and dotted with ponds, rough farmers, proletarians of the land, eked out a scanty living. Hard long winters, six months of snow upon the ground, Siberian temperatures, then suddenly almost without a spring, the torrid blasts of New England summers. Taciturn, repressed, stoic, with sharp explosions of humor and practical horse-sense on all occasions, these Concord people were pure-blooded Yankees, Franklin's Poor Richards.

Concord, when Emerson settled there, was a town of scarcely two thousand inhabitants which spread its white wooden cottages beside the lawn of a common shaded by elms, magnificent and poetic (*ulmus americanus*), all in garlands, in festoons, in harps, in plumes, in lyres. From afar with its white steeples among green leaves Concord appears like a fresh water-color painting. In spring when the maples are in bud, the landscape is pink. In autumn it is a mirage, a rainbow of violet, crimson, and gold. The forest "turns" and during Indian Summer an iridescent mist of mauve and blue floats over the countryside awaiting its thick ermine mantle of snow. Concord is not great in size but it is rich in memories, heroic memories. It was celebrating its second centenary when Emerson went there to live, and it was he who delivered the oration in the city hall of the historic village where ten years before the return of Lafayette had been hailed with ovations.

Two centuries of history had passed since Peter Bulkeley and his pilgrims had slipped into the forest among the odors of the ferns, two centuries since the pact of peace—Concord!—with the Sachem Tahatawan. Long years of Puritan theocracy, of land clearing, of plowing, of building churches and schools. Concord Common, sheltered behind its palisades, had seen Puritans go by in pointed hats with full floating capes. Four-hour sermons in the icy meeting-house with the tithing-man sticking his long staff into people who succumbed to the temptation of sleep. Terrible sermons with hell yawning and imps grinning in the pastor's anathemas. They struggled, they labored, they lived, they organized. The people of Concord were of good English extraction. In 1835 for the celebration of the second centenary, the old families of the seventeenth century were still there, their names had been perpetuated, and Emerson who had dug into the city archives proudly enumerated them in his speech. The old colonists had not grown rich. From squires they had become tenant farmers, artisans, shop keepers, but there is no degrading work in America and all remained gentlemen and ladies nor lost an ounce of their self-respect. Concord is proud of its past. It has its river and its bridge, its column on the battle-field where fell the redcoats come from Boston to seize the revolutionists' supplies. Lexington and Concord that day grimly peppered King George's mercenaries on the bridge and along the hedges of the Boston road. It was from Concord that re-echoed round the world America's salute to the Rights of Man and the Citizen. It was followed by many others.

Concord was a democratic town and equalitarian. Its people were not rich and every one worked with his hands, lived on from day to day satisfied with little in his small domain. There were moreover highly cultivated individuals in the village, these self-taught dynasties which one ran into in those days in the land of the Puritans. There were the Hoars, the Ripleys; soon came the Hawthornes, the Alcotts, the Channings, and, unknown to all, a young student freshly graduated from Harvard, Henry David Thoreau, with the ardor of a Bonaparte, meditated over his map upon the annexation of the rivers, the woods, the ponds of the surroundings. Boston was not far away. The stage made the trip in three hours. Emerson had been a sensation in town, too much so for his taste, and admirers, curiosity seekers, disciples flocked to him. It was the beginning of an inner circle whose circumference would spread. Toward 1840 all that was needed to make a Weimar out of Concord was a duke friendly to letters.

Emerson came to Concord instinctively, impelled by atavistic influences. The family and clan spirit was always lively in the Emersons. A roof was needed for Mrs. Emerson, his mother, and for Charles, the inseparable brother, who wished to open a lawyer's office in the village and who was engaged to be married. Emerson was about to wed a second time. He had just inherited from his first wife a small capital which made him independent, the income of which he calculated with joy, practical Yankee that he was. In 1835 a chance appeared and he bought, at the edge of Concord on the Boston road, a large square house with a garden and fields sloping down to the Musketaquid, which means in Indian "Grass River." The spot was damp but the house was in good shape and well built and the garden faced the west. It was isolated but the stage passed before the door. Emerson was proud of his place and of his four acres of land to which he would join the woods of Walden. Along with his house had he not bought the mysterious essences of the soil, the secret marvels of the sap, the essence of apple, of pear, of corn, of flower, a whole stretch of sky above his orchard, the sunsets, the moonlight and starlight, the illusions of the frost, the snow, the song of birds, the beasts, and insects? *Multum in parvo, Il più nel uno, All in each,* as he liked to say.

His wife Lydia was not satisfied. She would have liked to keep Ralph Waldo in her native Plymouth, but how resist the caprices of a poet? The snow, the north wind, shelter him so well from intruders and he needs the sunsets, the river, the woods, and the mirage of Concord. So be it. There he was to stay. His income was modest but he had the fees from his lectures and his muse was Economy. Let us admire the abnegation of this man whose voice had resounded in pulpits and meetings, whose heresy had set tongues wagging, who had interviewed Coleridge, Wordsworth, and Carlyle, who had seen Naples, Rome, London, Paris, and who shut himself up in a town of two thousand souls in order to follow the call of wisdom, to obey his inner voice, an adventure so impractical, so inglorious, it seemed, when expanding America surged forth in the gold rush. Emerson found Concord, Peace, solitude, silence, the woods, the sky, the waters, the night, the day, the seasons, and he found himself. It was from this calm dwelling leased from Fate that went forth the oracles of his speech on the American Scholar and the storm of the address to the Divinity School of Cambridge. Nothing thenceforward would trouble the security of the sage and America began to listen to his voice.

CHAPTER II

Idealism Let Loose

Emerson did not invent transcendentalism. For years everything boiled and fermented about him and America was in the birth pangs of an ideal. The mystic wave had not ceased to foam since the arrival of the Pilgrims. For these incorrigible visionaries the ideal was real, present; there was but one law, the inner law. Conscience! Conscience! It was to conscience that they related all. Upon it they had founded Church and State. But human reason has always some shortcoming. The Pilgrims had to live, to found and organize the state, to colonize, to trade. The Puritan had turned pioneer; his faith had become sectarian; his theocracy had melted into the state. Political constitutions had replaced the covenant and revolutions had been fought and won. Men no longer sought salvation but ran after happiness. How far they were from the days when from the depths of a burning bush the Eternal talked to man, when each man was a temple, when there were as many churches as souls. . . . But faith was not dead and the mystics had not capitulated.

The fire had been smouldering under the ashes for two hundred years. At each turning point of history, when fervor languished, suddenly surged forth a cry of awakening, a wave of conversion. The most practical men lost their footing in the ideal. Religious truths which had become dead letters for them suddenly kindled anew and impressed themselves upon them with the force of an hallucination.

There were sudden awakenings; there were attacks of collective hysteria. Jehovah was speaking; lightning flashed on Sinai and, under the breath of the Invisible, souls trembled like leaves in the wind. The desert was peopled with voices. Evenings along the water one felt the divine presence in the flowers, in the breeze, all around one, as if the soul in nature were God, and the forests were singing the Song of Songs. The soul felt itself free, gushed forth, leaped in the air, fell in trances. After having brandished the

Devil's pitchfork over the heads of terrified sin-
ners, Jonathan Edwards, the implacable Puritan,
met the Master in the woods and he saw His
visage in all of Nature. . . . Aspirations, in-
stincts had remained repressed and there existed
countless souls in hunger. The sense of individual-
ity was taking its revenge. All was related to the
soul. Should the church and society happen to fall
short of their aims, it was the right and the duty
of each to recall them to their original purity, to
the canon of justice and charity. The pioneers
were conquering the world, the saints were seeking the kingdom of God. Unitarianism had succeeded in withering faith only for a handful of
rational people; the crowds demanded emotions.
Adventists, Quakers, Perfectionists, Quietists,
numberless sects, believing only in the light of
the heart, daily awaited a Messiah and kept themselves in a state of grace. The day was coming
when God's children would have wings and would
fly toward the Eternal. . . . Meanwhile they
must follow the Voice, speak not, and listen in
trembling silence.

What a fervent and serene countenance did
these idealists present to their compatriots already

in the grip of the strenuous life. It is in the ranks
of these saints that reformers and utopians would
be recruited, it is among them that the Transcendentalists and Emerson first of all would come
to temper their fervor. In vain did they live in
contemplation, on the outskirts of society; let the
social institutions crack, let crying abuse appear,
let a cause be given them, and they would throw
themselves into action. It would be seen in the
great days of abolitionism, when the Quaker shoe-
maker of Haverhill, Whittier, would compose his
inspired songs, lashing the politicians, exalting
the lowly, and denouncing the reign of hypocrisy.
It is the function and duty of mystics to compare
ceaselessly the real with the ideal, the social state
of man with his immortal destiny. They dream of
a better man; they wish him to be as perfect as
the Heavenly Father, and they are there to assure this perfection, throwing themselves into
campaigns in favor of temperance, of freeing the
slaves, of abolishing war, of emancipating women
and laborers. Nothing in this world avails for
them against the impetus of the Spirit. The soul
is mistress of the universe. Exasperated by their
utilitarian epoch, angry to see traders and poli-

ticians corrupt the image of God, these mystics bring pressure to bear from all sides and it is from them that starts the enthusiasm for reform.

New England is a nursery of visionaries and wonder-workers. On the mountains, in the wood-lands, in many a distant hamlet there are seers and prophetesses to whom God talks face to face, to whom He has given a mission and who leave all to follow Him. Beside all them there are the inspired laymen impelled by the desire for better things, for progress, another form of perfection. These non-conformists wipe out all traditions and established institutions. They have an ideal in themselves, a message to broadcast, a mission. They thirst for sincerity, for unity. They de-nounce the duplicity of existence, religion on the right, civil affairs on the left. They protest against two-faced morality, against the substitution of human goals, utilitarian and selfish, for ends which are divine. They take the ideal literally and refuse all compromise. They mean to fashion their conduct on their beliefs and, if the world refuses, they are willing to be wise alone. Then there are the utopians, the eccentrics, the un-bridled queer ones. . . . About 1840 America,

New England in particular whence they swarmed, flowed over with them. . . . The Church, the State, education, the family, commerce, labor, manners, the ways of living—they wished to reform all. Drunk with sincerity, with reality as they said—was it not wrong to cast upon them as an insult the epithet of Transcendentalists? They knew clearly where to aim. This one wished to reform religion, another the schools, a third refused to pay his taxes, a fourth to take an oath. This one was against money, that one against war. In private life there were enemies of luxury and apostles of the simple life, those who wished to forbid the employment of servants, those who prescribed the use of alcohol and meat. Even among the vegetarians there were groups and subgroups. There were partisans of unleavened bread and partisans of bran bread, adversaries of tea, milk, coffee. There were those who forbade themselves the use of wool and cotton, those who let their beards grow, those who went barefooted. It was a veritable Babel, but these saints were authentic Americans. They dreamed of returning to the Golden Age *via* reform and prohibitions.

Emerson knew them well, these utopians. It

was he who let them loose. They were at bottom his disciples and his spiritual children. It was for them that he threw down the gauntlet to the age, that he opened the doors of the future, that he preached the gospel of self-reliance, of sincerity at any price, that he affirmed the identity of the soul and of God. And they believed him upon his say-so. Emerson fumed when they camped upon his doorstep. His eye never left the clock when he was obliged to harbor them, but the Spirit breathes where it will. He loved their sincerity, their enthusiasm, the new worlds they carried in their glance.

~~~~~~~

CHAPTER III

What Time Is It?

~~~~~~~

THE dissenting movement born of the unitarian schism was not cut short. People of
culture and gentlemen too were in effervescence.
They were looking for a reasonable faith outside
the churches and nourishing doubts touching the
social institution. The time had come, they were
thinking, for a return to sincerity. They must put
the axe to the roots of the tree and radically reform the existing order. The world as it had been
made by the cold reason was untenable and current morality was only a vast hypocrisy. Society
must be reconstructed from the ground up. But
the reformers were not agreed upon the method
to be used. Some held for the spirit, others for the
letter. Many took a sheet of paper, a quill pen,
and drew up on the spot the plans of the ideal city.
They reformed the world with ink and paper,

165

hic et nunc. These constituted the left wing. The others—and Emerson was their spokesman—followed the ways of the spirit. They wished for radical and universal reform but were suspicious of utopias. They expected salvation not from plans no matter how beautiful on paper but from the inner work of the soul upon itself. If their tactics were less sensational, they were not less redoubtable. Beneath each institution, beneath each of our acts, they placed new thoughts. They invited their fellows to transcend themselves. They shattered nothing; they provoked no one; but they turned the inner being, states of mind and ideas, inside out like a glove. They took refuge in a respectful silence; they made no scandal; but the moment was coming sooner or later when the edifice would fall, thanks to their subterranean labor. Then the conflict between the ideal and the real became inevitable as one saw it during Emerson's schism and was going to see still better, this time tragically, during the war against slavery. That ideas were dynamite, had to be believed that day. Twenty years of palavering—and the guns went off by themselves.

Emerson was in this camp and it was he who

gave the commands. The paper utopias inspired
him only with distrust. He wished to renew the
whole moral being. Let us reform our thoughts
before we reform the world. Let us return to
fundamental principles by dint of sincerity. Let
us know ourselves. Let us compare the world such
as it is with the world as conscience tells us it
ought to be. This will enlighten us upon our
duties and our rights. . . . Self reliance, sincerity! . . . But at length Emerson welcomed and
encouraged the innovators. He smiled at the
utopians, and misanthrope though he was, he
loved the company of gentlemen. It was in his
study in the autumn of 1836 that the idea of the
Transcendental Club was born.

Pronounced and traditional as was the taste of
Bostonians for hyperbole, the gentlemen gathered
about Emerson were too modest to inflict upon
their informal meetings the yard-long title which
history has wrapped about them. The huge sign-
board ran the risk of concealing the whole pedi-
ment of the temple. The club in reality was called
more simply and not less poetically the "Symposium," a strictly Puritan symposium or banquet,
where no wine was drunk in beakers wreathed in

roses. The idealist, according to Emerson, quenched his thirst with cold water in a wooden dipper. The members of the Symposium met informally at one another's houses. There were women of culture, artists and poets, but especially philosophers and theologians: George Ripley, philosopher and fervent spiritualist; Orestes Brownson, ardent *polémiste*, a man of sudden changes, who passed one day from transcendentalism to Rome, burning behind him all that he had adored; Theodore Parker, the fiery apostle, always battling, always charging, whose brain was an arsenal of erudition, a polyglot library; Alcott, the soul of the circle and sharp-shooter of the ideal; Freeman Clarke and William Henry Channing, adepts in the religion of humanity; Elizabeth Peabody, importer of ideas and of European books, whose bookshop in Boston was the headquarters of these gentlemen; Sarah Alden Ripley, who combined with the cares of housekeeping the advanced study of Greek, German, and the differential calculus; and finally Margaret Fuller, the inspired, the stimulator, who had read everything, seen everything, and whom everything set in vibration. They talked of art and literature, but

MARGARET FULLER

especially of religion and philosophy. Everything took place in free conversations in the course of which they discussed Kant, Jouffroy, Cousin, Benjamin Constant, Coleridge, Carlyle. Parker thundered, Alcott uttered oracles, Margaret Fuller gave herself up to her familiar improvisations on art and the beautiful, exalting Raphael, Goethe, and Beethoven, whose symphonies were being played for the first time in America, commenting upon the last novel of Balzac or George Sand. From time to time the great preacher Channing, always enthusiastic about liberty, came to bless the assembly.

Emerson used to listen. He loathed verbiage and more than once he must have believed himself back in the Pythologian Club of Harvard, but the conversations excited him and in the Symposium one was among people who knew philosophy and letters. The rashest ideas became harmless in a gathering in which each believed only in himself. Was not the Symposium called the Club of Sister Souls, because, said a wag, there was no member of the group who agreed with any other? Besides, with Emerson present, the wildest fancies became reasonable. It was he at bottom who furnished the topic of the conversation. The polemics about the Cambridge address were not yet ended—infidel, pantheist, atheist, disciple of Kant, of Hegel, of Spinoza! Reluctantly he had unloosed a whole movement of ideas about which the adversaries waxed hot. The reviews, tracts, sermons re-echoed with the noise of his heresies. It was for him that his bodyguard, Ripley, Brownson, and especially Theodore Parker, broke lances, mobilized English, German, and French philosophers against the rough tilter Andrew Norton, defender of orthodoxy at bay. Thidoxy, midoxy—snickered Carlyle from across the water.

But as a matter of fact where were they? What was going on in the world? Whither tended the course of events? You can clearly imagine an absent-minded man like Alcott tearing himself brusquely away from his dreams—when Alcott was not talking, which sometimes happened, he was dreaming—and asking these gentlemen point-blank, "What time is it?"

No, gentlemen, do not take out your watches. Time did not exist for Alcott, who lived in the Heavens. He wanted to know the time as told by the stars of progress, of the idea, of truth, and of all these great words which he worshiped.

And you can again imagine the Transcendentalists of the Symposium all exclaiming together: "Alcott is right. We need a dial, an indicator, a clock." And the Symposium in delight decided to publish *The Dial*.

Emerson was not without a finger in the pie. For some time, since college days, he had dreamed of a review. The memory of Addison's *Spectator* haunted him. He had set himself to editing an imaginary gazette which would come out at five o'clock, between tea and cakes, to present to society, so to speak, the ideal upon a tray. There were the *Globe*, the *Revue des Deux Mondes*; there was above all *Blackwood's* and the *Edinburgh Review* from which he had first received Carlyle's electric shock. Substituting one romanticism for another, Americans needed a *Globe*. As editor Emerson had first thought of Carlyle, poor Carlyle already dyspeptic and rabid, pretty well taken up moreover with the conquest of London. His visit across the sea became more and more problematical. His room was always kept waiting for him at the Emersons, but Carlyle did not come and the scandal of the Cambridge address was to end his plans for the voyage. Emerson was perfectly willing to be stoned for his faith but he was not asking martyrdom for his friends. And what would that sarcastic Carlyle have cared for the transcendental *Dial* which he was always making fun of by himself and which he called the *Aurora Borealis?* What would he have done on this Himalaya among people whom he openly called fools and cloud-mongers? So Margaret Fuller was chosen as editor, the Muse, the inky-fingered Sybil, who had shown her mettle in Horace Greeley's workshop on the New York *Tribune*, which was completely won over to the new ideas.

A strange clock, this *Dial*. It told the hour, the months, the seasons, the present and the future, counted, preached, moralized, sang, played music, prayed, sighed, aspired, hoped, and was supposed at the same time to forward the progress of the world in each swing of its pendulum. *The Dial*, needless to say, was always ahead of ordinary time. But the machinery was complicated and one had to work in groups to make it go, to repair it, until the final catastrophe, which had not long to

wait. Mysticism, sociology, theology, metaphysics, literature, religion, fine arts, ancient,
modern, and foreign books, Platonism, Buddhism,
eclecticism, Swedenborgianism, mesmerism,
phrenology, novels, confessions, sermons, essays,
poems, all this in that inspired tone—how in-
structive, touching, generous, pathetic this *Dial*,
in which young America, now its own master and
tearing itself from its theological swaddling
clothes, threw itself bravely upon the Good, the
True, and the Beautiful with a conviction, a zest
worthy of a better fate. But does one ever know
what one sows? . . . Alas, they had to pack
their trunks after four years. *The Dial* had only
two hundred and fifty subscribers and Emerson,
who had tried to save it by taking over the editorship, had been out of pocket. He carried off the
remainders to his garret. . . . But the impetus
had been given, America had heard the new hour
strike, the hour of hopes, enchantments, prophecies, had heard the crowing of the cock perched
on this belfry of bountiful clouds. There remained only to put into deeds the program of the
idealists. It was the utopians of Brook Farm and
Fruitlands who took it upon themselves to do this.

CHAPTER IV

Revolution in a Skillet

B ROOK FARM had sprung fully armed from
the brain of the utopians. It was again at
Emerson's that the plans had been drawn up. The
philosopher once more had played at his favorite
game of being a spring-board. He kindled the
young, encouraged them, stuffed them with dynamite, and then, just as the bomb was to be thrown,
he stole away, prudent Yankee that he was, to
watch the fireworks from a distance. He loved
new and generous ideas and utopias held no ter-
rors for him provided that they destroyed nothing
about himself. He smiled at what was then called
socialism. It was the great era of the phalansteries.
The reveries of Saint-Simon and Fourier, later
those of Auguste Comte, were crossing the water.
America was a young country, spacious, malle-
able, the Promised Land of utopias. It was there

174

that the visionaries of Europe since Rousseau had situated the Golden Age. It was up to the Americans to take the hint.

The program of the Brook Farmerites was more practical and at bottom more selfish than it seemed. Doubtless they meant to teach the age a lesson, to give the world an example and a challenge, but they also thought of themselves. Life was sweet for no one in New England and still less for dreamers and intellectuals. One had to vegetate, cramp himself, limit his horizons, clip his wings, accept lowly tasks, struggle for his living. The luxury of heresy or eccentricity came high. It was a question of one's daily bread and every one did not, like Emerson, have an income to assure it. Or else one had to be a hermit, live meagerly on next to nothing, turn into a pedlar, woodcutter, day laborer, even, like Thoreau, flee to the woods. This heroism was without glory. Why not simplify the problem of existence and make a virtue of necessity in the literal sense of the word, affirming in the teeth of the world that it was not by constraint but by principle and free will that one was reforming his life, that one was espousing simplicity, that one was consecrating himself to manual labor? Yes, the world was ill made, especially for idealists and poets, for their wives and children. Against the insolence of the rich the proletariat of ideas must unite. For a world based on egoism, why not substitute one founded on fraternity and love?

In America the passage from idea to act is rapid, and certain of these gentlemen meeting at Emerson's had made marvelous dreams on paper. They would club together; they would buy a great tract of land; they would have orchards, fields, woods, meadows, which they would cultivate in common and farm with their own hands. They would build a big house, a school in which they would teach the children according to the method dear to Rousseau and Pestalozzi. Every one would work with his hands and share the fruits of his labor. In the intervals between work, each would be free to devote himself to philosophy, poetry, painting, music, or dreaming. . . .

One of the first to bite at the idea of the phalanstery was the bashful Nathaniel Hawthorne. Life was hard for him. He had been weigher in the custom house at Boston, but an election had lost him his place. He scraped along

on the meager products of his writings and, what
is more, was in love, engaged to the good Sophia
Peabody, whom he was impatient to marry. He
had been told that at Brook Farm he would find
a means of livelihood and a home. He had therefore risked a thousand dollars from his savings in
the venture and embarked for Utopia. He had
begun his journey on a cold April day in 1841 in
a blizzard and had arrived stiff with cold in the
great hall of the phalanstery where, thank God,
a good fire was crackling. He had been served a
steaming cabbage soup and had bent himself to
the rules of the house. . . . How little the
reality resembled his dreams! He had to get up
at break of day when the head farmer blew the
horn and set himself to manual work, sawing
wood, piling manure, looking out for the stock.
Then little by little he was initiated into the work
of the fields, digging, plowing, hoeing . . .
Hawthorne's martyrdom was to milk the cows.
He made an awkward milkman and he pretended
that the cows made fun of him as he milked.
There was in the stable a transcendental heifer
belonging to Margaret Fuller and this recalci-
trant animal threw the whole herd into disorder.

Hawthorne succeeded better as a swineherd. The *far niente* of the pigs committed to his care plunged him into Hamlet-like reflections on the rudimentary existence to which certain philosophers of his acquaintance were condemned.

Sensitive to the picturesque, Hawthorne was astonished to see himself in boots and a blue smock escorting to the fields his utopian brothers, a strange troop who looked more like a band of ragamuffins or guttersnipes than a school of idealists. Each had come to wear out at Brook Farm the relics of his wardrobe. There were city men in cutaways, clergymen in frock coats, with scanty trousers shiny in the seams, vests coming up to the armpits. . . . To spare their self-respect they had given the most repugnant duties to companies of children clothed in uniform. . . . The idyl was complete. There were amusements at Brook Farm. Puns and charades were favorite sports. Sundays they discussed Kant and Spinoza in the commons or read aloud the *Divine Comedy*. In fair weather matrons and maids posed in living pictures in the forest. They picnicked on the grass, they flirted, they loved . . . and there were cabals and dramas. Sometimes they danced and they made merry when clothespins fell from the pockets of the waltzers. . . .

During this time the crops grew as they could. The cows were not alone in laughing at the phalansterians. The fields could have imitated them. Not content with wounding themselves with scythes and pitchforks, the Brook Farmerites took weeds for vegetables, buried the sprouting plants under the compost or planted them upside-down. At the end of the month those who had watched the others work received the same wages as they. . . . In March, 1846, a fire burned the phalanstery to the ground during a dance and the members of the community lost their savings in the adventure. Hawthorne had escaped long since, with calloused hands, body tanned, swearing like the crow in the fable that he'd never be caught again.

Emerson had had a narrow escape. He had come to pay a formal call to Brook Farm and to take off his hat to the Ideal. He who had such difficulty not to hurt his foot when he dug and whom his little boy warned just in time, what would he have done among these improvised farmers? Above all, how would he have accommodated

himself to the promiscuity of the phalanstery, he
whom the shadow of an intruder sent back into
his shell? But Brook Farm was a paradise compared to Fruitlands, the *Nephelokokkygia* of Alcott the platonist and his friend Charles Lane. At
Fruitlands they had deliberately tried to square
the circle by combining humanitarian zeal with
agricultural ambitions. At Brook Farm the farming suffered from the distractions of the phalansterians. At Fruitlands it was the triumph of the
purest utopianism. All was transcendental. They
tried to make the crops grow without fertilizer
and without beasts of burden and plowing. All
was cultivated with the shovel and hoe and the
soil itself was put upon a vegetarian diet. As for
the inhabitants, the strictest Trappist monastery
could not touch the austerities of Fruitlands.
They were systematically forbidden for reasons
of religion and principle, sugar, tea, coffee,
chocolate, wine, spices, rice, meat, fish, fowl,
eggs, milk, butter, cheese. They were fed on
coarse bran rolls cooked in the shape of animals
—those animals whose flesh was taboo—and on
vegetables. But a distinction had to be made between those vegetables which were called noble

and those called vile. Only those which ripened
in the air were tolerated. Tubercles were taboo.
Out of humanity for the beasts, they forbade the
use of wool nor did they permit that of the cotton cultivated by the slaves of the barbarous
southern states. They were dressed exclusively in
linen and no stockings were worn. . . . But as
far as the spirit was concerned, there was no
mortification. The phalanstery put at the dispo-
sition of its members an esoteric library of a thousand volumes, Plato, Plotinus, Jamblichus, and
their commentators. While the crops waited, they
discussed metempsychosis, the pre-existence of
souls, the origin of the ideas, and the procession of the Logos. Our seers were pious anarchists.
As they prohibited meat and stimulants, so they
condemned private property, the state, the school,
commerce, medicine, the arts, the sciences, and
family affection. It was the return to man naked
as he stepped forth from the discourses of Rousseau. Naturally Fruitlands failed and poor Alcott
fell flat. Here again Emerson had seen clearly.

CHAPTER V

Wisdom

D URING this time the sage was cultivating his garden. He was full of sympathy for the innovators but for reasons and in ways which remained foreign to them. Between them and him there was first his prudence, his timidity, what he called his laziness. He lacked ardor. He distrusted impulse. Nature had allotted him only a certain stock of force and he intended to economize it. And then too the intellect separates. Between the subject and the object it puts the interval of a thought. Illusion, illusion. The idea is fugitive, the spirit changing, the universe fluid. *Panta rei*, all things flow. He who was afraid of men, who declared that man is insulary, that each man is a globe with infinite force of repulsion, who bristled over a nothing, how could he have had confidence in phalansteries? The man of

182

genius lives alone and, like the mountains, the snow and silence are the tax he pays for his elevation. In society, despite his outer coldness, he grew warm, gave of himself, then reproached himself for having done so afterwards. Emotions depressed him.

But his abstention was especially philosophic. Let us reform the world certainly. He was far from accepting society as it was and he did not spare it his sarcasms. He ridiculed those who feared to see the planet fly off in space and lose itself in the Absolute, who were leagued together to calk it, to bolster it up with buttresses and chains that the aged, children, and women might sleep in peace. Had he not preached the eternal youth of the world, the necessity of spiritual revolutions? Had he not in a moment of transcendental enthusiasm in his Dartmouth and Cambridge addresses given a new and virgin universe to youth? If he was suspicious of the reforms it was not that they were too venturesome; on the contrary, he found them too fragmentary. The reform maker is not such and such a man, such a group of men in particular, such a program; it is the universal Spirit, the all-powerful rhythm of Nature in perpetual evolution. To this impulsion of the world one abandons himself consciously and completely. The universe reaches its ends in spite of us. It is a system of self-executing laws, of compensations. The Spirit, the world tends toward Unity, toward union; the particular is integrated into the Universal; but the ways they follow are mysterious. What use is such and such a reform, such and such a panacea? It is life entire which must be transformed. But that is the work of the spirit, of thought. It is by a renewing, a rejuvenation, a conversion of all being, a complete revolution in our thoughts and our states of mind that the reform must be accomplished and on that day there will be neither reformers nor phalansteries.

The world does not hear the cock crow. It does not see in the east the gray track of the dawn. At the first ray of light it grows afraid. Who has opened the blinds? Bad luck to him! But the wild horse has heard the call of the trainer, the maniac has caught the eye of the guardian. The Dreamer appears, and sects, universities, churches, statesmen are in alarm. The soul drags all in its train. It is the spirit which must be liberated. The reform of the world is an individual and mental reform. One must learn to see, to feel, to love, to think. One must harmonize himself and unite himself to nature. Generosity, but prudence. Life is short. Time, the little gray-beard, draws our fate from his pocket amid numberless illusions. The world is an arrangement of means and ends in equilibrium, but we must not let the arrows make us lose sight of the target. To each his destiny, his calling, his duty. What we need is not acts but men. You cannot raise man by modifying circumstances. Circumstances are diversions, illusions, dreams. At the wakening causes alone satisfy us. Philanthropy, charity, duty, clouds which the wind sweeps away! It is in and about the self that each of us has the chance to save the world, to rejuvenate it, to recreate it by substituting new thoughts for old. . . .

That is why Emerson stood aloof and remained calmly at home with the Cause of causes. He was afraid of alienating himself in giving himself, and he had, alas, but one existence. He would not expose himself to the chance of missing his destiny while seeking the Golden Age. His laziness was calculated. The indolence which the re-

formers condemned in him Nature welcomed and
tolerated when he went into the woods. The
leaves which trembled on the water, the fleets of
gnats on the pond, the deep sky loved him and
accepted him. With them no distrust, no constraint, no remorse. Yes, to be sure, he had an
income and could indulge in isolation and
procrastination, but he had principles also. Rich
or poor he remained faithful to his dream. It
was he and not his twelve hundred a year who
sought God. Why should he leave his little prison,
if prison it was, for a vaster jail? He had not finished the capture of his poultry yard and he would
go to lay siege to Babylon! Enough Don Quixotes
were on the road. His liberty was dear to him, a
liberty without end. The universe is a federation
of autonomous monads. *E pluribus unum*, as the
motto of the United States goes. Each individual
is his own universe. To bind oneself is to lessen
oneself, and the fusion of man to man is impossible. The universe is given as well as duties and
ends. One has only to fulfill his function, follow
his destiny, get the best out of the present moment, make of necessity a virtue. Self-reliance!
The Great Spirit will take care of the rest. Emer-

son was a spectator, not an actor. His temperament like his philosophy was transcendental.

He was moreover afflicted with the gift of second sight. He felt the distance between realization and principle and this distance touched upon the comic. To go barefoot, to live on unleavened bread, to let one's beard and hair grow, what had that to do with the ideal and how did that contribute to the world's happiness? Neither water, nor vegetarianism, nor abstinence, nor refusal to take an oath or pay taxes, nor prison, nor the community of goods aided man to be free. There was liberty only in self-obedience. Let us be fully ourselves and the Angel will come to snatch us out of the hands of our jailers. Union, yes, but solitary, silent, and ideal in the conduct of daily life. Family, friends, cities, the world is full of phalansteries. Fourier saw no farther than the end of his nose. He was a French sensualist whose famous Harmony was only a hugging premium. There was union only between perfect and independent unities. Emerson was willing to abstain from drinking wine, from lying, from committing adultery, but as soon as one ordered him to, he itched to break the rules. Liberty before all and free initiative. The utopians would forbid him the use of his sword and his gun. But why take from him the sole refuge of his weakness? . . .

Emerson did not shout all this from the house-tops, but between conservatives and reformers he found no sufficient grounds for choice. Compensations! For him the four walls of his home were the safest of institutions. His transcendentalism remained practical. After all, hurrah for reform if it wakes human beings out of their torpor and recalls them to the reality of an always changing world. But he distrusted Peter and Paul. He was waiting for Him who will come and Whose coming he prophesied, the Superman who would pierce and overthrow all with a look. While waiting he adapted himself to the course of things. This was no small affair. The Ideal is in the humblest aspect of the real. Each instant expects a plenitude from us. His family, his friends, his house, the woods, the waters, Concord was a microcosm, a universe in epitome. The world was waiting at his door with duties and infinite relations. To conciliate himself, to unify himself, to adapt himself, to discover the infinite in the hol-

low of an atom and from all that make wisdom
and poetry, such was the career of Emerson.
Antique phantoms, builders of illusory palaces,
utopia makers, why encroach upon the repose of
the sage? Nature preached his duty to him. His
vocation was to be professor of the Joyful Wisdom, to celebrate truth, knowledge, nobility, to
proclaim the Law—but by music and the dance,
priest of the soul, in joy, health, and harmony.
The sky is blue, the fields are green, the springs
are cool, joyous the rivers, friendly the light of
sky and stars. Ah, leave then the Sage in peace,
leave Saadi, leave Osman. What interest to him
your theorizings, your institutions, your laws? He
is free; he lives his own life; his life is a May
game.

CHAPTER VI

The Charm of Concord

E MERSON arose early. He watched the daybreak on the hills, the dawn, primrose in
the river of Time. He felt the world in its new-
ness and freshness. A short walk in the garden to
see the tricks which the magician hidden in the
flowers and plants had played him during the
night. His trees which he compared to the tree
Yggdrasil, support of the world, bear their secret
like a sphinx. The bluebird has gone back to his
nest, the friendly turtle meditates by the brook
side. The day will be fine and Emerson will have
it all to himself. No lectures in Boston, no visitors
on the calendar. If only no tramp from the land
of the Ideal comes knocking at his door! But he
has the refuge of the woods. It is sweet to belong
to oneself, to worship silently the invisible Presence, to feel Thoughts coming to birth within

one, to listen to the music of the Hours. . . .
Each hour has its morning, its noon, and its night.
Another mysterious day coming softly like a cat,
hooded like a dervish, presenting its offering to
him who knows how to receive it. . . .

Here is Emerson in his study, his thinking-
room, among his books, universal books which are
his relatives, his friends, books rich in passionate
experiences and which cure, spur on, command.
It is the Soul of the World which they express
and it is the Soul which wrote them. . . .

He dreams, he muses. He is in no hurry. He
has Eternity before him, about him. It is useless
to rush inspiration. The gods arrive unaware. To
attune the soul there are the pacifying influences
of the night, moonlight, the stars, and during the
day, Plato, Plotinus, Goethe, Montaigne, Plutarch, Shakespeare. All is calm about him. A carriage rolls by on the Boston road. In the house
he hears the quiet coming and going of the servants. . . . Of what does Emerson think? He has
his course on human life in preparation, his lectures here and there. . . . Lectures, lectures! He
has to earn his daily bread . . . but to be alone,
to wonder, to weave his web in the Eternal, indif-

ferent to chance events, there is perfect joy. . . .
When will he finish his corrections of Montaigne?
When his *Essays*? . . . His "Wide Worlds" are
ranged around him. For more than twenty years
he had been jotting down his thoughts, daily, in
these schoolboy copy-books, his savings bank, his
treasury. It was there that he had been establish-
ing his co-ordinates, noting the position of the
Soul in the firmament of ideas, the sublime and
the holy side by side, his reading, his conversations, his meetings, his walks, his intuitions. . . .
Guido Reni's *Aurora*, which Carlyle had just sent
him, drove her chariot above the mantelpiece.
The portraits of Shakespeare, Montaigne, and
Swedenborg looked down upon him——these sages,
these seers, his immortal companions, his true
hosts. . . . He was lodging At the Sign of the
Three Fates and under the protection of Isis, goddess of illusions. . . .

Emerson is seated in his rocking chair, by his
table, with a writing pad on his knees. His mind
wanders. The breeze stirs the tops of the pines, a
cloud passes, the shadow of wings. . . . Does
any one know whether the bluebird has nested in
the cage that John Thoreau built him in the

garden? Emerson rocks in his chair, he dreams, he works, he waits, and from time to time, he reaches into his "savings bank," into his notebooks, for fine purple patches, fragments of mosaic which he will have to put together and cement. In matters of style as in matters of idea, Emerson was a fatalist. He took what the gods provided. Thoughts are sacred. They float down to us mysteriously in the coolness of the inner life. Style is our intellectual voice. It is only in part under our control. It is a tone of voice which we adopt without thinking of it, a road toward the Infinite across Chaos and dreadful Night. Language is as the air which clothes the earth; as the atmosphere it lies upon contours, objects, and takes on their forms. Style is the alchemy of thought, the result of the subterranean work of the spirit. One writes by the grace of God. . . . There are dead words, mummified and living words, initiators, fecund, prophetic, virile, those he loved. . . . Write as the dew falls on the leaves, as stalactites grow on the walls of caverns, as flesh drips blood, as the woody fiber of the trees is formed from the sap. . . . Style is a crystallization. Thoughts adhere to one another. No order, no method among them, it seems. Where begin, whither go? Let them go by themselves, tame your thoughts, take them up and, behold, they organize themselves. . . . Style is the divine order, the architecture of God. Style should be natural, spontaneous, expression inevitable. How did Montaigne put it? Ah, yes, speak on paper as with the lips. . . .

Emerson stands up. He has taken from the shelves of his bookcase his Montaigne in the savory translation of Cotton. He loves Montaigne, the pyrrhonian, the sceptic, but so lively, such a good fellow, so natural, the friend of years and forever. For twenty years he has cultivated his friendship, has quoted him, has made him his own. It seems to him sometimes as if it were he who had written the *Essays*. He says so fully, so frankly what he thinks, Montaigne; witticisms, poetry, theology, philosophy, humor, anecdotes. With his whole heart Emerson embraces the great man without shame, this pagan who makes virtue possible without Christian discipline. The panegyric of Cato and Socrates winds up the loosened springs within him. The heroic note is struck in it, the sound of the warlike trumpet

which sets the blood to vibrating. Nature abhors
an author, but she loves Montaigne. So much the
worse if Emerson steals his thoughts from him.
. . . He has riddled with notes and cross-refer-
ences the fly leaves of the *Essays*. He has marked
in pencil dozens of passages on rhyme, eloquence,
books, friendship, the education of children,
which he will lift bodily into his own *Essays*
when he needs them. . . .

Emerson puts back the volume between Plutarch's *Moralia* and his great Plato of Basel, near
the numberless little volumes of the Stuttgart edition of Goethe—Goethe, whom he read in the
German text to please Carlyle, whom he pillaged,
whose universal intelligence he admired, but who
was not quite his man, whom he found too
courtly, too worldly. . . . And here is Swedenborg, who put the world in pictures, Shakespeare,
magician in words. . . . In the realm of the
Spirit all roads lead to Rome. And what did that
inspired apothecary of Boston, the Swenden-
borgian Sampson Reed say of style? That poetry
is a growth, a flowering in the soul, that to each
image corresponds a natural object, that nature
and language hold together, call each other, that

words are beings and images truths. . . . Emerson will go for a talk with Reed again. . . . In the meantime here are rich gleanings and an essay all ready on the poet. . . .

But here is Lydia, his Asia, entering on tiptoes. She approaches, takes his pen, inscribes three names on the blank page, Ralph Waldo Emerson, Lidian Emerson, Waldo Emerson . . . and goes away. . . . Lidian, his Lydia, is accustomed to do things like this. The other day while he was accusing himself of misanthropy and bewailing his sins in his *Journal*, Lydia in his absence had left this short maxim in his notebook, "If you wish men to love you, love them." . . . A well of wisdom, Lydia, who put between him and the storm her serene optimism and her good sense. . . . Women are not writers but they are born inspirers. . . .

Before lunch ten minutes of gardening to make him fit. He had so often sung the praises of manual labor, and the gentlemen of Brook Farm and Fruitlands made him ashamed. Well, let's try . . . A little of everything . . . But there is gardening and gardening . . . It depends on the inspiration of the moment . . . Meanwhile manual labor is play, a sport, a salutary exercise, but let us not exaggerate and go too far. . . . Emerson is not rich in animal spirits. . . . He reserves the hoe for dark days, when he has suffered from an intruder, for instance. Then, yes, he runs to the garden and hoe in hand he wears down his ill humor, tears out his weeds, but he is quickly tired and his enthusiasm does not burn long. . . . To each his own garden. His is the garden of ideas. . . .

Lunch time. Emerson has Brook Farm in his mind . . . Suppose they tried a bit of vegetarianism and in the way of revolution Lydia invited the servants to come and eat at the master's table? . . . Lydia has done the errand; the servants prefer to eat in the kitchen. They have not read Fourier and the phalanstery does not appeal to them. . . . Emerson smiles. He has tried an idea by the test of experience. The meal is over and he takes up his stick. To Walden. Emerson is going into the woods, his woods, on a tour of inspection. . . .

It is a fine afternoon in early summer. All the farmers of Concord are in the fields to watch the growing crops and calculate the promise of the orchards. Emerson sees George Minot, his neighbor, and waves to him. This caustic Minot, half poacher and half farmer but expert gardener to whom Emerson owes more than one useful bit of advice. Emerson loves these nature's gentlemen in worn-out hats and spotted blue blouses. Nature has formed these rough Anglo-Saxons in her image. They are the Cæsars, the Alexanders of the soil. Napoleon won sixty battles, they have won thousands. Alchemists of the seasons, their sure instinct is privy to the mysterious laws of the universe. They are secret as nature and padlocked in taciturnity. They resemble their houses whose doors are attractive but shut and which one enters only from the side. Architects in compensations, they are the true supermen, the heroes whom Plutarch forgot, the true representative men of Emerson. There now is Edmund Hosmer in his field. Emerson greets him and approaches him. Has Hosmer read the last bulletin of the Massachusetts Agricultural Society? What does he think of it? Ah, what are these Boston fellows mixing in for? Advice to farmers on how to build, to get the wealth out of their land, to bring up their daughters! Hosmer has only one professor, experience; one master, necessity; and all the rest is literature. . . . Whoever thought to make a fortune farming? "A bit gruff this good Hosmer and devilish stubborn," thought Emerson, going away. "But who hears only one bell hears only one sound and thy wisdom, Edmund, puts ours to shame." During this time Hosmer, half respect-ful, half mocking, watches the tall outline of the philosopher disappear round the bend in the road. All idealists from father to son, these Emersons. . . .

On the way Emerson amuses himself picking wild blackberries. Beware! There is a mosquito on the watch on each berry and Emerson's hands are scratched on the bush . . . Compensation, one has nothing without difficulty . . . He came for blackberries and he had picked philosophy . . . Here is Walden . . . The pond is like a sapphire lying on moss. The water is blue, the sky the color of amber, the clouds float softly. Emerson sits down and contemplates . . . The water, the clouds, the woods, he has all that for himself alone. The water-spiders make merry, the frogs jump up at his approach and dive. Emerson is amused at the almost human fright of these creatures . . . Three strokes and the frogs briskly turn about, let themselves float, staring at the philosopher with round fat eyes . . . What are they looking at, how far do they see, these frogs? . . . The rhodora spreads her purple petals, the bumblebee, philosopher in yellow breeches spotted with pollen, skims the flowers and passes his life amid pure essences and aromas, violets, daffodils, heather, and clover. Free, nourished on nectar—carefree, happy bee . . . Emerson envies him . . . A squirrel leaps from tree to tree as if he carried with him all the joy of the forest. If Agni, the Fire, and if Water did dispute the beauty prize at the tribunal of the gods, it would have to go not to them but to the squirrel . . . How vast and profound the slightest stretch of water with rings and ripples driven before the wind! It is surely for the wind that water was made and the wind for the water. . . . Emerson cuts in two some oak buds. In each there is a star . . . All in each, *il più nel uno*, all contains all . . . Learn the history of the bilberry, note the day when the pine-cone and the acorn fall. If his life were long enough, Emerson would like to make up a calendar of the seasons on which would figure at such a day and such an hour, the birds, the insects, the plants, and the animals, all astronomy, botany, physiology, meteorology, the picturesqueness and poetry of the woods . . . And the trees, what enchanters! "Thy life," they murmur to him, "is measured in a few swings of our crowns, but the forest sprouts forever, forever our force re-forms its buds, its shoots, its roots . . ." The wind soughs in the pines, or is it the voice of Nature, the song of the Causes, of the Destinies, the hymn of the world in its becoming? Space and Time were born, the nebulæ begin their pilgrimage in the blue, the globes proceed one from the other, what *is* melts into what *seems*, the eternal Pan runs from metamorphosis to metamorphosis. The pine sings and the universe is born in the heart of the poet. . . .

The sparrows, the finches, the bluebirds, the blackbirds reply to the murmur of the pines. The oriole, the red bird, the bobolink hold forth. . . . Suppose Emerson should go to meet Thoreau or Ellery Channing at the bend of the path? No, something tells him that the day will be all his own. . . . He skims stones on the water, he watches the ripples spread, grow wider and wider like a lotus flower, wave upon wave, circle upon circle. . . . Thus the concentric laws of the universe. The pines, the pond, the mysteries of water, of stone, of resin, of sap, who will relate this tale? These blocks of granite are contemporaries of the Flood, petrified forms of a once fluid universe. . . . There are no more miracles, you say. But what about the crow immobile on his branch, the lizard on his dead tree trunk, the rat in his hole, the squirrel staring at you with his little stubborn eyes, what do we know of these vital worlds? How beautiful are the movements of animals! "Nature," suggests the inner voice, "is only the flowering, the efflorescence, the fruit of the soul. Of the soul all in Nature is a sign and an emblem."

The peace of things envelops Emerson. Just now on the edge of the pond he had a great moment of ecstacy, of rapture, of thrill. His feet on the ground, his head bathed in the fluid air, lifted into infinite space, he felt the universal affinities. It seemed to him that he was becoming something cold, damp, that nature was crowding in on him. The frogs piped, the waters gleamed, the dead leaves hissed, the grass shone and rustled, he was as dead, he felt only a vague sympathy, a strange existence, cold, aqueous, ethereal. He was dropping the sun and the moon . . . These sunsets, this starlight, these swamps, these rocks, these bird songs, these animal forms, all this charm floating about him like moths about a lamp—did not all that conceal the religious and divine history of the universe? Would one not say that to tell man her secrets Nature awaits him at his apogee?

* * *

Emerson has returned home. The day has been perfect and he has sucked out its nectar. The evening is beautiful and the night will be still more so. He has gone back to work under the protection of the Fates, sewing, cementing, patching together the day's discoveries, face to face with his "Wide Worlds," that other Infinite of thought. The Evening Star is kindled on the hills, a sparkling meteor plunges straight into the summit of Monadnock. The tardy gleam of twilight, twinklings above from Venus and Jupiter . . . Nothing in nature has the mellowness of shadows. The sublime light of the night is exciting; its charm floats, stirs, disappears, comes and goes, and then dies out. The murmur of the wind is the murmur of the stars. . . . The pungent odor of the fields and ferns mingled with that of flowers penetrates to him. . . . The fire-flies, like Psyches, carry their little lamps and the moon, chaste, virginal, rises and dominates the sky. . . . Moon, air, plants, hills, living geometry, animated mathematics, the plenitude and beauty of beings come from their obedience, their self-abandonment to the universe. . . . Night. Progress. Ladder of four rungs . . .

After the family dinner and a walk in the night, Emerson has taken his old Plotinus bound in black sheepskin and all marked with blue bookmarks . . . Like the Montaigne it is covered with cross references and notes. Prometheus, the legend of Typhos, the Sphinx, Hermes Trismegistus, the beatitude of the gods . . . At random he draws out a sentence, then another. It is his bedtime draught. "For those that live in solitary places are the saviours of themselves, so far as respects human causes . . . The worthy man perceiving himself beautiful, rejoices and is delighted, and producing in himself beautiful conceptions, gladly embraces an association with himself . . . This, therefore, is the life of the Gods, and of divine and happy men, a liberation from all terrene concerns, a life unaccompanied with human pleasures, and a flight of the alone to the alone."

And now Emerson goes to bed. He worships Sleep . . . Let us hope that he will have no nightmare this night, that he will not hear the ghost who saws wood in the garret, that he will not see the bewitched cradle rocking all alone, nor the devilish imps in the muff running off with a snicker at his approach. A little time to sleep and then death. But the morning will shine again upon the hills and the day will smile at the universe forever young. . . .

* * *

Thus pass the days, the nights, the months, the seasons. In summer Concord burns and smokes like a censer. There is a hot mist on the river and the meadows. Emerson dives joyfully into its drift. He reads the *Vedas*, sublime as midsummer heat in their imperturbable peace. Nepenthe! Nirvana! The summer makes a Brahmin of him. Moonlight nights Thoreau takes him boating with Margaret Fuller. Their oars glisten and the water lilies are heavy with scent. Autumn, the evening of the year, Indian summer. Illusions rain down upon them in the multicolored forest. The winter, the snow, the long Northern winter, the wind which whistles in the pines, the Æolian harp which laments like the spinning wheel of the Fates. There is skating on Walden—Emerson, Thoreau, Hawthorne—Hawthorne spectral in his floating great coat, Thoreau goatlike, sketching bacchic dances. Emerson, with his whole body bent over the ice, darts ahead—and sometimes the Northern Lights unfold their banners in the open sky and the snow-covered landscape glows red.

~~~~~~

CHAPTER VII

Margaret, or Love in Absence

~~~~~~

EMERSON did not shrink from society but had trouble getting used to men. Sociable in principle, he was misanthropic by temperament. Possessed by the torment of unity, avid, as he said, to conceive the universe without contradiction, he made praiseworthy efforts to get out of himself, but humanity was less welcoming than the Concord woods and rubbed him the wrong way. When he had in prose and verse sung the praises of solitude, he reproached himself for his apathy, his coldness. He sadly meditated upon his lack of natural sympathy and accused himself of egoism. For after all humanity also was a part of nature, and for a philosopher who celebrated the universal affinities and compensations it was logical to include human beings in his affections. Emerson set himself to it without much success. He made

207

a duty of social life and of friendship an idea like that of the ancients, but the theory of the autonomous monads restricted his flight toward the Over-Soul, the universal all-containing Spirit. Everything tended to give him confidence in men and he loved them in theory. He had the calling of an apostle. From a preacher he had become a lecturer and still occupied a pulpit. He was still a director of souls. People came to him for guidance, for advice, impelled by curiosity or admiration, but those who approached him did not hesitate to complain of his coldness, his indifference, that icy draught which discouraged and held at a distance those who came to him with the best intentions. Emerson in many ways was a man of snow, an egoist who feared to lower himself by love. His admirers themselves admitted that Bacchus had forgotten the drop of wine at his birth. And then too there was his taciturnity. Except with a few privileged souls, his conversation was full of reticence; he did not give of himself. He welcomed one with a sunny smile but it was sunshine without warmth. Even his perpetual smile seemed like a mask, an alibi, a rampart behind which he was intrenched. He put on an air of innocence which ended by mystifying one, and his callers left disappointed, believing that he was making game of them. This man had nothing to give them and some even wondered if he had a conscience. . . .

Emerson suffered from all that and he was the first to complain of it. He passed long hours in self-criticism, in stimulating himself into love of his neighbor. Why did he act the porcupine? Why did he not break the ice? . . . He was thus even with those who were dearest to him and whom he saw always across a gulf. . . . He was always caught striding over Lethe. . . .

Incapable of reforming himself, after long resistance he had erected his coldness into a philosophy. It was without any doubt his natural impotence to attach himself to others which inspired that strange essay on "Friendship," all recantation, evasion, paradox, in which he framed with his particular type of epigram a portrait which is certainly his own. He had read and reread Montaigne; he was full of Plato; he was attached to Murat and Carlyle; and he despaired of friendship. He wanted all or nothing. Beyond those rare beings, those exceptional spirits, those

divinities, he declared that friendship was impossible and he slipped it out of sight. The law
of nature is perpetual change. The soul produces
friends as a tree its leaves, dropping them when
the first new shoots appear. Friendship is a spider
web, a continual disillusion. To bind oneself is
to abase oneself. Friends cost too much, the gift
of you is paid by the gift of me. Friendship is a
paradox, it gives more than it can receive. True
friendship does without friendship. A friend
after all is only a spectacle. If he binds us to him,
he betrays us. Let us hold our friends at a distance; let us treat them as fair enemies. We are
alone in the world. . . . And Emerson gave
thanks to his natural apathy and his shyness which
sheltered his delicate organism from what he
called a premature blooming. . . .

Toward love he was a bit more courteous. It is
a beautiful illusion of youth, but after thirty one
loves no more. . . . Love is a trick of Nature
. . . Eros scatters roses and illusions over the
universe. He must indeed; it is the only way to
hold together by the chimney-side people who
daily discover each other's faults. . . . In the
sphere of the senses love is a degradation. Bodies

touch but not souls . . . Love is an inaccessible ideal. No possession, no embrace is possible, the cup is always far from the lip. . . . One always loves oneself alone. Love is a prison. The sage will unmask the illusion. He will pretend to play with a whole heart, he will cover the loved one with gifts, he will give her all but will beware of giving himself. . . . Upon which Emerson covered the little god with compliments and flowers. He slipped away, took refuge in irony upon the heights of joyful wisdom with Ariel.

He had then never loved? Ellen, the frail bride of twenty, had alone touched his heart? He had loved women only in idea? His biographers are very chary of information on this point and to read them is to feel that they too evade the issue. There are many notes in his *Journal*, several passages in his poems which one would gladly give to Dr. Freud, and we have not all of his *Journal* and correspondence. Who was this Rhea, this Hermione, this Una of whom he despaired and whose aims he frustrates? Who inspired the verses on Initial, Dæmonic, and Celestial Love? To whom was that "Ode to Beauty" dedicated, which ends on a tragic appeal and in which the poet asks

beauty to give herself to him or to let him die?
And here and there, these profound insights into
woman, these sarcasms on marriage, these fears,
these hopes deceived, this remorse, this short
poem on "Grace" in which he thanks God to
have saved him from temptation and sin, to
have stopped him on the edge of the pit? Were
these only poet's play in the manner of Dante,
Petrarch, and Shakespeare? . . . Or is all that
a holding of secret inhibitions in the unconscious?
We are reduced to guesses. It was Emerson's habit
to transpose his hidden thoughts into the transcendent and to distil, to evaporate his repressions
in poetry. Lacking other evidence, let us then accept the hypothesis of the man of ice. But after
all ice has its limits and it should have melted
at the contact of Margaret Fuller. Whose was
the fault if no such thing occurred? Not Margaret's certainly.

A queenly carriage, a broad brow, a thick twist
of blond hair, dreamy eyes, an energetic chin, a
pout of disillusion, a way of always snapping her
eyes, and a soul afire. An ironic god had brought
this sister of Corinne and Lélia to birth in the
country of the Puritans. All her life she had to

beat her wings, ruffle her feathers, wound herself against reality. Her tragic end seemed foreshadowed in that existence full of contradictions. Margaret was self-taught. From infancy she had been a voracious reader. Greek, Latin, German, French, Italian, fine arts, philosophy, politics, history, she had learned all. While yet a child she had had to be put on dry bread to tear her away from Shakespeare. She copied in her Bible the Hymns of Novalis; she addressed passionate prayers to Rousseau and wrote imaginary letters to Beethoven. She pressed flowers on her heart, she spoke to them, envied them. She loved to mask herself, to split her personality. She believed that she had been born an Italian princess. She tricked herself out in a thousand imaginary names. In one of these fictitious portraits she changed herself into a Mænad, raced through the forest in the moonlight, bathed in the icy pools, enticed men the better to repel them. In her Bacchic frenzy she indulged in a taste for murder, for sadism. She felt within her an enormous force which she had not enough senses to express. She took refuge in art. A picture, a statue threw her into transports, and she adored music. Ah, to leave

this land of the Puritans, to go off to the country
hymned by her dear Goethe in the song of
Mignon . . . Italy! Italy! Her life was a series
of ecstacies, enthusiasms, prostrations. And she
dragged all hearts after her. The young women
worshiped her. She had built up in Boston a veritable court of admirers before whom in great
pomp she delivered her improvisations on beauty,
love, religion, genius, like Corinne at Cape
Misène. She set all Boston running. . . . Margaret was a poet, art critic, journalist, feminist,
and Emerson had given her the editorship of *The
Dial*.

He had met her in 1835. She was twenty-five,
he thirty-two. A common friend had shown him
Margaret's translation of Goethe's *Tasso* and she
had come to spend two weeks at the Emerson's.
Emerson was at once her god. She had prophesied
him, expected him. The Boston lectures had struck
her like a thunderbolt and Margaret was one of
the earliest habitués of the house at Concord.
They saw each other frequently, wrote to each
other, took long walks together. She taught him
to speak German—purposely, that he might be
under an obligation to her, he pretended in a

moment of ill humor. She introduced him to the
fine arts, lent him albums of the old masters. He
guided her in the reading of English authors of
the good old times: foreign writers she knew
already.

That Margaret may have tried to throw herself
at Emerson is beyond doubt. She laid siege to him
according to rule. Emerson himself admitted that
she neglected nothing to seduce him. She studied
his tastes, goaded him, amused him, met frankness with frankness, dizzying him with her stories,
with her flashes of wit. She had an amazing need
of expansion. She was lively, malicious, overflowing. All that he lacked, she made a great show of
—ardor, enthusiasm, the passion for the beautiful, the gift of effusion, that way of losing herself in all she loved. Ah, how he envied her this
genius of perpetual youth—her *Nuovissima Vita*,
as he called it. She reminded him of the ideal
forms of the world in full flower. He compared
her to the goddesses, to Ceres, Minerva, Proser-
pine. But all that remained platonic. She would
so much have liked to conquer the sage, to break
his ice, to draw him out of his crystal cell, to
succeed in kicking away his stilts from under him,

and she spared no pains to do it, neither sallies nor sarcasm. He played dead, the idiot, according to his own say-so; he grew angry and brought tears to his friend's eyes. She stung him, nagged him, stormed, reproached his coldness. "Adieu, my dear positive," she wrote him, "Believe me superlatively yours." Emerson did not know what to do. He snubbed her, scolded her, held her courteously but firmly at a distance. She had promised him to be good, but he did not trust her. It was understood that he was icy, dumb, uncommunicative. She must take him as he was. He besought her not to go on talking about himself. But she continued and frightened him. She encroached upon him. She enlarged the lobes of his brain and of his heart, dazzled him, but when he went home, these lovely fireworks were nothing but straw fires. Then too, Margaret was malicious; she had a wicked tongue. Leaving her, he still heard, he said, the thorns crackling under the pot. She made him superstitious and he felt in her what he called a potency of catastrophes.

What would he have made of this Mænad who expected all of the universe? He needed in those he loved a calm mirror of himself—Ellen, Lydia, as serene as the sapphire of Walden. . . . And so he was but half saddened when in 1846 the Mænad set sail for Europe. Margaret had realized her dream. She was in Europe; she had found George Sand, Chopin, Lamennais, then Italy, the Lakes, Florence, Rome—Rome where her destiny was sealed, where she had met the prosaic but devoted Ossoli, where she was united to him, where she had given birth to a son in circumstances which set all tongues wagging in Boston. . . . Then one day Margaret re-embarked for America with husband and child. . . . She was going to recommence the siege of Boston, find her court again, see her sage once more, quite harmless and chastened now, but these dreams had foundered when the vessel on which she was returning went down with all hands, one sad dawn off the coast of Fire Island. Emerson remained to pronounce the funeral oration of the Mænad, to write her life, and probably to think of her until his death as of his Egeria, his Inspirer, his Muse. How often must he have recalled her visits, their conversations, their walks, that amber glow she spread about her. She expected something of him which he, alas, could not give. She had seen through him. This man who adored the universe did not know men and was not interested in what was before his eyes. A great cause, a great love, she thought, would have pulled him out of the ice. If only she had found in him a brother; but he had been only a critic. He had taken her only as a magic lantern, as a spectacle . . . Margaret exaggerated. She had produced a deep impression on Emerson. She had revealed to him the Eternal Feminine, the splendid virtue of the Form. It was indeed she he had in mind when he spoke of the mystery in the depths of a woman's eyes, those eyes wherein the sculptor sees his statue, the architect the form of his temple, the poet the anticipation of his odes, the woman whose love colors and animates all about her, tragic, always on the edge of tears, consoling herself by devouring her emotions.

Poor Margaret! Instead of a Puritan she should have had a Goethe, a Liszt, a Chopin, a Wagner. She had mistaken her latitude. When she laid siege to her sage, had she not read his essays on "Love" and on "Friendship"? If hope remained she would have lost it surely in re-reading the peroration of these celebrated pages quite in the tone of the discouraging epistles which Emerson sent her. He could have cut out these lines and slipped them in the letter-box. She would have read what follows:

My dear Margaret:

I do then with my friends as I do with my books. I would have them where I can find them, but I seldom use them. We must have society on our own terms, and admit it or exclude it on the slightest cause. I cannot afford to speak much with my friend. If he is great he makes me so great that I cannot descend to converse. In the great days, presentiments hover before me in the firmament. I ought then to dedicate myself to them. I go in that I may seize them, I go out that I may seize them. I fear only that I may lose them receding into the sky in which now they are only a patch of brighter light. Then, though I prize my friends, I cannot afford to talk with them and study their visions, lest I lose my own. It would indeed give me a certain household joy to quit this lofty seeking, this spiritual astronomy or search of stars, and come down to warm sympathies with you; but then I know well I shall mourn always the vanishing of my mighty gods. It is true, next week I shall have languid moods, when I can well afford to occupy myself with foreign objects; then I shall regret the lost literature of your mind, and wish you were by my side again. But if you come, perhaps you will fill my mind only with new visions; not with yourself but with your lustres, and I shall not be able any more than now to converse with you. So I will owe to my friends this evanescent intercourse. I will receive from them not what they have but what they are. They shall give me that which properly they cannot give, but which emanates from them. But they shall not hold me by any relations less subtile and pure. We will meet as though we met not, and part as though we parted not.

Yours ever—or never,
Ralph Waldo Emerson.

And he could have added as a postscript that as for him he was getting along very well with this absentee friendship. He said that the sun is not troubled to know where his rays may fall so long as he shines. True love dwells in the Eternal and lets the objects of its affections tumble like masks. It then feels its independence the surer.

Poor, once more poor Margaret! What would she have said could she have discovered in the *Journal* of the man of ice this thought about his dear Plotinus which he wrote one day in his notebook and which gives us perhaps the key to the whole mystery, *"Plotinus pudore quadam affici videbatur quod anima ejus in corpore esset"*— which means in plain English that Plotinus was ashamed to think that his soul inhabited a body, and that he did not like one to remind him of it?

CHAPTER VIII

Thoreau

HE KNEW the age and the size of all the trees
of Concord, the name of all the flowers, of
all the plants in English and in Latin, he had
ferreted out all the nests and warrens. He used
to tame the turtles and the snakes; he would track
down the foxes; he played hide and seek with the
squirrels; he pulled the woodchucks out of their
holes by the tail; he had only to scratch the soil
with the end of his stick to unearth Indian ar-
rowheads. One day he stumbled in the mountains
and fell upon a variety of arnica for which he
had been looking for days. He knew by heart the
Greek Anthology and Virgil; he translated Anacreon, Persius, Æschylus, and Pindar; he played
the flute; he surveyed land; he made pencils—
the best in the world, as they say in America; he
knew how to build houses, make boats, make trees

221

grow, repair walls, and he found time to be a philosopher. He was consulted upon glowworms,
fishes, turtles. He was a walking natural history
museum. In coarse gray trousers, with an old
straw hat, thick shoes, an old music box for a
herbarium, a spyglass, a notebook, a knife and
string, punting, swimming, climbing trees, he
journeyed toward the ideal, indifferent to the
heat of summer, to rain, to snow, from the edge
of Walden to the forests of Maine and to the
coasts of Cape Cod. The calendar of the seasons
which Emerson had planned, Thoreau had passed
thirty years of his life in composing. From it he
drew the horoscope of all that bore fur, feathers,
leaves, or scales. He knew the exact time when
the flowers opened; he watched their birth, today this flower, tomorrow that; he was there on
the dot as if to catch a train. The water lilies, his
favorite flower, unfolded in his hand. Why didn't
he have a motion-picture camera? He had built
himself a yawl, painted blue and green, the
Musketaquid, and he sailed up the rivers in her
with his Greek and Latin poets. He passed his life
in the woods or on the water and he had the scent
of an Indian or a trapper. He said his prayers to

Diana, Selene, the moon with which he was in love, like Endymion; he was passionately fond of a beautiful heifer; he would have liked to press the young oaks against his heart. But he fled from men; he was an enemy of the law. Society inspired in him only sarcasms; he preached passive disobedience to the state. So much the worse if they put him in prison, as happened.

Emerson had sold him a bit of ground in Walden and he had built himself a cabin there. For two years he played Robinson Crusoe. He had settled the social problem by asceticism, doing without practically everything. He was satisfied with the sunlight and a handful of nuts. He maintained that with six weeks' work a year one could fulfill the needs of existence. His stay at Walden cost him in all twenty-five dollars for eight months and he had the world for nothing. His gospel was simple: Be what you are, live in the present, do what you like, do not be too moral, the essential thing is to live. Simplicity! Simplicity! Do not be melancholy. Do not read the papers. And above all, one world at a time!

He loved using his hands, nailing, planting, measuring, building. His gods were the hammer, the hatchet, the hoe, the trowel. He was an artisan inspired, a transcendental geometer. When he surveyed with the chain and the rule, he seemed to be playing with Space and the Numbers. He had put all his ideal in the real, all eternity in the present moment. He believed in the world's salvation by the redemption of the senses and he had consecrated his to solitude and nature. Others sought the idea in the clouds; he found it by his side in the animals, the plants, the stones. He worshiped the elements. He would have liked to kiss the earth, the naked earth, inhuman, sincere, and rough like himself. The Transcendentalists dreamed, discussed, made plans for the reformation of the universe. Thoreau was content with existing, with feeling himself being, happy by himself, savoring the sweetness of his breath. What cause would he have had to be gloomy, he who had never stopped wondering? Of ambition he had none outside himself. He was uninterested in the result of his acts. He had attained the perfect Buddhist peace of Yoga.

He was a marvelous image chaser. All his life was concentrated in his vision. What was idea for Emerson became form and color for Thoreau.

The plants, the animals, the waters, the sky, the seasons, these were his ideas, his images, his idols, an endless film which he passed his life unwinding. The Over-Soul for him was not a dream. He saw it in the brilliance of a flower, the flight of a bird, the leap of a squirrel or a fish; he heard it in the noises of the forest; he breathed it in the odors of the earth. Seeking everywhere the traces of the Ineffable, Thoreau photographed the universe, but in his images, however precise they might be, there was always a beyond, a transparence, an influence, an effluvium, something which brought him back to the Fortunate Isles in the open sky or on the summit of the mysterious mountain Ktaadn, which he saw in dream sleeping or awake. Like a true Puritan, he abhorred art. When one spoke to him of painting he took a sheet of paper, smeared it with ink, folded it over and across, opened it, and said, "There's your picture." Great men left him indifferent. He was his own great man and he despised history. Time for him had only one dimension; he held all in the present.

Thoreau related everything to himself. The seasons were his seasons, the weather his weather.

The noises, colors, odors, enriched and explained to him his states of mind. The real was his poetry. He loved nudity, simplicity, the pure triviality of things, the gray, the brown, the dun. . . . The ugly was beautiful in his eyes, an abandoned road, a deserted pasture, a ruined farm, a crow, a snake, a mole, the lichen on a worm-eaten fence, the dried seaweed and the refuse on the beach. He abandoned himself with delight to the appeal of the savage and the primitive. The more savage one is, he used to say, the more alive. Give him the blackest wood, the most sinister swamp. When he left on an outing his compass led him always toward the west, turning his back on civilization. "Go fish and hunt far and wide, day by day; and rest thee by many hearthsides without misgiving! Rise free from care before the dawn, and seek adventures! Let the noon find thee by other brooks, and the night overtake thee always at home. Lead such a life as the children that chase butterflies in the meadow. There are no larger fields than these, no nobler games, no more extended earth. With thy life uninsured, live free and forever as you were planned. Grow wild according to Nature, like these ferns and brakes, which study not morals or philosophy; nor strive to become a cultivated grass for cattle to eat; or like these bulrushes, behind which you see the reddening sky over the lake, as if they were the masts of vessels in a crowded Venice harbor. Let the thunder rumble in thy own tongue; what if it brings rain to farmers' crops? that is not its errand to thee. Take shelter under the cloud, while others fly to carts and sheds. Enjoy thy dominion, and waive men, the fowl and the quadruped, and all creeping things. Seek without toil thy daily food; thy sustenance, is it not in nature? Through want of confidence in the gods men are where they are; buying and selling, owning land, and following trade—and spending their lives ignobly."

Such was the credo of a free man.

He had been brought to Emerson some time after the latter had settled in Concord. Thoreau was twenty, fourteen years younger than Emerson. He was fresh from Harvard where he had been fractious but scholarly. He had written many essays and had come out a fervent humanist, fed on Greek, Latin, and English classics. Thoreau kept a journal and so well imitated the master that Emerson had been told about him. Thoreau had come. He was not a beauty; he had blue eyes, chestnut hair, a large crow's beak for a nose like Emerson's, but nothing suave or angelic about him. Quite the contrary. Hard and prominent features hacked out as with a knife, and set awry behind a beard, a great mouth which took on in time a twist of bitterness, something imperious and aggressive in his looks, not an angel but a Viking (his father's people had been Norman). As soon as he set himself to writing, one would have taken him for a double, for a reflection of Emerson, the same ideas, same style, but with movement and passion. Emerson moved in circles, played the squirrel in his wheel; Thoreau sped straight ahead before him to the end of his ideas, without recantations, without evasions. He was authoritarian, dogmatic, and purposely paradoxical. But in the average calmer portions of his prose, it was impossible to distinguish him from Emerson.

At twenty Thoreau had no longer any ambition. He had espoused Concord, had put it upon him as a garment. Emerson had tried to tame this savage. He had opened his house to him, had taken him as a man of all work, as a Jack of all trades, leaving him long periods of leisure. When Emerson was traveling, it was Henry who was in charge of the house, nailing, hammering, repairing, gardening. He played with the little Emersons, carried them on his back, made them toys, told them animal stories, led them off into the woods or sailing. Henry had been in love only once and he had sworn not to begin again. Was it not said that he had withdrawn in favor of his brother and that he had suffered ever since in secret? He brusquely pushed aside the young ladies who would have fallen on his neck, saying that they would ruin his career—his career as a woodsman. Like Emerson, he had transposed, sublimated his love into the transcendent. Between man and woman he declared he could not discover any essential difference. All that he ever knew of love he learned from the plants and animals and the only wedlock he knew was that of the flowers. But he used to read Anacreon, and however savage he was, his soul was delicate and tender. He had dedicated an altar to Lydia Emerson, whose house he guarded. Once when far from each other, they corresponded. Lydia confided to him her troubles. She encouraged him as a sister without succeeding in curing him of his misanthropy.

The man of ice saw himself with amazement in this sublime youth who seemed to him to return his ideas with a vigor which he himself could not give them (in flesh and blood, he said, and with Saxon ruggedness), this candid youngster, this child who did not hesitate to answer back. Thoreau had a soul but also senses, a very lofty soul but equipped with arms, hands, claws, tentacles, the image of Emerson but of an Emerson with muscles, who knew how to nail, build, measure, plant, run through the brush, climb trees—and who knew better than he all the byways and hidden corners of Concord? Henry taught his host to garden without hurting himself with his hoe; he taught him the names of the plants, the flowers, the ways of the animals, and, thanks to him, the philosopher's thoughts took on form and body. Thoreau propped up his dreams with facts. He had taken Emerson's lessons literally. He had reduced his needs to a minimum, embraced poverty and solitude, but without sprees in Boston. He was not married; he had never had a legacy;

he did not eat meat, smoked not, and had never drunk wine. He had never used a rifle, refused to pay his taxes, never went to church even to bury himself in his overcoat collar. All this not for the sake of a pose or because of utopian dreams but by temperament and principle. Thoreau was individualism sovereign, self-reliance incarnate. And their temperaments were very different, not to say contradictory—Emerson, calm, prudent, long suffering; Thoreau, full of the spirit of contradiction, authoritative, paradoxical; instead of waiting for the universe in his chair, he bravely dashed off to meet it and challenged it.

Henry like Margaret had had a beautiful dream. He too had knocked at the secret door of Emerson. The sage had opened his house to him but had jealously barred the entrance to his inner chambers. Henry like Margaret had been confronted with the placard on the door of Emerson's heart: No trespassers! It had required several years to admit the evidence. It had begun by harmless tiffs over certain manuscripts which Thoreau had submitted to *The Dial*. Emerson reproached him for his affectations, his mannerisms; he meant his paradoxes. Thoreau had a grudge against him for these evasions. In the long run their characters clashed like their tastes. Emerson maintained that he would have shaken hands with a tree as willingly as with Henry. Thoreau felt that he was talking to one absent, that he too was taken by Emerson for a magic lantern, a spectacle. Emerson was not always just toward him in his *Journal*. He called him a general without soldiers and went so far as to confer on him the title of "captain of huckleberry parties." . . . Emerson had never taken very seriously this man fourteen years his junior who posed as a philosopher, who took his ideas without great originality, he maintained, whose strong muscles he secretly envied, sometimes with a touch of bitterness, and whose paradoxes seemed in his eyes to be conceit. . . . At the point we have reached, however, the effect still lasted and Thoreau had not lost his illusions. He was still dreaming, he too, of a great and beautiful friendship in the antique manner with the sage whom he frankly admired without none the less ever calling him his master.

Thoreau had an *alter ego*, Ellery Channing, married to the younger sister of Margaret Fuller

Henry D. Thoreau

From "The First and Last Journeys of Thoreau,"
The Bibliophile Society, Boston

and nephew of the great Unitarian preacher.
Channing had had his attack of romanticism. In
"The Youth of the Poet and the Painter" which
he had given to *The Dial*, he had like René
called upon the longed-for storms. He wished to
be all or nothing. He threw down the gauntlet to
society. He mingled his feeling for the antique
with that for nature. Then he had calmed down.
He had poured out upon the trees and the fields
his excess sympathy. He had let himself be captured by the charm of Concord and had consecrated his life to solitude. He was a prisoner in
the golden rays of Emerson. Poet and fervent
peripatetic, he too paced upon and down Concord,
haunting its retreats, without herbarium, without
notebook, without compass, like a capricious spirit
amused by all about him. He guided Emerson
toward lonely places on the edge of the woods,
pastures reddened by red sorrel, wild gardens
where apples grew, apples to which he gave
comic names—the "Touch-me-if-you-dare," the
"Seek-no-further-of-this"—the beds of wild
flowers known to him alone, admiring all, wondering at all, launching himself apropos of everything and nothing into fanciful improvisations

adorned with quotations from Crashaw, Vaughan, Herrick, old savory poets whom he awkwardly imitated in his odes. He had put all Concord into fairly prosaic verse which Hawthorne in one of his tales tossed into the fire unceremoniously and by allusion. Emerson was at his ease with Ellery who did not try to force open his secret door. He had only to lend an ear to his poetic paradoxes, to his capricious and often bizarre associations of ideas. Channing had the eye of a painter. He gave the signal, the curtain rose, and the landscape grew colored and animated. He was an excellent telescope for Emerson. When Margaret Fuller had left and Thoreau began to grow in upon himself, Ellery Channing remained the faithful and official companion, the Eckermann of Thoreau, the quintessence of whose poetry and thought he gave us in a beautifully chaotic book, in which Concord, the walks, and the conversations of the three philosophers come to life again.

CHAPTER IX

Master Skylark

EMERSON confessed the simple truth when he admitted that his way of enjoying the Universe was to look at it through the prism of a hundred different mentalities. This prudent Yankee knew how to use men and he should have added to his famous essay on "Friendship" a chapter on the utility of friends. Thoreau, Channing drew him out of his cell, revealed to him the external world by relating to him those analogies, those secret correspondences in the exploration of which he had specialized. They did better than that, they inspired him. The bee takes his honey from all the flowers and keeps no account of his booty. The honey alone counts. Returning from their walks Emerson carefully collected in his notebooks the remarks, the witticisms, the discoveries of his companions. Of what they had thought aloud before him he took good care to lose nothing. All was sewn into the *Essays* without a trace of the seams remaining when the work was done. He made no alliances, but he made annexations. . . . And perhaps his friends were wrong about him. He admired and loved them after his fashion. They were "almost dear" to him—admire this "almost." In a moment of enthusiasm he had even dreamed of decorating his hall with portraits of Henry and Ellery, beside those of Franklin and Washington, and he added Bronson Alcott's to theirs. This repaid a debt.

Thoreau had revealed man to him, Alcott would open to him the seventh heaven of the Idea, the platonic universe. He did not go to the Ideal by cross roads. He did not track it down in hiding as Thoreau tracked the fox. He did not discover it like Emerson in zigzags. Having plunged head-first into the occult, he had never come up. Having chosen to dream, he had never awaked from his dream. The transcendent was his natural element. He pulled worlds out of his head as a pastry cooks pulls cakes out of an oven. He passed his life ruminating on the banks of the Absolute. It was not the soul whose existence had to be proved to Bronson Alcott. It was the senses. He was saturated with mysticism.

He had begun his life as Rimbaud finished his, in business, and he had ended it in poetry. He had started out as a pedlar to pay his family's debts and he succeeded. Then the demon of analogy caught him and he had lost his footing in the world of dreams without renouncing his ambition of assuring the happiness of mankind. He had opened a transcendentalist school in Boston which Emerson had often visited and where he had received the magnetic shock. It was a fine school such as had never been seen until then, full of light and air, furnished with *objets d'art* and antique busts. Alcott maintained that to be a good teacher one must first be a philosopher. He gave Plato and the Gospels to the children as their primer and he acted the Socratic midwife. At his word and contact—he was kindness incarnate— the little boys and girls uttered prophecies. Give him a group of children and he took it upon himself to draw all Plato out of them by questions and answers. The Neoplatonists and Gnostics had gone to his head. He had taken up his observation

237

post in the clouds, and as soon as he opened his mouth, the Universe turned to steam. He took over the most ancient doctrines, marvelous thaumaturgies. He said that the Soul had pre-existed in a better world where all was beautiful, pure, and good; that it had fallen; that from fall to fall it had been reincarnated in the beasts, the plants, the stones, that all the apparatus of law, institutions, society, the family were only like the sensible universe, the waste matter, the dross of the Spirit, illusions; that one must save the world, return to the Gold Age, to original purity. And he, Alcott, offered himself as guide for the return journey. The Soul was petrified upon the surface; it must be re-won, brought back to its primitive fluidity. To save the world from its errors, it must be reabsorbed in intuition, in the Idea, and the road which he followed to that end was the Word which draws the soul out of its depths. He was a spiritual midwife, a Saint John Chrysostom—John with the Mouth of Gold—an incarnation of the Logos. As soon as he began to speak, he refused to stop. Gilded atoms fell from his lips; he drowned you in a sort of mystic haze, an aura in which all sense of reality evaporated.

He made one dizzy. One seemed, his listeners confessed, to sail heavenward in a swing. No practical talent, no concrete fulfillment. He was, according to Emerson, an intellectual torso, without arms or legs. Alcott passed his life going into bankruptcy. One idea made him forget another. Upon the slate on which he wrote the sponge rubbed off as fast as pencil could write. They sold his pamphlets to the trunk makers and, when he published in *The Dial* his "Enigmas" and his "Orphic Sayings," they were greeted with shouts of laughter. People chuckled over these sublime tautologies. But Alcott went on all the more. . . .

Emerson, who admired him but whom he exasperated often, would have liked to get rid of him by shipping him off to Carlyle. (Alcott had fervent admirers in England.) Teufelsdroeckh must have been highly amused to see good Alcott appearing with his razor-blade face, his graying temples, his hang-dog but luminous expression. Here was the man who wanted to save mankind by making them eat acorns as in the Golden Age. Then Carlyle grew angry. He could not swallow what he called "the Potato Gospel," and one day he brought his visionary into the heart of the City of London. Striking his cane on the pavement and showing the substantial houses of the rich about them, he addressed Alcott: "Do you see this, man! This has stood for a thousand years, and will stand when you and your dam'd potato gospel have gone to the dogs. . . ." But Alcott crushed it all to powder with one glance and Carlyle could not help liking him. The American friends who had clubbed together to send him to England (and Emerson was a good first on the list) had lost their trouble and their money. Soon Alcott came back, this time with reinforcements, flanked with an esoteric library of a thousand volumes which was to be the basis of Fruitlands. Idyllion! as Carlyle said.

After the rout of his phalanstery, Alcott had settled in Concord, a sublime parasite, needy, in debt, scarcely feeding his family in which Louisa was growing up and whose charming and homely novels struggled to pay the expenses of the poor Don Quixote's dreams. To follow a new Utopia Alcott would not have hesitated to leave his wife and children. Thoreau said that the rats and mice nested in him. Emerson came to his assistance, defended him, offered him even the hospitality of his home. He had taken his measure at the first glance, full of nonsense, of bubbles, but one inspired, a true seer. Alcott was a poet, a poet who believed in his poetry. Reading him one thinks often of Mallarmé, but for him the Penultimate was not dead. He went to the Idea *via* the word; he had reduced the Universe to a Vocable without ever being satisfied and putting to himself along the road very subtle and profound problems on the relationship of words and thought. Suffering from the torment of unity, always on the point of reaching his dream, always disillusioned, he took refuge in the apology of Silence as the only transcendental means of expression, or in oracle. The world was a forest of symbols across which his soul was groping to find herself. Instead of pretending to reduce the world to his categories, it is too bad that Alcott like Mallarmé did not know how to put his intuitions to music. Emerson had suggested it to him, but Psyche eternally slipped away from him without moreover any ridicule being able to lay him low. At eighty years he still tramped the roads, peddling his clouds, delivering them for nothing, for the fun of it. . . .

Emerson admired this metachemist, as he

called him. He sometimes got on his nerves; he joked at him gently, but the abstractor of the quintessence inspired him. He owed much to Alcott, perhaps more than is admitted. He was deep in the reading of his *Journal*, he took part in his conversations, read him his essays, his poems, discussed with him his doctrine, and he planned to write his life. The main transcendental initiatives, the Transcendental Club, *The Dial*, Fruitlands, the project of a transcendentalist university at Concord, all that was due in large part to the inspiration of Alcott whom many considered as the soul of the movement. All of Emerson's philosophy is to be found in *Nature*, and the reveries of Alcott certainly colored this essential book, the bible of absolute idealism. Emerson again took up in it the Platonistic and Swedenborgian views of Alcott on the genesis of the world by emanation. The Over-Soul, representative men, the spiritual laws, there is Alcott in all that. In his most cryptic poems, "Brahma," "The Sphinx," "The World-Soul," in the inscriptions and mottoes which decorated the title page of the *Essays*, Emerson took on even the tone of voice of Alcott, whose "Enigmas" and "Orphic Sayings" have left an echo in his golden verses. One finds in them the same hovering of thought between earth and sky, the same gaps of silence between the idea and the word, the same mythology of the abstract. At his extreme and purely transcendental end Emerson made but one with Alcott. There must have been between them a real transfusion of blood.

Emerson went to the Idea as to men, shyly, prudently, with a kind of false shame as soon as he reached the heights. He surrounded himself with reticences, allegories, subterfuges. He was afraid of being too wise. He was grateful to the Over-Soul for having put him near men of originality and eccentricity whom he laughed at, these people who discussed their own breath and who speculated while contemplating their navels. Several of them were his guests and companions; Sampson Reed, the Swedenborgian apothecary, fertile in original intuitions, explorer of the secret ways of the spirit, Bergsonian before Bergson; King Newcomb, inspired æsthete, who sang all alone the litanies of the Virgin at night in his cell at Brook Farm, and who had put the portrait of Fannie Elssler, the dancer, between Saint Francis Xavier and Saint Ignatius; Edward Palmer, who refused to use money when he happened to have any—which was rare—and who paid his bills at the inn with prose and verse at the risk often of dying of hunger; Charles Lane, the oracle of Fruitlands, ascetic and convinced nihilist, who grew angry when he had to eat flesh at the Emersons; above all, Jones Very, who took the *Gospels* literally, preached the return to absolute sincerity, took Emerson to task and interrupted the preacher in church. Very had given up his free will; he hesitated when it was merely a question of leaning his arm on a table; and he lived as if disincarnated. . . . These gymnosophists put oxygen into the air, as Emerson said. They carried out their ideas—his ideas—to the bitter end, and projected them in full light upon a sometimes absurd background. Emerson experimented and watched them making at their own expense the trial of complete transcendentalism. The art of writing was unknown to them. The intellectual torsos could not hold a pen. It was he who fixed their dreams, clarified them, humanized them, and gave form to their visions. He made them speak, listened to them, sifted out all they said through his good sense and changed the nonsense of these dreamers into verse or maxims rich in wisdom. These visionaries inspired him with a respect analogous to that which primitive people accord to the simple and the feeble-minded. He felt them by obscure channels to be in direct communication with the soul of the world; he consulted them as true mediums.

CHAPTER X

Home, Sweet Home!

AND the days of Concord flowed on all alike. The sage divided his life into two parts, dream on one side, action on the other. In the woods and over the fields he followed the inner music; in the village and at home he took men as if they were real—perhaps they were, in fact. The world was a theater and he conscientiously played his rôle in it. It was the effect of deep prudence. He was not sure enough of his dreams to sacrifice simple duties to them, not sure that the real world was identical with the world of thought, and he took his precautions; he did not wish to miss anything. . . .

Concord had adopted him at once and he showed himself to be the most accomplished of its citizens. This man who broke everything up into clouds, who put between him and his fel-

246

He loved the Sabbath calm, the wooden church, bare, white, the clock in the steeple which took the pulse of Time, the naïve liturgy, the rustic music, the humble soloist, the blushing young girl who offered the bread and wine to the communicants. As at the town hall, he came there the better to observe the groups at the foot of the pulpit. Ah, if the orator of the day could have seen the image of himself engraved upon the blue eyes of that imperturbable man seated below him. . . . If he had read the commentaries on the sermon which Emerson pinned into his *Journal* on reaching home . . . Emerson trained himself there, so to speak, by default. He felt the gaps in the sermon and he made it over by himself. Was not all Concord seated there below the pulpit? He recognized merely by looking at their faces the farmer, the apothecary, the book dealer, the barkeep. All humanity was there with its needs, its eternal aspirations, the cobbler whose daughter had gone mad, the poor school teacher abandoned by his pupils, the woman of bad reputation in the town, the stage-driver who was with difficulty recovering from an illness, X——, who had just failed in business and who was not yet back on

his feet . . . All had come to the Temple to beg
of their Father their daily bread, a bit of comfort
and hope, while there floated high, so high, above
them the indifferent words of the man in the
black gown. . . . It was there that Emerson understood men, that he loved them, that he com-
muned with them, and prepared for them who
suffered his lay sermons, his compensations. . . .

He went frequently to Boston. Two or three
hours in the stage. This promiscuity did not
alarm him. There too he hit the target, he met
his fellows, notaries off to court, circuit preach-
ers, shopkeepers off to buy goods, ladies a-visit-
ing. . . . He loved the animation of the suburbs,
the coming and going, the off-handedness, the
motley of the crowd. He felt them to be more
sincere, more real than society folk and he was
at ease with them. He felt awakening within him
a taste for form and color. He was very sensitive
to the beauty of the human form; there was not
a trait that escaped him—children, young girls,
young boys, old folk. In everything he had merely
to open his eyes to discover expression. It is the
charm and as it were the balm of life to see shining on all sides in the common people those ma-

jestic traits which make such a striking contrast with their trivial occupations. . . . Everything instructed and diverted the gentleman in the black coat and high hat who was going to unveil the mysteries of the Over-Soul in Boston, Baltimore, or Philadelphia.

Concord was a universe in epitome, a *piccolo mondo moderno.* . . . The fools, the clowns, the charlatans, he could adapt himself to all of them. They were the fringe of the tapestry of existence and gave reality and snap to the picture. Emerson accepted all—the shops, the bar-room, the poor house. Walking he would stop to talk with the habitués of the tavern, the fishermen, the woodchoppers, the shepherds. The sight of an humble woman behind her window curtains brought tears to his eyes. No pretensions, no hypocrisy here. It was the freshness or, as he said, the milk of life. . . . Then, too, Concord had its festivals, reviews, commemorations, the Fourth of July, the parade of the militia, music, uniforms, the sham battle on the parade ground, the open-air ball . . . The enraptured philosopher forgot nothing.

His favorite theater was his home. . . . In this

domain once more his life was a masterpiece of prudence and he redoubled his efforts to belong to himself more surely. It was there that he played the rôles of master of the house, host, husband, father. It was his laboratory, the test-tube, according to him, of the true sage. Life is short, so are human forces; the universe is wide. Let us not fail in our experiments; let us not cheat the ideal and let us try to make the infinite our own. Ends are transcendent, but destiny is all about us. The dearest beings were seen by Emerson across a gulf. All the more reason to cling to them. Left to himself, he dreamed, he floated, he broke loose, he dissolved; all the more reason to be attached to something solid. . . . To live between earth and sky is good for utopians. The prudent aviator does not travel without a parachute. At home, in his house, dreams took on the shape of friends. . . . There as elsewhere he put his wisdom into practice, and his philosophy of human relations did not vary. His scepticism about friendship and love, he extended to family affections. There again he was at least in thought distant and detached. Above all he must keep his fine independence, defend his autonomy, his and that of others, live without alienating himself, respect in himself and others the rights of sovereign personality. Wife, children, guests, friends, he received them with gratitude as presents from the supreme Soul but with the freedom of God's children. . . . Human contact is only possible in respect to very lofty relations. Emerson consented to play father and husband, but always at a respectful distance. This detachment he pushed sometimes a bit far, so far that he might well have been taken for an immoralist. It seemed to him sometimes that if the great Universe remained his, he would yield up without too great regret what was dearest to him. . . . His city, his home reattached him to the real and fastened him down. In the city council, in court, in town meeting, Emerson played the statesman; at home with the ashes, the soap, the beer, the vinegar, the manure, the household remedies, he played chemist; and he had indeed to turn into a naturalist to treat with the trees, the hens, the pigs, the horses, the fish, the bees, the worms, the wood, the coal. . . . "Honor to the house where they are simple to the verge of hardship, so that there the intellect is awake and reads the laws of the universe, the soul worships truth and love, honor and courtesy flow into all deed." If the world was so wide, it was probably to permit each one of us to own his house in it. . . .

Near 1840, just before the publication of the *Essays*, the band of Emersons was no longer complete. Mrs. Emerson, his mother, was still there, finally recovered from her fears and coddled by the best of sons. Aunt Moody—Tnamurya—still as fanciful and impulsive, ran from boarding house to boarding house and came from time to time to burst in upon her nephew. Her austere lessons had borne their fruit and she could be proud of Ralph Waldo. Lydia, dear Lydia, was the soul of the house, devoted and gentle, defending and shielding as well as she could the solitude of her philosopher, very sensible, very sweet, very wise. He called her his Asia, but more familiarly and more tenderly by the pet name of Queenie. "And Queenie says . . . and Queenie says . . ." His *Journal* is all strewn with the oracles of this exquisite wife, whose natural wisdom and strong goodness protected him against many a storm, especially at the critical time of the Cambridge address when the sage, angered by the criticisms, lost his patience and prepared to sharpen his pen to answer his opponents. It was Queenie who disarmed him and taught him self-reliance, perfect self-confidence. Emersonian wisdom thus owes more than one thinks to the homely oracles about him and to daily experience.

The brilliant fraternal Pléiade was broken up. Of the four brothers there remained only Ralph Waldo and William. The two close friends, Edward and Charles, had died young. Edward, handsome, fluent, elegant, eloquent, military, carrying his head like a young proconsul, brilliant, more brilliant even than Ralph, they said, and who had begun in the office of a celebrated lawyer, Daniel Webster, a career rich in promise, Edward had died of hereditary consumption in Porto Rico after an attack of insanity. There had also died at thirty Charles Chauncy, the talented younger brother, stoic, pantheist, humanist, hellenist, poet, full of whims, full of life, deeply misanthropic, self-reliance incarnate. His loss left Ralph Waldo inconsolable. They would no more read together the Greek tragedians; they would no more commune in nature. . . . There remained William, the eldest, magistrate in New

York. He too had had his religious crisis. A student of theology at Göttingen, he had lost his faith as a result of religious scruples, which he went to submit to Goethe. Emerson had buried his dead with fine ceremonies in thought; he had laid them to rest with great Greek orations, while waiting to resurrect them in the soul of his representatives of humanity of whom like Murat, they had certainly given him the idea. . . . He remained haughty, serene, despite these blows of fate. He plunged more deeply into the Nirvana of great books. He continued to declare that death did not exist for him, that he would remain untouched and unshakable under the ruins. . . . But Nemesis was preparing to strike him a blow in the face.

CHAPTER XI

O Child of Paradise

SINCE 1836 Emerson had been father of a
delightful little boy who had been named
like him Waldo, the little Vaudois. He was enraptured with the adventure; he never got over
it. Father, son, what did all that mean? With a
little obstinate expression, a broad forehead, big
eyes which devoured the whole heavens, the child
made one think of a dreamer and a precocious
philosopher. The father was filled with joy before this being who came to him from heaven,
from the depths of the Unconscious. The child is
closest to nature; he incarnates her mysteries, impulses, secret wills, caprices, in his cries, laughter, tears. Emerson was dumb before this little
man who slept in his cradle like some one who
had returned from a long journey. He adored the
child Waldo; he adored himself in him. He com-

257

pared himself to Pygmalion infatuated with the statue of Galatea. He so distant, so aloof, set himself to writing charming things on children, things very profound, very simple which he could not prevent himself however from framing in quotations from Milton and Coleridge. Thus he received into his house this present from the Fates, from Fatality, that unknown guest. . . . He had connived with the Universal Spirit to produce this miracle which is a human person, a life. The supreme Soul had reincarnated itself before him, through him. Childhood foretells man as the dawn foretells the day, a perfect harmony of soul and senses. The little Waldo astonished the big. One would have said that they played secretly together, the child all mystery, Emerson all astonishment. He watched him grow, spread out, acquire confidence bit by bit with picture books and toys, conquering the household while waiting to conquer the universe. He noted his deeds and gestures, his words. It was an idyl which lasted six years. Thus Providence had brought him, to enrapture him, reinforcements for the bluebird, the tree, the flower, the æolian harp, the changing skies, the surprises of the day

and the night. And the little boy was of an astonishing foresight, with his grave and sovereign
ways, his perfect gentleness, his divinations, his
unconsciously prophetic words, his baffling images,
his instinctive poetry.

The house was from then on peopled by the
little peaceful being who was everywhere, who
invaded the sage's study, built houses of cards on
his writing table, mobilized the whole house, the
chicken yard and the garden, cooing like a pigeon,
speaking to all, loving all. Lydia also madly loved
her little one. She kissed his houses of cards, ran
to hug him in the nursery, retailed his sayings, his
finds. The child Waldo was a poet in bud, an imagist without knowing it. Emerson noted from
day to day his remarks in his *Journal* between
meditations on great divine and human themes.
The dead bird was not dead for little Waldo; "he
was broken." The old gentleman did not smoke;
"cobwebs were going up out of his mouth." The
cover was not the cover of the box; it was the
cover "which lived in the box." Waldo had a
whistle that Thoreau perhaps had cut him from
the willows along the brook, and he said during
the thunder storms, that it was his whistle "that

made the thunder dance," that his bell when he rang it would be heard over the whole world, before breaking into pieces like a great glass thing, into thousands and thousands of pieces. "Pussy-cat, come see Waddo! Liddle Birdy, come see Waddo! Fies! fies! come see Waddo!" When his father took him into the woods, the little boy knelt down to kiss the violets, taking care not to pluck them. And how nicely he imitated his father's voice, humming and whistling gently. And when he was ill, or coughed, what a nice little goody-goody he became, what a delightful little Phari-see! And when he prayed that God make beautiful the ugly woman who took him to church . . .

Ah, may God keep his little son for him! Suppose his angel should fly away . . . Even rough Thoreau was full of kindness for the child. He carried him on his shoulders, made boats for him, told him stories of the battle of the giant turtles and that of the red ants. Luckless Emerson, who in a moment of transcendentalism had declared that even if his wife or son should die, he could not weep. (There are tombs under churches, but

the Intellect is joyous.) It was a challenge to
fate. . . .

After an illness which lasted four days, the
27th of January, 1842, at 8:15 P.M., little Waldo
died of scarlet fever. He had just written to a
young cousin who had sent him a magic lantern.
He breathed his last breath like a bird, said his
father; like the mist which rises from the brook,
said Thoreau. This time death existed and the
heart of the sage bled. In vain did he seek refuge
in the transcendent. The little traveler from the
beyond had disappeared as mysteriously as he had
come and Emerson sought him at his side and
could not find him. The brightly colored sled, the
bluebird's nest, the dog-house, the sticks which
held the snow-man up, the hole in the sand, the
garden, the brook were there, but the little boy
with the deep glance had gone.

> O child of paradise,
> Boy who made dear his father's home,
> In whose deep eyes
> Men read the welfare of the times to come,
> I am too much bereft.

It was high time, O philosopher, to step into
your balloon and find refuge on the heights of

the Idea, up there, way up, on the summits of the Invisible, to find him who had disappeared. . . . Fatality? Compensation? Did you think of Waldo, your dear shade, when under the title of "Brahma" you composed that cryptic poem:

> If the red slayer think he slays,
> Or if the slain think he is slain,
> They know not well the subtle ways
> I keep, and pass, and turn again.

The sun flooded the blinds, the dandelions and the violets sprouted on the edge of the pond, the bluebird returned to his nest, spring was there, but the child Waldo did not keep the appointment. The sage meditated upon Proclus, the Vishna Purana, the Bhagavat Gita, but he could not forget. When two years later Lydia, looking at him from the depths of her eyes, murmured to him, "Two years ago . . ." his heart still bled. Yet two gracious little girls had been given him. To the first Lydia, with a touching thoughtfulness had given the name of Ellen, in memory of the frail bride of twenty. Soft, peaceful, brown little creature, sacred child, little winter bud who also came to try her luck in this great world and make her choice among the things of God. To Edith the younger he gave this greeting:

"There came into the house a young maiden, but she seemed to be more than a thousand years old. She came into the house naked and helpless, but she had for her defense more than the strength of millions. She brought into the day the manners of the Night."

Edith was born two months before the *Essays*.

CHAPTER XII

The String of Beads

EMERSON had by now been giving lectures for six or seven years. Upon his return from Europe he was full of his subject. He had begun with natural history, then English literature, the philosophy of history, culture and life, the present time. Emerson taught what he called "first philosophy," the science of that which is as opposed to that which seems. He preached the religion of the spirit; he opened up wide historical perspectives, infinite horizons of the universe, the better to exalt the individual soul. He affirmed the presence of the divine in us, the unity of each spirit, of each instant, the sovereign duty of fidelity toward oneself. With the intuitive and penetrating look of a poet, he enunciated beautiful and austere compensations which, he believed, made of ethics an exact science. Nothing is given;

all is bought; love compels love and hate hate; action and reaction always are equal; no evil exists but has its check; the physical and mental form a *plenum*; it is impossible to harm the universe or oneself; the flood in one place produces an equal ebb in another; there is no freedom, no chance; our will is submitted to general ends; punishment accompanies crime. . . . He called these familiarly his "old saws."

From the sublime heights of the *a priori* he criticized society and religion and abandoned himself to great mystic transports, to Carlylean apostolic fervors.

"What shall be the substance of my shrift? Adam in the garden. I am to new name all the beasts in the field and all the gods in the sky. I am to invite men drenched in Time to recover themselves and come out of time, and taste their native immortal air. I am to fire with what skill I can the artillery of sympathy and emotion. I am to indicate constantly, though all unworthy, the Ideal and Holy Life, the life within life, the Forgotten Good, the Unknown Cause in which we sprawl and sin. I am to try the magic of sincerity, that luxury permitted only to kings and

265

poets. I am to celebrate the spiritual powers in
their infinite contrast to the mechanical powers,
the mechanical philosophy of this time. I am to
console the brave sufferers under evils whose end
they cannot see by appeals to the great optimism,
self-affirmed in all bosoms."

Such were the themes and such the state of
mind of these lectures which he gave somewhat
against his will, to earn his bread, he said, to pay
his debts and those he had contracted in order to
publish Carlyle in America. History, self-reliance, the Over-soul, compensations, the great
essays were there in germ, and he had already expounded the doctrine of representative men.

In spite of his doubts and his discouragements,
his lectures had had a great success and all Boston had run to hear them. No one had ever heard
the like before. For any one else the road would
have been dangerous, and Emerson himself was
conscious of the looseness of his subjects. He
might have poured out platitudes on the declamatory scale then in vogue from which his eloquence,
prodigious as it was, had hardly saved the great
Channing. But Emerson drew wisdom at its foun-

tain head; he substituted facts for words; he re-
lied upon the very constitution of man; his
transcendentalism was practical and he went
straight to the soul. He had given up rhetoric,
and the logic of his teachers; he spoke from the
fullness of his heart, but from a poet's heart
watched over by jealous thought. No declama-
tion or sentimentality. He threw his auditors
into a mist of golden atoms. Listening to his in-
cantations, his oracular symphonies, it seemed as
if one could sin no more. One perceived bits of
blue sky, fields eternally green; one heard the
beating of wings, one followed until lost to sight
a glance that melted into the skies with Ariel.
. . . Then, suddenly, a cymbal clash recalled you
to reality. The orator had a barytone voice to
which in striking moments succeeded the clear
and silver notes of a trumpet. His voice was full
of modulations and it made one think of an instrument which had grown mellow and as if softened from playing. Some compared it to the song
of the logs in the fire on a calm evening.

As for his expression and action, look at this
face, calm, grave, collected, bent over the paper.
Not a gesture, except, at intervals, the hand, fist

closed, which rises and falls. All the force, all the brilliance, all the emotion are in his eyes. From time to time, to make contact, his eye fastened upon the audience, or perhaps it would wander into the distance to interrogate the future. Emerson refused to lower himself to go to meet these people; he resolved to treat his audience like an assemblage of demi-gods; but every one understood and every one was at his ease. Those over whose heads his ideas flew were happy enough to be there seeing him. In the heights of transcendentalism, he was friendly, fraternal; he gave to the lowliest the impression "that they were as good as he."

In the audience there were friends and enemies, people whom he delighted, others whom he stupefied and mystified, cultivated people who criticized him, simple souls who admired him. His strength of conviction was contagious. He stirred people, he troubled them, he excited them, he drew, as he said, the electricity out of his listeners. What he read seems often intangible; one would say that he was chasing shadows, that he was besieging Aladdin's palace, that he was playing hide-and-go-seek. When one left him, one was a bit disappointed; he seemed to have lost his time, to have sent one off with empty hands; but the depths of the heart still trembled at the sound of his voice. What anxious looks stretched toward him, old and young; what faces in expectation; but the trumpet sounds, a shiver passes, they quiver at the voice of the Inspirer, of him who brings Life.

Emerson, always scrupulous, was not very proud of his lectures and he was often worn out by them. He called them "Eleusinian mysteries for marionettes." He reproached himself again and again for his lack of emotion, his coldness. He would have liked to commune with his audience, to possess it, to give himself fully, and still more to renew himself. Time was lacking as well as strength, and he had to go full force. If we are to believe him, he became a lecturer for want of something better—half-heartedly. The great subjects were forbidden him; he felt the uselessness of those he had. It was not his fault if he had fallen back upon poetry and ethics. Topics of the day would have brought him ill luck. He

had as much horror of polemics as of utopias, and
the fracas of the Cambridge address continued to
ring in his ears. Prudence, prudence. He had
therefore taken refuge in idealism. . . . Moreover he was a born painter, not a realist nor a
reformer, but a painter. He was a simple experi-
menter. Those who expected him to reform the
world were mistaken, like those who asked him
for guidance. He was a painter, an experimen-
talist, priest of the Soul, yes, but only by means
of music and the dance, in good health and harmonious energy. He spoke aloud his secret
thoughts, come what might; the supreme Soul
held all in all; it was up to men to understand.

But he was often very disheartened and he
swore never to begin again. His lectures caused
him little joy and he did not succeed in breaking
the ice. He would have liked to be eloquent, to
give himself over to the force of things, to the
beautiful ideas which he was exploring, but he
was cold, strained, solemn. Pretty things, wise
things, but neither arrows, nor axes, nor nectar,
nor roars, nothing which might enchant, seduce,
for lack of love. He did not know how to exteri-

orize himself; he husbanded himself, economized
—always that sinister apathy.

He was exaggerating and such was not the
opinion of his auditors, but he sighed for solitude,
the tête-à-tête with his treasures, the free exploration of his "Wide Worlds". . . . His vocation
was to pry into and describe in silence the occult
harmonies, the unknown beauties, the mysterious
progress of the soul, the correspondences, the secret analogies between nature and the spirit, the
awe-inspiring compensations, the Laws, the Ideas.

. . . He had remained faithful to his Voices. He
wanted to write at their dictation, beyond all
chance contacts, a book which would be his *Genesis*, a book of good faith composed for himself
alone but which would serve the same function
for all, a book in which would be found the pris-
tine and sacred character of thought, thoughts
emanating directly and magically from the secret
life, a hymn to Sincerity. He would take up his
"old saws." He would put together what went
together. He had explored the woods, dreamed
beside the waters, teased the Muse, listened to

271

Pan's flute, the song of the pine. For a number
of years he had been reading and making Montaigne his own. Why should he not correct him?
Why should not he too compose his *Essays?*

So he had gone to work, robbing his "Wide
Worlds," grouping, cementing, sewing, concen-
trating, a bit from here, another from there,
without method, upon the great themes which
sang in his mind. As early as 1835 the idea and
the plan of the *Essays* had been found. "When
will you mend Montaigne? When will you take
the hint of nature? Where are your Essays? . . .
Have you not thoughts and illustrations that are
your own?" And at the same time that he cher-
ished the idea of his book, he sketched its outline.
"The parable of geometry and matter; the reason
why the atmosphere is transparent; the power of
composition in nature and in man's thought; the
usefulness and uselessness of travelling; the law of
Compensation; the transcendent excellence of
truth in character, in rhetoric, in things; the sublimity of self-reliance, and the rewards of per-
severance in the best opinion." He was then
going to write for himself, for himself alone; it

was up to men and to the future to understand his message.

His *Essays* Emerson scraped and polished, drawing his material both from the arsenal of his lectures and his *Journal*, arranging, matching, without subjecting himself to any rule. He was very much at home this time; he could bring out his secret thoughts, go to the end, to the very limit of the idea, boldly. To the essay-lectures he added others which had never been delivered or which were not until later, which for the time being could not be, the most personal essays, the frankest, the most transcendent. It made a piquant mixture, extremely various in appearance and tone.

What did these *Essays* resemble? Nothing. It was entirely Emerson, the soliloquies of a soul who thinks and speaks aloud, variations on a single theme: the cult of sincerity. No logic, no structure. They begin calmly, rise bit by bit, leap, fall, dialectical, oracular, anecdotal, ironical, by turns sententious, poetical; quotations, proverbs, maxims, portraits, whimsies, great musical moments, landscapes, elliptic glimpses which open immense horizons of thought. They go, come, return, turn, seem to end nowhere. Each essay complete in itself floats, wanders, holds to nothing, but in appearance only. All holds together, adheres by an inner logic, through subterranean ways, thanks to a hidden rhythm which is that of Emerson's deepest thought: the particular, the universal, rest and movement, concentration and expansion, the rhythm of the world. One essay excites, pulls one along; another moderates and calms. Emerson rocks himself, swings himself as in the rocking-chair in his study; he abandons himself to delightful recantations. The essays are opposed to one another, flee one another; one would often say that they contradict one another, but compensation is near by.

In the first *Essays* Emerson's plan is clear enough. He begins by snatching us away from the contingent. He rids himself of the past, annuls history with a stroke of the pen; decrees the eternity of the present moment, the eternal youth of man and of the world ("History"). Then he affirms the autonomy, the individual's sovereignty, and gives us as master only Destiny ("Self-Reliance"), whose mysterious laws he pronounces ("Compensation"). From the height of this pinnacle, after having brushed aside the problem of evil with a fine ease, he proclaims a universal optimism ("Spiritual Laws"). He puts us on our guard against subjection to other persons ("Love" and "Friendship"). He recommends prudence to us ("Prudence"). After which we plunge into the heart of the Absolute, into the unconscious, into the world of infinitely expanding circles ("The Over-Soul" and "Circles"). Finally he announces the decisive authority of thought, of the spirit ("Intellect").

The second collection of the *Essays*, published three years after the first, in 1844, is looser, but from essay to essay the same alternate rhythm is found. The individualism of the essay on "Character" is compensated by the pantheism of the essays on "The Poet" and "Experience." The rhapsodies of the piece on "Nature" balance the views of the moralist touching "Manners" and "Politics." In the finale, "Nominalist and Realist," he takes up the antinomy, ideal and real, thought and action, and resolves it once more in a purely subjective sense.

Each essay has its distinct physiognomy, its atmosphere, its ring, its color. The essay on "Self-

Reliance" is hard, authoritative, dogmatic, imperious; the "Compensations" unroll a litany of examples, laws, proverbs, and Destiny passes as in a theogony. In this central essay, key to his philosophy, the circular thought of Emerson is all in recantations, in detours. How could it be otherwise? He cavalierly attacks the redoubtable problem of good and evil. A logician would stop him at each step, but he has abandoned dialectic for intuition and he would break away in sharp about-faces or simply shut his eyes. The essay entitled "Prudence" is very Emersonian, in the homely and intimate note of his later days. "The Over-Soul" is a rhapsody, a revery, a poem in prose.

As a whole the first essays are asymmetrical. All the weight is borne by the first part, the rest floats; and the second collection is still more disconcerting than the first, but there are gems of ideas in "The Poet." In "Experience" Emerson has put himself entirely, honestly, rashly, like Nietzsche. The essay is full of "perverse thoughts," penetrating and subversive insights of which Carlyle used to speak. Inside each essay there is no more cohesion than outside. Emerson did not construct; he juxtaposed, he diffused. He began and finished *ex abrupto*, sought no effect; he was didactic, sententious, lyrical, without transition, but one always felt in him the hidden rhythm, the piercing insights.

The beauty of the *Essays* is not their structure but their plenitude. Emerson had no illusions about his faults of composition. The book was not so harmonious as he would have wished; his *Essays* were only "boards and logs tied together," a log-house in the middle of the forest, not at all an edifice but a brick-kiln. But his sincerity made up for his lack of logic and there is always enough logic where there is truth. He left to the readers the care of binding his thoughts together. Each spontaneous thought took no account of the thoughts which followed. It was their affair to find their predecessors. He replaced logic by passionate repetitions, by sublime tautologies.

The string of beads was tied together, a necklace without architecture. Yet each gem shone rare and isolated, without eclipsing its neighbors, heightening them, on the contrary, by its own brilliance; each beautiful in itself, heavy and perfect, like an independent monad, a universe in epitome, a microcosm.

Had he mended Montaigne? In any event he had imitated him with genius. Montaigne can be found in Emerson's sallies, his anecdotes, his quotations, his strokes of wit, his maxims. Emerson embraced the reader more shyly, more courteously, but the Ego did not seem hateful to him. Like Montaigne he was by turns moralist, poet, and anecdotist; like him he lost man in the infinite, in the illusion of vast nature; like him he saved himself by tact, prudence, sublime familiarity; like him he gave himself to men under his universal form and his book was indeed his portrait, his and ours. But there the resemblance stopped. Emerson doubted, but by an excess of faith. In the dilemma of good and evil, he bet *boldly* on the good; he saw the grandeur and not the misery of Man and, a thing which would have seemed a sacrilege to Michel Eyquem, he allowed himself to deify man. He held reason to be sacred and asserted the goodness of nature in an absolute sense which his *alter ego* could not have approved.

. . . Then, too, Emerson was a stoic; he did not know how to be epicurean.

The book was a great success. The traditionalists, the classicists did not understand a word of it; they remained overcome by it. No one had ever thought or written like that. It was German, that is, jargon, or Hebrew; and they tried to crush Emerson under the name of the great heretics, Spinoza, Kant, Coleridge, Carlyle, Shelley, the school of infidelity. They wondered how the man who had composed "The Over-Soul" could have written "Prudence." He made the people of good sense dizzy. He abjured the art of transition; he did not let them breathe. He was declared to be unintelligible, mannered, archaic, obscure in his dogmas, fantastic in his style. They pointed out the contradictions of "Compensation," the divagations of "The Over-Soul." What good these beatings of wings, these Œdipus-poses before the Sphinx? He was illogical; he spoke for the sake of saying nothing, now writing like an angel, now pouring out sheer nonsense. His doctrine of giving in to instinct was anti-social. . . .

The soberer people were more just. They admired his practical sense and were not wrong in putting him halfway between Addison and Carlyle, between the pole of classic reason and that of romantic effervescence, between understanding, reason which reasons, and intuition, feeling, which he tried in fact to conciliate.

Carlyle judged these essays with his customary roughness. He made short shift of their metaphysics but he frankly admired "this soliloquy under the stars." Emerson was a solitary on a mountain top, a Himalaya on which he spoke alone, an occidental gymnosophist (others compared him to Saint Simeon Stylites). His essays were not as "a beaten ingot but as a beautiful square *bag of duck-shot.*" He complained of their excessive compactness, of Emerson's lack of order, and that need not surprise us from him who was passionately devoted to fine movement, who carried all with him in the torrent of his *verve*, who brought violence to bear on his readers. . . . Emerson followed another method.

And it was he indeed who had the last word. To excuse it as laziness, cold exhibition of dead thoughts, was easy. But no, he was a painter

and he was still more a musician, as his auditors
had felt. The essays were a poem in praise of the
Absolute, a moral and orphic poem, an offering to
the Muses and to the Graces. He leads us to the
"day without night, the fair Ocean without
tides"; he walks us in the fields of the soul, in
the novel and radiant regions of life. His essays
were the book of his Solitudes, his *Forest Essays*.
Not a dream on which the breath of the pines had
not blown and their shadows waved. His book was
sprung from him as the bud, as the new leaf from
the stem, and it was thus that he meant to be read
and loved. "I would have my book read as I have
read my favorite books, not with explosion and
astonishment, a marvel and a rocket, but a
friendly and agreeable influence stealing like the
scent of a flower, or the sight of a new landscape
on a traveller. I neither wish to be hated and dei-
fied by such as I startle, nor to be kissed and
hugged by the young whose thoughts I stimulate." *Ne quid nimis*, prudence, prudence, and let
us not startle the still small voice within us.

PART THREE

The World's Destiny

CHAPTER I

Young America

WHILE Emerson was reading Plotinus, Proclus, and the Bhagavat Gita, while he was stringing beads in his cell, the giant America was stretching his heavy limbs. Like the sage, America was trying to grow unified and drifted between the One and the Many without succeeding in reconciling them. The geography of the United States was sublime, but how little men were! The Over-Soul, the Good, the True, and the Beautiful, what had they to do with all that? Puritan New England still emitted her generous utopias in continual spurts. She exported apostles, pedagogues, visionaries. Boston with her Brahmins was still the Athens, the holy navel of the United States, but there was not only one America. There were several, scattered regions, floating, disparate, with neither common ideals nor

285

will to live. In the South, near the Gulf of Mexico, the black belt, the feudal system of the planters, fierce autonomists, people and manners of former days, loafing, duels, and junketings, manor houses with Doric columns overlooking Uncle Tom's cabin; along the formidable rivers, the Ohio, the Mississippi, a swarming of adventurers, ruffians, squatters, tramps, ebony traders, the democracy of the woodsmen, frontiersmen in coonskin caps.

Emerson's New England was transforming itself before his eyes and becoming frankly industrial and capitalistic. Cotton mills and factories along the peaceful valleys, swarms of Irish navvies, paddies, come to construct the railways. From the windows of his study Emerson heard the whistle of the first locomotives which tore open the silence of Walden. "Whew! Whew! Here I am! Down with that forest on the side of the hill. I want ten thousand chestnut sleepers. I want cedar posts, and hundreds of thousands of feet of boards. Ho for axes and saws, and away with me to Boston! Whew! Whew! Whew! I will plant a dozen houses on this pasture next moon, and a village anon; and I will sprinkle yonder square mile with white houses like the broken snow-banks that strow it in March." Thus spoke the new Cassandra, the locomotive, the voice of the nineteenth century and the future. It was not to the stars but to the steam engine that new America hitched her wagon. And here were enormous territories, wheat and corn granaries, Aladdin's caverns larded with gold, silver, and copper opening up before Yankee cupidity, and the lakes, the deserts, the forests, Kansas, Texas, Oregon, California, New Mexico . . .

In this fury, this anarchy of covetousness, Washington ran as well as it could the police and liaison services. The Capitol was besieged by rival factions, by jealous autonomists and regionalists. It was not the Boston transcendentalists who held America's destinies in hand. There were arising strong men, practical unscrupulous men, opportunists, cunning politicians. The far-sighted politics of the founders of the Republic had miscarried. . . . Whigs and Locofocos were no longer fighting for principles but for spoils. The Rights of Man had given way to those of the landowner and the first settler. It was a long time since ideologists had been replaced by adventurers, village lawyers, squires, partisans, and bosses. After Jackson and his happy warriors, appeared the Calhouns, the Clays, the Websters, utilitarian, realistic, tightly riveted to the present. In the height of the romantic effervescence, the United States was governed by the Harrisons, Van Burens, Zachary Taylors. . . . Get rich quick! That was the motto. As for the problems of the hour, they were no more transcendental—canals, railroads, tariffs, banks, the adjudication of the new territories, the opening of markets . . . Let the North make its spindles turn; let the South pour out its cotton, its sugar, its tobacco; let the West subdivide its lands—those were the problems of America while Emerson was lecturing on the Over-Soul and Compensation. The United States was still in "the quadruped stage."

The effervescence was contagious and the sage too was going through his stage of Nietzscheanism. He had forgotten the serene indifference which had flowered in the two series of essays. To act, he said, is to descend. The wise man takes nothing seriously. "I am a spectator, not an actor . . . I experiment . . ." He had changed indeed. Here he was now wanting to play a rôle, to act, to accomplish, not to let go the substance for the shadow. Forty years old, forty-five, soon fifty, in full force, in the height of ambition. The swinging of the compensations, the dizzy acrobatics on the transcendental trapeze, all that was far away. Down with these conventions, these restrictions, these prohibitions—march, bite, fly, dance! Above all express oneself! Give one war and alcohol, clashes, antagonisms. Anything to escape boredom. The world is flat. Let us change all; let us have a complete revolution. He had a grudge against the philanthropists for their cowardice. Instead of drawing up beautiful manifestos, why didn't they make a revolution? The ideal of the conservatives is the world in slippers and flannels, with a bib and a nursing bottle, potions and pills, a hospital, an invalid home. No, put dynamite under the table while the bourgeois dine . . . Less goodness and more tomahawks. The highest virtue is always against the law. The hero has only to create his own laws. Rather lie with dying Desdemona, assassinate with Timoleon, perjure oneself with Epaminondas, commit sacrilege with David, and glean on the Sabbath day—before all else live and put oneself into the hands of a transcendental conscience. Life is incessant metamorphosis; so much the worse if to erect a New World one must destroy the Old. Ah, let Bacchus madden humankind; let him inebriate with eloquence and poetry this mob of vagabonds.

There he was envying men of affairs, strong men whose absence of a moral sense he had been flagellating, those rough workmen, those political paddies who were stirring the world with their shouts. Eloquence, action! He would give all his *Essays* to become a John Quincy Adams, a Garrison, a Wendell Phillips, a Webster. . . Webster, especially Webster, that "steam engine in breeches," Webster whom he was soon to pillory, but whom he never stopped admiring. He envied the somber man, the long-faced man with cinderous eyes, his coal-black hair, impassive as a rock on the top of the world, master of facts, emperor of men, a cannon loaded to the muzzle's tip, carrying without weakening his cares as an elm its caterpillars, triumph of the practical reason, of the Understanding. The word "liberty" had no more sense in his mouth than that of "love" on the lips of a courtesan. Providence had refused him a heart. He who might have been the darling of America was at bottom only an ambitious vulgarian, a Metternich, a Castlereagh, a Polignac, but what force, what majesty! And Carlyle who admired also the Hercules, the colossus with feet of clay, joined the chorus from afar. . . .

Emerson had never lost faith in the ideal destiny of America. He had celebrated her genius. Land of free men, land of possibilities, of infinite creation, which he opposed to feudal Europe. He expected everything from this sublime geography. Ah, if he could wake up the sleeping giant, give a soul to this immense floating body, enormous, diffuse, confused, America who had grown too quickly. Liberty, virility, self-reliance, sincerity! Practical, to be sure, but let us first be poetical. What importance have numbers? Let us live for quality and not for quantity. America's problems are not political, they are moral. To solve them, one must see them from above, from far above, as a philosopher, as a poet. One must choose between the Whigs and God! The basis of our hopes is the world's infinity which reappears infinitely in the least of its parts. Against all appearances, there is a remedy for all wrongs and all walls are doors. Why tackle one abuse where there are thousands? It is the whole moral being, the very conditions of man's existence which must be changed.

And thereupon Emerson set himself to composing eloquent, hearty exhortations into which he put himself entirely, at once lyrical and satirical, the Transcendentalist, the Reformer, the Young American. Under the pretext of exciting the enthusiasm of his compatriots, he deluded his ambitions, his fallen hopes. He denounced false prudence, utilitarianism without heart or horizons. No, America had not said her last word; no, practical men would not cause the great men to be forgotten. Still more than money, America was in need of ideals. It was not the best cotton which she lacked but the best men. He showed the tedium, the despair of the young. He celebrated the return to the ancestral virtues—simplicity, poverty. He took up the cudgels for the solitary dreamers who found the world too small for their desires, who refused to act from a worthy cause, noble strikers. He declared that society was rotten; he denounced conscienceless lucre, cursed the rich, sang the praises of poverty, of the simple life. Self-help, self-reliance! Cut down our needs, help ourselves, count on no one but ourselves, be frankly what we are and reorganize society, beginning with the moral reform of the individual. Americans lack faith and hope. Let them be saved by charity and love. Treat men like gods and there will be no more slaves. . . .

In "The Young American" he recovered the enthusiasm of the great days, the glow of Dartmouth and Cambridge. He intoned a veritable hymn of confidence. He embraced the present, saluted commerce and industry, the railroads, the arrival of the immigrants. He celebrated in prophetic accents the expansion of America from the Atlantic to the Pacific and the colonization of the Far West. America would emerge from her isolation. From being provincial, she would become world-wide. She would make herself a new soul by contact with the soil, institutions as vast and majestic as the world. Commerce would establish peace. The captains of industry, the great individualists would replace the politicians and the government would be useless. Washington would

EMERSON

be nothing but an Intelligence Office. Every one
would be able to sell and buy freely. *Laissez faire,
laissez passer.* No more custom houses, no more
army, no more navy, no more war, no more slavery. Hurrah for Commerce and Liberty!

Once in Utopia Emerson did not loiter on the
way. He sang the praises of Fourier and the
phalansteries. He insisted on the moral rôle of
riches, praised the great speculators, the adventurers who would replace the State fallen into
contempt. He prophesied government by the
élite. He saw America, New England at the head
of the nations. His heroes would be great philanthropists. He ended by denouncing the servility
of the New World to the Old, and particularly to
England.

One could not be more optimistic, more modern, nor more naïvely hold out whips wherewith
to be whipped. A strange sight, that of our idealist putting the captains of industry and the mag-
nates of finance in the rank of representative men.
The day was soon to come when he would change
his tune, but like America Emerson was moult-
ing and he sang before Walt Whitman the song
of the Open Road, his hymn of faith in man and

294

the universe. . . . His optimism was in reality poetical, pantheistic, and mystical. In "The Method of Nature" he called the whole universe to witness and guarantee his prophecies. The rapt saint was the true logician. Forget means for ends, abandon ourselves to mysterious impulses. Man at his apogee is the inspired poet. The imagination needs immense and eternal objects. The only way of annexing nature is to put our highest intuitions into action. Adore the all-powerful and transcendent Soul. Let the feeling of the divine Presence tear from us cries of joy and exultation. Look in the sky at the stars of possibility, over there on the glittering mountains of the West. Upon which Emerson chants this pæan: "I praise with wonder this great reality, which seems to drown all things in the deluge of its light. What man seeing this, can lose it from his thoughts, or entertain a meaner object? . . . All things are known to the soul. It is not to be surprised by any communication. Nothing can be greater than it. Let those fear and those fawn who will. The soul is in her native realm, and it is wider than space, older than time, wide as hope, rich as love. Pusillanimity and fear she refuses with a beautiful scorn; they are not for her who puts on her coronation robes, and goes out through universal love to universal power."

O irresistible magician! how the practical men would have been amused if they had come to hear you. They too loved hyperbole and they would have joined in with joy in their hearts acknowledging you as a brother. "A chatterer, a transcendental chatterer, but still a chatterer." Do you hear the thick laughter of the Philistines?

CHAPTER II

We Live in Lilliput

PROFOUND discouragement followed these ardent effusions. His skyrockets burned out and Emerson woke up among the dwarfs. America lacked force, nerves, power; it had been emasculated, sweetened. American democracy! Banks and churches. Outside—a market, a Stock Exchange; inside—an oven of conventions and hypocrisy, a flame smotherer. The Americans were either too young or too old. Ah, these Yankees, greedy for gain, gossips, braggarts, rapacious, whom nothing can force to let go what they have seized! Give them a rope's end or a spar, they will make it carry them. Give them a tree trunk or a log, they will whittle out of it a house and a barn, a farm and stock, a mill seat and a village, a railroad and a bank. Ardent, yes, lazy, yes, and they make use of the elements to save themselves the trouble of working. Their practical horse sense is equaled only by their cupidity. Their god is the sacrosanct dollar. In each Yankee village there ought to be an idol, an enormous gold or silver dollar to which one would bring as offerings one of those pots of fat baked beans which the natives love so, but it would be prudent not to forget to set a watchman. . . . America, shingle palaces and shingle cities, picnic universities, an extemporized state, fruits admirable in looks but not a sound ripe apple on the tree. Nature, as much in a hurry as they, has never had time to finish the Americans, and they finish nothing themselves. Their leather is not tanned, their white lead is whitewash, their sulphuric acid half-strength, their stone is well sanded pumpkin pine. Not from old oak but from refuse sapling have their knees been sawed out. America, a wilderness of capabilities, of versatile and vagrant culture, enormous, formless, cringing country. Leaves, tendrils, tentacles, and no fruits, a brute which has grown too fast. Democracy: the government of brutes tempered by that of newspaper editors. Public spirit: boasting and bluff. The majority: the argument of fools, the strength of the

weak. The rulers: knaves and idiots, puerile utopians, short-sighted politicians. How enter politics without besmudging one's name with infamy?
America—a country without a conscience. My
country right or wrong! America is damaged
goods, the City of Hypocrisy, the country of
dwarfs, Lilliput. Franklins, Washingtons, cold,
practical, phlegmatic men without fire . . .

That is what Emerson wrote as footnotes to his
enthusiastic harangues. The *American Notes* of
Dickens were being collected at the same time.
Though they irritated him so much they were not
much more cruel than his own. Nor did Fenimore
Cooper satirize the country more malignly when
some years earlier he wrote of the Monikins. The
Idealist, the Transcendentalist in disillusion was
taking his revenge. But if he had been ambitious,
what rôle would he have liked to play? He who
lived on the mountain tops, who dreamed of
Alexander, of Mohammed, of Napoleon, should
he have fallen to the level of the Calhouns, the
Clays, the Websters? Once in politics he would
have had to make concessions, compromise himself, wobble from side to side without being sure

of coming out anywhere. What would he have done in the ship of state? Does Nature worry about Whigs and Locofocos, conservatives and democrats? This Constitution to which the parties appeal when at bay, what is it after all but a worthless scrap of paper? He despised democracy. He was for culture and not for number. He loathed crowds. If there is nothing to admire in one man, what is there to admire in millions?

His views on government were gently anarchistic. He put his confidence in men alone, in great individuals, in heroes. The State was he. The sage was the State. A single king and a single subject, himself; that was his dream. The less the government governs, the better it governs. But what would he have done in the full triumph of industry with his Arcadia, his naïve communism, his idyllic physiocracy, his return to nature in the epoch of the railroads? And how would he have chosen between conservatives and liberals, between the cat and the mouse, he, the man of all the contradictions? Either the revolt of the masses or the government of gentlemen, and if both are impossible, abstention and evasion in dreams.

The wings fall from him; politics holds nothing for him. The sky and its clouds alone are open to idealists. America does not want great men. He would return then to his lamp, his pen, and his books. He would meditate upon the divine compensations. The man of genius is always alone; like the mountain, he pays for his elevation a tax of snow and silence. The poet does not descend into the present without abdicating his throne. To retain his electricity it is better to remain upon a tripod of glass. Why go to war against a hostile world? Can one resist the law of gravitation? The scholar, the man of thought, escapes by subtle ways, by marvelous alibis. That is better than to complain. The intellect intervenes and puts its length between the subject and the object, thought and act.

Would Emerson pass for a fool? So be it. Better to be the fool of virtue than of vice. If he cannot act, at least he will not lie. He will keep his soul fluid. Identity! Unity! And he began to scoop out abysses of scepticism between the world and himself and to abandon himself to hidden forces. "He lurks, *he* hides—he who is success, reality, joy, power, that which constitutes

Heaven, which reconciles impossibilities, atones for shortcomings, expiates sins, or makes them virtues, buries in oblivion the crowded historical past, sinks religions, philosophies, nations, persons, to legends; reverses the scale of opinion, of fame; reduces sciences to opinion, and makes the thought of the moment the key to the universe and the egg of history to come." All is naked Buddhism. And Emerson buried himself again in meditations upon the Vishnu Purana, Confucius, and the Vedas . . .

But how useless one can be then with a wonderful string of beads about the neck, a golden fleece like the *Essays*—and how unhappy one can be. The wisest man in America was also the most lonely, the most idle, and he suffered from it. Washington Irving had been ambassador to Spain; Fenimore Cooper had filled official positions in Europe; Hawthorne was made United States consul at Liverpool; James Russell Lowell was ambassador to Spain and after that to London; Longfellow occupied a famous chair at Harvard. He was nothing. *The Dial* had crumbled to bits for lack of subscribers. In vain had Emerson tried to resuscitate it by giving greater room to questions of the day . . . Suppose he founded a university, another great review, a club; suppose he solicited a university chair? . . . He felt the need of renewing himself, of recharging his batteries. . . . He dreamed of exiling himself in the Canadian woods with his books, like Thoreau in Walden . . . At any cost to escape from Lilliput. But no, he would not be a hermit. Solitary, yes, but not a misanthrope. He would rub up against people. Leaving the house in charge of the faithful Thoreau, he embarked for England October 5, 1847, on the *Washington Irving*.

CHAPTER III

At John Bull's

H^E HAD been invited to lecture before the
Mechanics' Institutes in the north and
center of England and in Scotland. Instead of
Milton this time he had taken Alfred de Vigny
as his traveling companion. His notes on England
open upon the famous apostrophe of Chatterton
to the English vessel. Emerson copied the piece
in his *Journal* in full. " 'But, my boy,' cried fat
Beckford, 'what the devil has the poet to do with
running the ship?' He said, 'The poet seeks in
the stars the road which the Lord's finger indi-
cates.' " Replacing the vessel of Albion by the
covered wagon of the Yankees, here was the first
version of Emerson's famous verse, "Hitch your
wagon to a star."

At the gangplank in Liverpool Emerson found
a letter from Carlyle. He had still a week before

304

him and without delay he took the train to London. At ten o'clock at night he knocked at Teufelsdroeckh's door in Chelsea. It was Jane who came to open for him. Carlyle was behind her in the hall, a lamp in hand. "Well," said Carlyle, "here we are, shovelled together again." Carlyle had not changed. It had been fourteen years since they had seen each other, fourteen years of an imperturbable friendship between them protected by the gulf of the ocean. Carlyle still wept at the memory of the appearance and disappearance of "the Angel" on the heath at Craigenputtock. Emerson had published *Nature*, the *Addresses*, the *Essays*; Carlyle, *Sartor Resartus*, the *Essays*, *The French Revolution*, *Heroes and Hero Worship*, *Past and Present*, *Cromwell*; Carlyle's essays all full of capers, shot and shell; Emerson's serene and musical as a pastoral symphony . . . Their friendship had been transcendental but also practical—proofs, editions, checks, plagiarisms, and pirates of his books whom Carlyle would have been so willing to hang. Carlyle had written a preface for Emerson, had praised and advertised him; Emerson had published Carlyle. Teufelsdroeckh—ay me!

—was not blind to the charms of fair good dollars. Uncle Sam's teapot was really inexhaustible. Did he ever suspect that Emerson had gone in debt to bring him out? In their correspondence, at first frequent, then little by little and inevitably thinned out, they sent each other faithfully the echoes of their lives, the years of the lean kine in Scotland, the march on London, the accident of the manuscript of *The French Revolution* inadvertently burned at John Stuart Mill's, poor Teufelsdroeckh grumbling and setting himself to work again on it like an old Vulcan, toiling and moiling at his forge, beside Emerson—calm life, serene life, publication of books, lectures, childbirths, Transcendentalism, *The Dial*.

In their letters the contrast between the two men is complete: Emerson always good, condescending, optimistic, admiring; Carlyle, hypochondriacal, misanthropic, sardonic. Emerson confided to him his spurts of enthusiasm, his doubts, his dreams; Carlyle rebuked him, stung him, recalled him to a sense of reality, made fun of him, threw great buckets of cold water upon his flames with the help of Allah Kerim, Allah Akbar, Ach Gott! Silence, silence! Beware of

dreamers, of poseurs, of fools and fanatics . . .
The misanthropic Carlyle, who took the London
salons by storm, preached solitude to the suave
Emerson, who found his Concord somewhat
small. Both would gladly have changed rôles, but
what would London have thought—and Concord? At bottom they resembled each other as the
trip-hammer resembles the Æolian harp . . .
Emerson had sent ambassadors to Carlyle: Alcott,
Henry James, the elder, Margaret Fuller; but
Teufelsdroeckh, who needed a new victim each
day to devour, had turned up his nose at these
anæmic Yankees . . . The *Essays*, we have seen,
had not made much of an impression on him; they
were even a disappointment. Emerson's Milky
Way was too far from his Sinai, from his thunders. . . . Emerson's admiration was not blinder
than Carlyle's and it was more and more qualified.
At the time of the publication of *Past and Present*,
he had put a long article in *The Dial*, all feints
and nuances, which Carlyle had found "dangerous." Emerson found the book juicy and substantial, heavy and nourishing as an egg. He
showed Carlyle playing football with the most
venerable British institutions and capering about

the bishops and lords. He called Carlyle "a sick giant," a teamster who amused himself cracking his whip. He did not speak of the oaths. But what fire, what a wealth of images, what verve! A veritable Field of the Cloth of Gold. He who never laughed compared Carlyle's bursts of humor to an earthquake, a bacchanalia of vituperation. But when all was said and done, Carlyle was a poet, an inspired Cockney, a Gulliver among the dwarfs, an avatar of Thor and Odin, a Viking . . .

Just before Emerson left for England, they had exchanged portraits. The abyss which separated them was legible even on their faces: Carlyle with his broad forehead, his head strongly molded, his eye sockets bushy and cavelike, his bitter underlip, his scrutinizing eye that of a judge before the reading of the verdict, and in spite of that nevertheless a great air of diffused kindness; Emerson, on the contrary, angelic, benign, debonair, but with the side-whiskers and the look of a country doctor making his rounds—an Emerson who had hardly pleased Carlyle.

The great shovel of destiny had then once more thrown them together. Carlyle was fifty-

Thomas Carlisle

one, Emerson forty-four. The apologist of silence
was still the most inexhaustible of gossips. When
he had finished throwing vitriol on his victims,
he beat them with great whacks of the mallet:
"donkey, monkey, wind-bag, bladder, poor devil,
etc." The litany was endless. Carlyle was a
living paradox. Alone in the very heart of London, the misanthrope was the idol of the salons.
There was something tragi-comical in the sight
of this thunder-bearer, this Prometheus letting
himself be spoiled by the gentry. Did his admirers take him seriously? They paraded him
about society like a scarecrow to scandalize the
bishops, the courtiers, the writers, and the dons.
This guest of the aristocracy preached the gospel
of the people and hailed the coming of labor's
nobility, but he was above all a geyser of paradoxes. Were one speaking of liberty, Carlyle defended slavery. With the partisans of free trade,
he was invariably a protectionist. To the vegetarians he sang the praises of roast beef. With the
philanthropists he chanted a eulogy of murder,
capitalism, and the death penalty. He praised the
Tzar of Russia. Send him to Parliament and he
would immediately suppress the freedom of the

press and reporters; he would shoot the poor who refused to work. Paradox upon paradox . . . His enemies to shut him up proposed to send Carlyle to the House of Commons and to reduce him to silence by putting him to the test of facts. . . .

Emerson did not let himself be taken in, as he soared high above this volcano. If he loved his sick giant, he also could criticize him and with a criticism a bit unjust. Poet, imagist, wonderful word-juggler, but not a prophet. He envied him his Saxon vigor, this overflowing life of which destiny had cheated him. Carlyle had solved the dilemma; he knew how to be at once modern and transcendental. Emerson would have liked to imitate him, but not in that way, not by force of paradox and sarcasm, not with that satanic laugh, that demoniacal fury which made a "dangerous madman" of Carlyle . . .

The great cities of England, Liverpool, Birmingham, Manchester, frightened Emerson. The streets were full of the jobless, drunks, and prostitutes. He found Scotland gray and dirty, Edinburgh provincial. Where was his idyllic Concord, all clean and white under its elms? He lectured on "Great Men," "Socialism," "Politics," the

"Powers and Laws of Thought," before audiences of the people. In the spring of 1848 he was in London, the London of gas, omnibuses, steam ferries, the first postage stamps. He landed in the middle of the Chartist agitation. All England was stirred and the lords trembled on their seats. The French Revolution of February was making its reverberations felt. Louis-Philippe, the last king of the French, had just arrived in London and he set the court laughing as he told of the incidents of his flight. Emerson was present at a Chartist meeting and at the return of the delegation which had gone to France to congratulate the Second Republic. They sang the "Marseillaise" and the "Hymn of the Girondins." They shouted, "Every man a ballot and every man a musket." One would have said that England was on the eve of a revolution. The aristocrats would take care of themselves, but does one ever know? Carlyle himself had his doubts.

Carlyle did things up well in London. He introduced Emerson into society. Everyone wanted to see the Massachusetts Indian, the worshipper of the Over-Soul, the Jean-Jacques from over the Ocean. So there was the hermit of Concord in the salons. He seems to have moved about at his ease, a born gentleman and aristocrat. Receptions and dinners. He was in the *Almanach de Gotha*, at Lord Ashburton's, at Lady Palmerston's, at Lady Morgan's, at Lady Molesworth's, at Lord Lovelace's, at Lady Baring's—London's most witty woman. He admitted that he wanted oxygen. It was almost as tight and stuffy as Concord. Ah, if Thoreau, Alcott, and Ellery Channing had seen their walking companion strolling in evening clothes among these titled people under the chandeliers. He went to learned lectures, to meetings of Parliament. He was introduced to the celebrities: Stephenson, the builder of the first locomotives, the anatomist Owen, the physicist Bunsen. He met Dickens, whom he had not pardoned for his *American Notes*; Macaulay, the endless talker, full of anecdotes, humor, witticisms, but whose works Emerson did not care for; Prince Albert and Disraeli, whom he called a *chiffonier*, a waster of talent, a man without elevation of character who, instead of a planet under his feet, had only his pumps, his fine dandified pumps. He was presented to Byron's daughter . . .

In the Lake Country he had gone to see Wordsworth again, Wordsworth at seventy-seven, with his big nose and his face tanned and leathered by the wind, Wordsworth the impenitent Tory, who had quite forgotten his revolutionary escapades, and who railed against the France which he had, however, loved so well, too well . . . He went to Oxford where Froude found he had a striking resemblance to Newman. Froude wondered what would have happened if Newman had lived in Boston and Emerson in Oxford. But do not all roads lead to Rome? . . . Emerson envied the dons, the lettered monks of Oxford. He could be easily imagined among them, under their full red gowns with tasseled caps, in a solitude full of history, before a learned audience, surrounded by disciples, crossing the lawns after his courses at Oriel or Magdalen, along the beautiful Gothic quadrangles where Walter Pater used to walk. No doubt but that he dreamed a bit of that.

On the road to Stratford-on-Avon he had come across a young woman who told him abruptly and openly of her admiration for Rousseau. Emerson scarcely associated with Rousseau but he was polite and approved. He made a very deep impression on her. He was "the first real man" that she had ever met. The young enthusiast was George Eliot.

His brightest impressions were of De Quincey and Tennyson. It was in Edinburgh at the home of a friend that he met one evening the author of the *Opium Eater*, the Homer of drugs, he who for stimulants knew only pure water, the wind in the woods, and at long intervals a cigar. De Quincey arrived late and soaked, after having come miles in a shower and let his umbrella be stolen by some women of the street. The incorrigible bohemian was under the orders of a shrew who pursued him and stole his manuscripts. He lived at Lasswade with his three charming daughters, shy, nervous, like a perpetual sleep-walker, a veritable waking dreamer.

At Coventry Patmore's, the poet, he met Tennyson, Tennyson always in black, untidy, with his glasses, his cigars, and his port, a great diner, always absent-minded, an eternal child, one day here, another there, always about to go somewhere, and jealously cloistered in his dreams. Emerson found him of the earth earthy, but was not untouched by his extraordinary music, and he frankly admired the *Idylls of the King*. With Dickens and Thackeray he had had during an evening an *a parte* which had left him much perplexed. They were discussing chastity, and his puritan ears rang when he heard Dickens declare that if his son remained chaste he would believe him to be sick. The morality of the English was evidently not that of the Americans. He was shocked.

Meanwhile Emerson was photographing John Bull, qualities and faults, mentally and physically. He found among the English something animal which was confirmed by their love of horses and dogs. The women were thick-set and negligent about their persons. They did not conceal their gray hair like Americans. When it rained they tucked up their skirts without shame and showed their petticoats—what did the Bostonians do in such a case? The English were people who stood firm in their boots. They had their eyes screwed in their heads and were great mainly by the thickness of their necks. A stocky people full of sap, broad of chest, gorged with beer, a bit too heavy in flesh. Their genius was good sense, practical sense. They would kiss the dust before a fact. What had given them the empire of the world was their self-respect, their faith in causality, their realistic logic, the art of uniting means to ends. They had a passion for the useful. The French invented lace; the English added the shirt.

The English struck him as sincere, practical, and friends of facts. They detested equivocation in business. They were realists brutally frank, clean, methodical, truthful, proud, obstinate, loving comfort, industrious, great hoarders, fine sailors but without sunshine, without love, a bit sad. Emerson admired their fine manners. One would say that every Englishman was a lord, that every British subject was in himself the House of Commons.

The reverse of the medal: insularity, eccentricity, selfishness, and above all hypocrisy and cant, their earthiness, the lack of elevation in their ideas. Their social system was artificial, their legislation a network of fictions. They abhorred change and held on grimly to tradition

316

and decorum. They were exclusively English and hated foreigners. Their national church was a fetich, a doll. They cared more for the Old Testament than for the New. The English were without imagination. Their novels despair of the heart. A horizon of brass of the diameter of their umbrellas shut down around their senses. In literature, in philosophy, as in science, no loftiness of view. These people who had put the universe in subjection to them were afraid of ideas. They dressed the soul in English broadcloth and gaiters. Practicality and comfort made them forget heroism. "The island is a roaring volcano of fate, of material values, of tariff and laws of repression, glutted markets and low prices." Their poetry was purely decorative. Wordsworth was conscientious, Byron impassioned, Tennyson artificial. (But what of Keats, of Shelley?) The English he felt lacked a sense of the transcendent, the genius for contemplation. No Englishman would eve write a Bhagavat Gita.

Conclusion: England was the best nation in world, the country in which the individual w sacred, but one would say that the English peopl were in a state of arrested development. . . . He would go to the land of lace, France or Urbanity. Tennyson would have been willing to accompany Emerson to Paris, but he was *distrait* that day and did not want to be shot by the revolutionists.

318

CHAPTER IV

Swords, Beards, and Blouses

～～～～～

EMERSON arrived in Paris in May, 1848. He
stayed at 15 rue des Petits Augustins
where he had a comfortable suite of rooms for
ninety francs a month. He came to perfect his
French and he went to learn it at the *table d'hôte*
of a little restaurant on Rue Notre Dame des Vic-
toires. He felt that they put a price on each
mouthful, but he had the nouns, verbs, adverbs,
and, above all, interjections for nothing. Once
more this serene man had landed in the middle
of a revolution. The mob was still in the streets.
Everywhere there were notices, proclamations,
meetings, people in blouses armed to the teeth,
a sword or a pistol in their belts, bearded
like goats, with a *carmagnole* or a helmet on the
head. The trees on the boulevards had been cut
down to build barricades. Emerson maliciously

319

wondered if in a year from then the revolution would be worth the sacrifice of the shade.

He went to the Louvre, to the theater, *en soirée*. He heard Rachel in *Phèdre* and applauded her when she sang the "Marseillaise." He admired the great actress's mixture of grace, youth, and tragic force. He took Leverrier's course at the Sorbonne; he returned to the Jardin des Plantes and to the Museum; was present at one of Michelet's lectures on the philosophies of India, but—Frenchmen have no head for metaphysics.

He was happy. One can live well and cheaply in Paris. He idled along the quais, frequented the book stalls. He preferred French wine to English beer. He liked the light, free, and equalitarian air of Paris, which made him forget British conceit. He loved the Seine, the fountains, the gardens, the Palais-Royal, the boulevards crawling with people, the Luxembourg, the Cluny, Notre Dame. Every one was happy, at ease, informal. In short he fell under its spell. Doubtless Paris, like all great cities, had its vices but they were hidden and there were after all compensations. Here there was no aristocratic pride. With a little tact one was received everywhere. In England one needed a fortune to live; here one was content with little. *Vive Paris*, then! And don't let us forget the gay cafés blazing with light where he went to read the papers, to forget, to rest.

But what interested him most was politics, the Revolution which was still sizzling in the streets. He read the papers, the posters, the proclamations; he went to the Clubs, the Club of Clubs, the Woman's Club, the Conspirator's Club. . . . At the *Club de la Révolution* he heard Blanqui, lame, with his ill-omened face. At the *Club des Droits de l'Homme*, Barbès. Blanqui and Barbès were laying plans for the riot which passed under Emerson's windows on the fifteenth of May and disturbed his reading. He heard the general alarm being sounded; he saw the streets bristle with bayonets, the cannons which were being drawn to the National Assembly, the gatherings at the street-corners. The tri-color was floating over the Tuileries. After a flaming sunset the moon arose upon the swollen Seine.

And he rejoiced at the shopkeepers' victory.

Then he went to the *fête nationale* at the

Champ de Mars on the twenty-first of May—
120,000 people, an immense family gathering.
He copied in his *Journal* the program of the fête
(and in French):

"*Fête* of the 21st of May. Tricolored balloon; 500 pretty girls, *vivandières* and *can-
tinières*, and little children of both sexes dressed
like soldiers or with festive ribbons marching in
the procession . . ."

He noticed the huge drum majors with their
batons and fur caps; the firemen, the children on
stilts, the merry-go-rounds.

The National Assembly pasted up proclamations which he copied:

"The reign of swords is done, Napoleon's was
impotent in his defense and ours.

"The brute force of sabres, of conquest, is
crushed: crushed that of the mob's muskets. Let
muskets, like swords, bow to-day before ideas.
Become the generals of the ideas of the century
. . . What remains to-day of Bonaparte's cannons is the grape-shot of ideas which they also
contained . . . His codes followed his armies, as
cotton follows the armies of England. ASSEM-
BLEE NATIONALE, May 23."

Hurrah for the Revolution of the poor, the Revolution of the Good God, Liberty-Equality-Fraternity. All that slightly intoxicated Emerson. At last here was some oxygen. Paris seemed to him a continuation of the theatres where he had just been. It gave him the effect of lemon soda, the equivalent of champagne for a Yankee . . . Blanqui and Barbès were incarcerated at Vincennes. "The old Revolution said, *What is the third estate? Nothing. What ought it to be? Everything.* The New Revolution read, the *producer* for *the third estate.*"

At the National Assembly he had been to hear the great Lamartine's speech on Poland, a fine head, a free and superior style of delivery, manly and cultivated. When Lamartine was tired the members cried out, "Rest!" . . . Ah, these French, always chivalrous, always the same, who in the midst of a riot find the time to interest themselves in Poland and Italy. In short he had completely changed his mind about the French. He had arrived with his Anglo-Saxon prejudices about them: gossipy, theatrical, immoral, with their subversive ideas, full of tact doubtless, of moderation, of wisdom, the great brokers of ideas in the world, friends of progress, but without imagination; the country, however, of the Fénelons, the Montesquieus, the Pascals, of Madame Guyon, and of Madame de Staël. . . . He now was putting France above England. He had exaggerated the merits of the English. The French rose in his estimation. They were more virile, more expressive, their heads were less round, less opaque. He found them better bred; he liked their informality, their good humor. . . . He found Paris more interesting than London. In London one does not see the Thames; in Paris one sees the Seine and there are trees, fountains, gardens. In short *vive la France*! If ever he were in quest of some refuge of solitude and independency, he knew where he would seek it. The French were much more influential in Europe than the English. England dominated by brute force; France reigned by sympathy and talent. He went to say good-by to Madame d'Agoult, who had been one of the first, with the Polish poet Mickiewicz, to make his *Essays* known in France, and he left for London regretting that he had missed Lamennais and Edgar Quinet.

CHAPTER V

We English, or Carlyle's Cigar at Stonehenge

A<small>FTER</small> a month spent in Paris, Emerson returned to London *via* Amiens and Bou-
logne. He was this time the guest of society and
he gave its people lectures which at first sight
seemed to be above their heads: "The Powers and
Laws of Thought," "The Relation of Intellect
to the Natural Sciences," "Tendencies and Duties
of Men of Thought." . . . But he treated the
lords and the ladies as his humblest auditors in
America. He gave himself as he was, without
compromises, without lowering himself. All that
was very transcendental, very stiff, very oracular,
but there was a trembling in the voice, a flame in
the glance. Carlyle was present, applauded, nod-
ding his head and grunting aloud his approbation.
And then Emerson had had a capital idea. He
had prepared a homily after his fashion on
aristocracy.

In this naïve, though well-meaning composition, he stripped the nobility of its prestige and
its historical privileges. He laicized it and reduced it to personal superiority and distinction.
All unawares, he too was a Chartist; he was carrying on his revolution. He uncrowned the lords
and ennobled the average English commoner such
as he had described him in his notes. He once
more apotheosized self-reliance and character.
He spoke of the nobility as an agnostic speaks of
God. Indifferent to the past, he maintained without a quiver before these titled Englishmen that
kings had lost their romantic halo, that a king
today is no more a king than our modern
consuls are consuls in the antique sense of the
word. To propose as he did to list in the future
directories "kings" as we do "physicians" and
"brokers," might pass for a somewhat coarse
American joke. The gentry could not have failed
to smile. Emerson obviously lacked imagination
on that occasion. No more in politics than in religion would he admit the survival of certain
symbols. He was unwilling to understand that an
ordinary man in the sense of nature might be very
really ennobled by time, rank and function.

Another fault no less grave was that he took it upon himself to scourge the aristocrats and declaim against what he called "aristocracy without duties." He added without ceremony that such an aristocracy deserved to have its farms burned by the peasants. The moment was ill chosen for such advice and Lord Morpeth requested the lecturer to suppress that passage.

This speech reminds one of Voltaire's *Ingénu* and Mark Twain's *Connecticut Yankee*. But he was sincere and meant no malice. For that matter he pronounced a panegyric of good manners, personal merit, individualism, which went right to the heart of the English. In the place of the noble he enthroned the gentleman. That was not calculated to displease the British.

His lectures obtained only a *succès d'estime*, which disappointed him a bit. He was more at ease with the popular audience which came to hear him at Exeter Hall. His London lectures had passed almost unnoticed. The time was not propitious to transcendentalism and the receipts suffered. People praised the nobility of his carriage, the elevation of his ideas, the charm of his voice, his evasive and distant air of a man who

has just met an angel. He had been made tem-
porarily a member of the Athenæum. He had
visited Turner's studio. The time had come to
return to his own people, to his Asia again, his
little daughters, Ellen, Edith, and his last born,
Edward, to go back to his study, his books, Proclus, Plotinus, the Vedas, and his favorite season
of all, late summer, rich in mirages, with sunsets
on the Concord. . . . Before leaving he wanted
to make a trip to Stonehenge with Carlyle.

Friday, the seventh of July, 1848, the two
friends arrived *via* the South Western Railway
at Amesbury in Hampshire, familiar country to
Carlyle, who had spent vacations there, and after
lunch they took the road for Salisbury Plain.
From a distance under the gray sky amid the
deserted downs, the menhirs and dolmens of
Stonehenge resembled a group of brown dwarfs.
The grass-grown barrows rose like bosses on the
plains where wandered here and there shepherds
and their flocks. A fine spot for a Carlylean meditation on Time and Eternity. There was the egg
from which England was hatched. Here were
ruins as antique as those of Ilium. Upon the mil-

lenary blocks eternal Nature had sewn buttercups, thistles, thyme, and daisies. In the sky soared and sang Shelley's larks—last year's larks in a wind as old as the world. What Mastodons, what megatheria, had piled up these gigantic stones? Ah, if the old sphinx would talk. If she would recount the history of Britain!

Carlyle who had not calmed down since their departure and covered with curses the globe-trotters, snobs, art, science, and artists, Carlyle drew himself together and softened. He remained there pensive, his head low. Ah, how well this spot suited him, he who planted cypresses wherever he went and who never went wrong when in search of pain . . . The mournful heath, the mysterious blocks of stone, the flight of time, the eternal vanity of things, history, religion, *ay me*! Silence, silence! Carlyle is thinking of the saints of Iona, of the old chroniclers, whom he evoked in *Past and Present*, of Abbot Samson, of the age of faith . . . How far was London with its paganism! Then suddenly interrupting his reverie, Teufelsdroeckh went to light his cigar in the leeward of a dolmen. . . .

The two friends left Stonehenge at twilight

to take tea at the inn. There was, alas, only a drop of milk for them both. Returning, Carlyle rode his hobbies again. He let loose against the landlords, who left thousands of acres fallow which might have fed the starving. They visited Wilton House, seat of the Earl of Pembroke; then Salisbury Cathedral. At an evening with friends Emerson was questioned about the future of America. He expounded to them "Boston fanaticism," renunciation of armed force, the coming of justice and love, abolition of war, simplicity, poverty, each for self and God for all. This little speech impressed Carlyle. When dinner was announced he refused to go in first, saying that "he was altogether too wicked." There followed a new series of questions on America, the landscape, the forests, the houses—Emerson's in particular. (In London some one had asked him if it were true that there were rattlesnakes in New York.) On the road to Winchester, they stopped at Saint Cross where, in accordance with an immemorial custom, the travelers were offered beer and bread. Upon which a new explosion from Carlyle against clergymen who, instead of feeding the poor, fatten themselves on their prebends. Another stop at

Winchester. The Viking Carlyle insisted on paying his respects to the tomb of Canute, of Alfred
the Great, and of the Saxon kings. Then they
took the train for London.

On the fifteenth of July, 1848, Emerson embarked at Liverpool on the *Europe*. He left
England with more esteem for the English than
he had had on his arrival. He pardoned them
their pride. Lacking sympathy for them he nevertheless did not spare his admiration. The dough
from which they were kneaded was unique.
English, Anglo-Saxons, after all, England and
America, were all as one. The English race and
tongue were still purer across the sea. It was the
best of himself that John Bull had saved in becoming Brother Jonathan. The melting pot had
not yet transformed the United States into an
amalgam of disparate races. Emerson remained
faithful to the voice of his blood. In his lecture
in London he had caught himself saying, "We
English," as if this descendant of the Puritans of
authentic British lineage, America, and above all
his native New England, were after all only a
sort of dominion. Emerson did not admit that the
two peoples were cut asunder. In the immense

and trivial continent of America, in the high pastures of the Alleghenies, in the prairies whose only frontier was the sky, survived the great Saxon mother-country, the common mother exiled now many years from the too-well-clipped hedges and too-carefully-cultivated gardens of Albion.

He carried off the realistic and practical England in 1848 with him in the *Principles of Political Economy* by John Stuart Mill.

CHAPTER VI

Diogenes and His Lantern

A N OPULENT soul fashions a universe to its size. What else had Emerson done up to this time? He doubtless pushed his philosophy of isolation to the point of paradox. But if he isolated himself it was the better to belong to himself. It was not he who would reduce the universe to the dimensions of his umbrella. He went beyond his tiny Concord in his balloon which soared over time and space. His dives into Nirvana were only subterfuges. He withdrew into Buddha when Brahma failed him. He soared, he plunged, he flew, but do not take him for a pantheist. He was rather a humanist. In the Concord woods he exalted and aggrandized himself, defied contingencies, became conscious of the universal affinities. In his study the work of annexation went on. He pillaged the historians and the philosophers. To beguile his solitude he bound himself to the great souls of all times. Like nature, history was his refuge, his alibi, his mask. Montaigne also raised himself thus to the height of his heroes.

Do not take his paradoxes on love and friendship too literally. Beware above all of making him a misanthrope. No one more than he found man to his taste or practiced the religion of humanity. But he was difficult, haughty, transcendental on this point as on all the rest. He needed all or nothing. It was long since, his lantern in hand, he had set out to find a man, like Diogenes. From childhood the names of the great had resounded in his ears. He had read and reread Plutarch, Shakespeare, Milton, Plato, Montaigne. About him he felt the superman, the central man, the new man, the plus-man: Murat, Webster, Everett, Charles Chauncy, his brother, Tnamurya, Margaret Fuller, Thoreau, Alcott, and still more, Carlyle. . . . Give him the man who knew how to reconcile the One and the Many and he would follow him as a god. "Of the universal mind each individual is one more incarnation."

He had given his choice to history as to nature. His philosophy of history, like his philosophy of love and friendship, is paradoxical and it does not seem romantic. The picturesque resurrection of the past had been imagined by dreamers at bay in order to forget the present and its pettiness. The past did not interest Emerson. He believed only in the eternal. Time and space did not exist for him. The centuries of duration held all in the present moment. All in each, *il più nel uno*. All the past was held in the present. There was no past; there was only the soul. Useless to resuscitate that which is not dead. To relive history was enough to take a new view of it. What Plato thought, we could think; what a saint had felt, we could feel. There was a relation between the hours of our life and the centuries of time. No one of us but had wide open before him the entire cycle of great deeds. It is for us to make ourselves Greeks, Romans, Turks, priests, kings, martyrs, or hangmen; for us to fasten these images in our secret experience. Hasdrubal, Cesare Borgia, Alexander, Napoleon, are ourselves. Greece, Spain, Italy, all that is in us. It was for us as much as for their contemporaries that Socrates, Saint Paul, Marcus Aurelius, Luther, Milton, had lived. It was our history that Æsop, Homer, Hafiz, Ariosto, Chaucer, Walter Scott, related to us. There is no history, there is only biography. All history becomes subjective.

Why do we not accomplish what we admire? Why do we not reproduce within us all humanity, the primitive world, the Golden Age, the garden of the Hesperides, the expedition of the Argonauts, the calling of Abraham, the building of the Temple, Christ, the Middle Ages, and the Renaissance? . . . Life is short; man endless. We have not yet taken the count, the inventory of our possibilities, of our potencies. Scarcely have we tried our wings. Revolutions, migrations, evolutions without end await us. Tongues, sciences, politics, music, poetry, explorations, let us live them all, let us try all. Why should there be only one Columbus, one Cabot, one Walter Raleigh, one Humboldt, one Pythagoras, one Napoleon? Why, in view of our enormous privileges, should we bury ourselves in a narrow domesticity? Why, instead of meeting each other from the height of our six feet, do we not make the Infinite and the Immense the basis of our relations and our duties? The fairest souls are always the most universal. To individualize all public facts, to generalize all private facts—that is the law of history.

The Superman was coming. Emerson expected him and prohesied him; history announced him. Genius and greatness are not the privilege of a caste, of an élite. Properly speaking, there are no common men. In principle there are only great men, more or less great, more or less universal, who call to each other, correct each other, complete each other. The domain of genius is not a monarchy, it is a republic based on universal suffrage. On the one hand, the body of electors, the constituents, all of us; on the other, the representatives of the people, our representatives, our great men. At a certain degree of elevation of thought all men are heroes. The great man is not the exception but the rule. Man, each man, is infinite. Let heroes be a mirror and a guide for us. In them let us contemplate ourselves and discover what we are, what we might be, and what we ought to be. Intercessors, stimulators, let us reach them by sympathetic imitation. Use them without becoming servile to them in the hope of surpassing them. No hero is final; all greatness is approximate. Self-reliance! Heroism consists in being oneself at any cost and fully.

Bovarysm, braggadocio, and bluff, protests the devil's advocate; desperate but vain efforts of a great soul to escape its limits and broaden its narrow horizon. Emerson sought to escape the mediocrity of his little city, to forget the Philistines who surrounded him. He freed his repressions. Alexander, Hasdrubal, Cesare Borgia, Napoleon! He who had never harmed a fly! His heroism resembles the sham battle on the Concord drill ground or the living pictures which the ladies of Brook Farm posed for in the woods . . . Carlyle had written his essays; Emerson had, of course, to publish his; Carlyle had published *Heroes and Hero Worship*, Emerson had to compose *Representative Men*.

Carlyle's famous book had in fact appeared before the Boston lectures on great men and once more the contrast between the two men was striking. Misanthropic and atrabilious, Carlyle called the demigods to aid him purge his spleen and empty his vitriol. Much cared he for the common run of man! In his colloquy with the Infinite, he defied men of action. "In the beginning was the deed." Like the *French Revolution*, *Heroes and Hero Worship* was a revolutionary hymn, a saturnalia. Thunder and lightning; great lonely statues appeared on a high mountain—Odin, Mohammed, Dante, Shakespeare, Luther, John Knox, Rousseau, Cromwell, Napoleon—gods, men, warriors, visionaries, fanatics, solitary geniuses.

With what dash, what verve, what irony did Carlyle jerk his marionettes to the front of the stage, spurring them on, curbing them. Forward march! Sublime marionettes, exceptional and yet so human, astonishing, moving, crushing. . . .

In the Hall of Fame Emerson chose not men of action (except Napoleon) but contemplators: Plato, or the Philosopher, Swedenborg or the Mystic, Montaigne or the Sceptic, Shakespeare or the Poet, Goethe or the Writer—in all six figures only, six portraits detached from their background which float a bit too much in the void. And these portraits proved a thesis, illustrated a lesson: the philosophy of representation. Emerson took up ancient doctrines, old myths on emanation, reminiscence, transmigration of souls, the microcosm. He called upon monists and transformists to contribute: Goethe, Ocken, Cuvier, Linnæus, Lamarck. He modernized it all by borrowing his title from the republican institutions of his country. Plato, Swedenborg, Montaigne, Napoleon, Goethe, were nothing more than representatives of the people, Congressmen in the Capitol of Humanity.

The book was largely autobiographical. His representatives were mirrors. He had been searching for his heroes for a long time: Plato, the Plato of the famous letter, the companion of his twenties, the inspirer, the model; Swedenborg, whom he had pilfered in *Nature*; Montaigne, his bedside companion; the inevitable Shakespeare; Goethe, read a bit against his taste to please Carlyle; Napoleon, the colossus on the horizon of his youth. Had not Emerson reached his twelfth birthday on the date of Waterloo, his eighteenth when the Emperor died at Saint Helena? Channing besides had preceded him in a famous philippic which excommunicated the conqueror. Through these portraits it is himself whom he is painting; his thirst for unity in Plato and Swedenborg, his tergiversations and recantations in Montaigne. When he did not paint himself directly, he is still recognized by contrast—his clear reason lined with humor in his criticism of Swedenborg, his puritanism in that of Goethe.

Of true portraits, of those line drawings of which Carlyle spoke, there are only three alive and picturesque in the whole book—Plato, Swedenborg, and Montaigne—and Plato is eclipsed before Socrates. Emerson's Plato resembles him like a brother. He is a man in quest of unity, the hero of "Compensation," he who can see the inside and the outside of things, the man with the two vases—the one full of ether (*i.e.*, ideas), the other of pigment (to wit "experience"); the rare being who reconciles the One and the Many, poet and geometer, mystic and dialectician. It is indeed he himself whom Emerson presents to us in this great average man, on the same footing as ourselves, triumph of nature and culture, practical, full of common sense, and prudent even in ecstacy, transcendent but always simple and natural, philosopher of lofty range but without a system. Emerson has strongly orientalized his Plato. He has seen him through Plotinus, Proclus, and the Buddhists, at a time when he deserted the groves of the Academy for the banks of the Ganges.

To compensate we have a delightful portrait of Socrates, one of the best which Emerson ever drew, a Socrates informal, Yankee, and Frank-linian; "a good old uncle," wily as one found them in Concord; a Socrates in slippers, simple and familiar, strong-minded and humorous, great cracker of jokes, whose ugly face the Athenian potters caricatured on their vases; a sly fellow who could back the craftiest talkers against the wall, a good drinker as ever had existed, who waiting for the hemlock never refused a glass, and always composedly leaving his companions under the table, went off to seek soberer opponents elsewhere; in short, what Emerson familiarly called an "old one," yet at the same time a martyr and a saint. . . .

In the Swedenborg Emerson outdid himself. He traced a haunting portrait of the man and the mystic. Mineralogist, chemist, zoölogist, mathematician, physicist, engineer, astronomer, anatomist, theologian, mystic, and visionary, Swedenborg in his velvet coat, sword at his side, traveled about haunted by the demon of analogy, of identity. What a nightmare, this universe! this mystic quadrant of which man and the serpent form the two legs, vertical and horizontal, and between which swarms the whole animal kingdom. The length of a fantastic dorsal spine, from the worm, from the atom, to God, climb all beings, pushing one another on, overlapping, coupled together, duplicating one another, in a whirlwind of angles, spheres, spirals, amid angels beating their wings and grinning devils, to infinity, each close to each. Geometry gone mad, a world opaque and black, fallen into epilepsy and trance, a lackluster landscape, gardens of the dead amid cypresses where never a bird has sung. A charnel breath mingles with the incense of the temple. "Except Rabelais and Dean Swift nobody ever had such science of filth and corruption."

Emerson did not let himself fall under the spell. He continued his optimistic pæan in terms as frank, as realistic as those used by the Swedish Dante. Our sins, what do they matter? The less we think of them, the better off we shall be. "The carrion in the sun will convert itself to grass and flowers; and man, though in brothels, or jails, or on gibbets, is on his way to all that is good and true." What stranger and more vivid words would Baudelaire have spoken? Yankee humor takes its revenge. Emerson jeers at the modern Rhadamanthus "who goes up and down the world of men . . . in gold-headed cane and peruke, and with nonchalance and the air of a referee, distributes souls." Swedenborg's Paradise amuses him highly. "These angels . . . are all country parsons: their heaven is a *fête champêtre*, an evangelical picnic, or French distribution of prizes to virtuous peasants." That is a veritable etching.

Montaigne, or the Sceptic, is the man who plays head and tails with the universe—the antidote of fanaticism. How Emerson loved his Montaigne, the frankest and most honest of writers, how often he read him and how, once he established contact with him, did he do his utmost to imitate him! With what joy he opposed him to the so-called "realists," those folks who believe that mustard bites the tongue, that pepper is hot, that matches are incendiary, that revolvers are to

be avoided, and that suspenders really hold up
pantaloons! Hurrah for Saint Michel de Montaigne, sceptic and man of prudence, who took
the world with a grain of salt, as an illusion and
perhaps a farce . . . but who did not doubt except
by an excess of faith!

The philosophy of representation triumphs in
the essay on Shakespeare and culminates there in
paradoxical conclusions. The man Shakespeare is
eclipsed before the author, the playwright before
the poet, and the poet before the thinker—the
greatest of all thinkers, in conformity with the
Anglo-Saxon tradition. Emerson, who totally
lacked theatrical sense, treats the plays very cavalierly. He lets one read them backward, beginning at the end. . . . Shakespeare is always
Shakespeare! He accommodates himself easily to
the mysteries which hover over the life and the
work of the great poet. His apocryphal and
anonymous genius thrills him. He had made the
acquaintance of the very erudite Delia Bacon, who
had attributed the Shakespearean dramas to her
great namesake. Delia's paradox fits in perfectly
with the doctrine of representation. The genius,
according to Emerson, was always and naturally

345

anonymous. The less he is original and personal, the greater he is. All great books are collective. That one is in ignorance of all that concerns Shakespeare is not astonishing. It was the genius of the Anglo-Saxon race who wrote these plays. It is of the essence of poetry "to spring like the rainbow daughter of Wonder, from the invisible, to abolish the past and refuse all history." He is just short of writing an apology of plagiarism. Thus was Shakespeare transcendentally juggled away.

Napoleon too was only a symbol. He was the man of the world, the man of the crowd, the incarnation of democracy, of the average man, of the bourgeois; a marvelous business man, the apotheosis of reason without conscience; a rogue, a liar, an actor; Jupiter-Scapin, Babbitt, the American Tartarin, but Babbitt armed to the teeth. We are far from the Arc de Triomphe and the Colonne Vendôme. . . .

Goethe also passes a *mauvais quart d'heure* in this portrait gallery. "He is the type of culture, the amateur of all arts and sciences and events; artistic, but not artist; spiritual but not spiritualist." Goethe was fragmentary! . . . But Emerson's transcendence has its limits and by dint of seeing high, he saw ill at times.

In short, three suggestive and well-drawn portraits; the others weaker and drowned in ideology. *Representative Men* was an uneven book, rich in ideas but without much relief, a precious book to know the thoughts and the secret tastes of Emerson but which paled before the *Heroes* of Carlyle. Carlyle was none too satisfied by it. He held its metaphysics and Emerson's optimism cheaply. Plato left him cold and he was cheated out of his dear Goethe. He expected better.

CHAPTER VII

Mammoth Cave

IN THE *Conduct of Life* Emerson came down from his ivory tower. He forgot the Vedas for Mill's *Political Economy*. He threw, as he said, cakes to Cerberus and flirted with the atheists. He preached the gospel of action. He was very frank, very realistic; the era of dreams was at an end. Transcendentalism had discharged its last flames; utopians, reformers, philanthropists were launched into the same mêlée—religious, political, and social. The party of pure intelligence was swamped. The whistle of the locomotive had blown away the mists. America had to be made. Emerson envied Carlyle his being at once transcendental and modern; here he was in his turn in the heights of actuality. No more swinging from side to side, no more wavering; the reign of action was beginning. The author of the *Conduct of Life* was a man for whom the external world existed. For the first time in his life one would say that he became aware of the obstacle, that he felt the resistance of matter.

The essay on "Fate" takes up the themes of "Compensation," but Emerson no longer plays blindman's buff with the problem of good and evil. He approaches it head-on without evasion. He draws up an implacable list of determinisms and no longer escapes it by bird's-eye views or long-term consolations, but by a direct appeal to the will, to energy, to action. To the determinism of Fate, he opposed that of human acts. Let us equal with our stoicism that of rivers, oaks, and mountains. The atoms which compose us can cope with the universe; they are as tough and savage as the world which assails us. Triumph over fate by submitting to it. A breadth of Will eternally traverses the world of souls in the direction of the Just and the Necessary. Fate does not exclude progress but implies it. It is the duty of each of us to create his reason for being, his destiny. Life is freedom although the world reaches its ends necessarily. There is a harmony between events and men.

349

The piece terminates on one of those great lyric bursts common in Emerson, on a prayer and a hymn to Blessed Unity, to the fair Necessity to which he wished us to raise an altar.

The essay on "Power" is Nietzschean. He compares the soul to an electric battery and celebrates the superman, whom he calls the plusman. He praises force, declares that a bit of wickedness produces better muscles, that the world could not get along without rogues, that a Judas is needed among the saints. He extols adventurers, soldiers, explorers, buccaneers. He would preserve in civilized man the primitive and savage element. He exalts war, the will to power, what he calls the "affirmative class." Savage force becomes sublime when it is united, as in Michelangelo, with art and refinement. He celebrates labor, technical and mechanical skill, organized and methodical power concentrated on one point. All is mathematical; there is no chance. Let us follow the way of machines.

It is a curious spectacle to see Emerson yielding to the call of the wild and reaching out his hand in anticipation to Jack London, to the Roosevelt of the strenuous life, discovering Efficiency.

Combining these declarations with the confidences of the essay on "Experience," we obtain an unpublished and paradoxical portrait of the sage beyond good and evil. Was it not these pages which thrilled Nietzsche on the heights of Sils Maria?

The considerations on "Wealth" make one think of Carnegie's *Gospel of Wealth* and Henry Ford's memoirs. The apostle of poverty and the simple life sketches a philosophy of money which amounts to a glorification of it. He takes the side of the promotors and speculators, declares that poverty is demoralizing, that property is a product of the spirit, that wealth is moral, that it gives us access to the universe, that everyone is created and put into the world to be rich, that the revelations of political economy are worth those of the Bible, that the dollar is a spiritual force. . . . One can read between the lines that in Emerson's eyes the poor, like the sick, are rogues, that the capitalists are the real "representative men," that all compensation which pays in specie is divine, and that Wall Street is the true temple of the Over-Soul. . . .

But Emerson's political economy is disarming

besides in its naïve optimism. It is based upon the play of eternal compensations, automatic adjustment of prices, of supply and demand, the futility of legislative interference, *laissez-faire, laissez-passer*. To realize his destiny, every man is and should be a capitalist.

Very American, very modern too, is the program of education expounded in the essay on "Culture." The Phi Beta Kappa orator, an overseer of Harvard College, does not hold the universities in good odor; the friend of books protests against literary education. He who had never run, never played, who was shocked by ballets, sang the praises of sports, shooting, riding, fencing, football, swimming, the dance. He had not forgotten his puritan childhood; he had not pardoned it. Montaigne, Rabelais, Rousseau, chambered scholars, were always sportsmen in imagination and as far as others were concerned; it was their revenge on life, the freeing of their repressions. Then Emerson sang of evolution and the survival of the fittest, like a man who had just read Darwin. He celebrated the ascent of creatures from the fossil to civilized man. Men really worthy of this name are rare. We all drag behind us vestiges of the quadruped. "We call these millions men; but they are not yet men. Half-engaged in the soil, pawing to get free, man needs all the music that can be brought to disengage him. If Love, red Love, with tears and joys; if Want with his scourge; if War with his cannonade; if Christianity with its charity; if Trade with its money; if Art with its portfolios; if Science with her telegraphs through the deeps of space and time can set his dull nerves throbbing, and by loud taps on the tough chrysalis can break its walls and let the new creature emerge erect and free—make way and sing pæans! The age of the quadruped is to go out, the age of the brain and of the heart is to come in."

All the essays are skillfully dosed and balanced. The chapter on "Behavior" constitutes a little manual on etiquette. Prudent Emerson takes his precautions against letting the savage bite. He gives recipes for civilizing the quadruped and putting a mute on the call of the wild. He mixes his honey with American vinegar, praises good manners; sketches portraits in the style of Labruyère. He is there with all his tact, his natural nobility, his pedigree. At the very moment

353

when there was appearing in the Middle and Far West a new type of man, this little treatise on civility was not useless to defend the traditions of the American gentleman against the adventurers and the cowboys of Bret Harte and Mark Twain.

In his "Considerations by the Way" Emerson deals in evasion and irony. These digressions once more betray the impenitent individualist. This time he is hardly American, or at least he is not a modern American. He denounces the superstition of the masses, of the majorities. He is not for number but for culture. Instead of flattering the masses it would be better to educate them. "Masses! the calamity is the masses. I do not wish any mass at all, but honest men only, lovely, sweet, accomplished women only, and no shovel-handed, narrow-brained, gin-drinking million stockingers or lazzaroni at all." Better to restrict than to multiply the population. Nature produces fifty bad melons to one good one. "The mass are animal, in pupilage, and near chimpanzee." But courage, good will be born of evil. Compensation! Nature lasts by antagonism. It is from the middle classes that the great men emerge. There are the men we need. A man who would not make life and the world happier would be better un-born.

Elevation and fine lyric rapture are not rare in the book. In the essay on "Worship," Emerson prophesied the church of the future: a new church founded on moral science, at first naked and cold like a babe in a manger again, the church of the man to come, a puritan church without "shawms, or psaltery, or sackbut," with heaven and earth for its beams and rafters, science for symbol and illustration, which would annex beauty, music, painting, and poetry. Emerson vowed his temple to "the nameless Thought," the "nameless Power," to the "super-personal Heart," to the good and consoling Laws, vague enough divinities, empty enough temple, but animated and peopled by his fervent heart.

In the essay on "Beauty" he was very poetic, very subtle, very platonic. He took up his lauda-tion of beauty and woman. He asked before all a beautiful and romantic life, protested against the bourgeois virtues, little lives, little people, narrow horizons, good husband, good son, good citizen. . . . He pleaded for the romantic in character. Let man adopt a real idea of self. Let his hands touch the stars, his eyes see through the earth, his ears understand the language of beasts and birds, let the earth and the sky speak to him by force of sympathy. . . . He celebrated the beautiful splendor of the true, the flower of perfect health, the unalterable and calm heaven in which are hidden all wisdom and all power. He found subtle and suggestive words to the glory of the Eternal Feminine, declaring that every woman is a poem, that the universal affinities bind the beauty of woman to that of nature, that lovers are right to compare their mistresses to moonlight and the stars, to woods and waters, to the pomp of summer. *Vis superba formæ*! The only beings who really belong to the horizon, he affirms elsewhere, are beautiful women. He tells us the story of the fair Pauline de Viguier whom the people of Toulouse made appear twice a week on a balcony that they might admire her, authentic forerunner of the Beauty Contests. He undertook the defense of the little god Cupid unjustly accused of being blind, the most perspicacious, the most clear-sighted of all the gods. Love is an eternal child whom Beauty guides, pilot of young souls. . . . Thus Socrates-Emerson, without seeming to, knew well the science of love, the most important of all, a secret difficult to discover, so profound is it, but disclosed by a glance. In a pretty conceit he puts all the philosophy of flirting: "It does not hurt weak eyes to look into beautiful eyes never so long." And he finely analyzed this wireless telegraphy of lovers who communicate to each at a distance and in a glance broadcast to each other all they desire and all they know. . . .

The book begun under the sign of "Fate" ends with an essay on "Illusions." So much reading of Plato, of Plotinus, so many dives into Brahma, have colored these final pages. Aladdin-Emerson has discovered Plato's Cave in Kentucky. In the Mammoth Cave which he had just visited he found the symbol of life. . . . In the subterranean shadows he glimpsed domes, unfathomable depths, he heard invisible cataracts, sailed up the River Echo, crossed Lethe and the Styx, awoke the echoes with shots and music. He saw icicles, orange flowers, acanthus leaves, grapes, snowballs, and shot Bengal lights into the vaults of the subterranean cathedral. In the Star-Cham-

357

ber, all lights out, he saw shining over his head the "night heaven thick with stars" and even a comet gleaming among them, while a chorus sang, "The stars are in the quiet sky." Splendor, lights, illusions, Maya . . . Our life is an ecstasy. It is the imagination, wonder, feeling which keeps us alive. The world is a carnival, a masked ball, in which no one drops his domino. To violate the unity and the fiction of the drama would be an impertinence. "Yoganidra, the goddess of illusion, Proteus, Momus, or Gylfi's Mocking, for the power has many names—is stronger than the Titans, stronger than Apollo. . . . Life is a succession of lessons which must be lived to be understood. All is riddle, and the key to a riddle is another riddle. There are as many pillows of illusion as flakes in a snowstorm. We awake from one dream into another dream."

In the Mammoth Cave Emerson left as an offering to Yoganidra the illusions of Power, Religion, Beauty, Love . . . but he did not lose faith. The Truth and the Right remained; there was neither chance nor anarchy in the universe; all was system and gradation. A god presides in every sphere. Illusions rain down like meteors; we feel ourselves transported, shaken up, duped in the huge phantasmagoria. . . . Then the sky is cleared; the clouds disperse; and the gods are there about us on their thrones, alone with us alone.

Carlyle preferred *The Conduct of Life* to Emerson's other works. He found in it an Emerson of his own size, harder, more incisive, more substantial, with lightning flashes of thought, and he admired what he called the "Fiat lux" of the finale. Let us agree. All of Emerson was in the book—the thinker, the poet, the humanist, the man of action, what he was, what he wanted to be, his desires, his ambitions, his hatreds, his repressions. His book is harmonious, well constructed, all of a piece, each essay leading to the next, with an ascending rhythm, a sustained allegro. Utopias, vigorous thoughts, audacity, prophecies, lyricism. This time he did not vaporize; he carved. *The Conduct of Life* is his masterpiece.

CHAPTER VIII

John Brown

1861-1865. The worshiper of the Over-Soul was to awake to the sound of cannon. For long the fire had been smoldering under the ashes. While he was adoring in solitude the interplay of the divine compensations, while he was celebrating the autonomy of every thinking being, the presence of the divine in the soul, the uniqueness, the infinite value of each man, the South bought and sold slaves and the North connived at it. If it did not practice slavery, it lived on it. The South for the North was cotton. What a lie given to the idealist's dreams, to his most peremptory declarations! But the conscience of New England was awakened. Philanthropic and religious to the quick, the country of the Puritans was launched in an anti-slavery crusade. Abolitionism had come out of the same smoky but gen-

erous heart as Brook Farm and Fruitlands, from
a soul always brooding reform. The Garrisons,
the Wendell Phillipses, stirred up the country and
Uncle Tom's Cabin made all eyes weep.

Emerson had slowly come into the movement.
A temporizer and a man of prudence as always,
he observed and let it come, confident in immanent justice. Had he not moreover like all of
us his own slaves to free in his inner life? Every
movement which did not start from the depths of
the heart inspired him with distrust and once
more he had translated the problem into the
depths, into those troubled regions of the soul
where the primitive beast struggles with the
angel. Slaves—were we not all slaves of cupidity
and egoism? Let him who was without sin cast
the first stone at the Southerners. It were better
then and ever to begin within, with internal reform. The problem of slavery was a moral
problem.

But events were soon to force his hand. An
outsider in politics, anxious above all to pursue
his meditations in peace, thinking was his profession, and he demanded peace of mind for himself and those of his caste. If he threw himself

361

into the battle, it was neither from sentimentality nor philanthropy, but from duty, impelled by self-respect. He must rout the nightmare. And then, however indifferent he was to politics, he was jealous of the honor of his little country whose glorious destiny he compared to that of Judea and Attica. It was there that his ideal of government had taken shape: a state to the measure of the individual, where the town meeting was the foundation of the republic, a government based upon referendum, the direct appeal to conscience, state, government, and law having no other mission than to defend the sacred rights of the individual. No morality, no law.

Little by little, then, he had made his decision, without directly allying his cause to that of the Abolitionists. But the moment had come to declare oneself, under penalty of being unworthy of the name of gentleman. In 1844 Great Britain had emancipated the blacks of the West Indies, while Massachusetts was letting its colored citizens be arrested aboard ships in southern ports. Emerson had pronounced on this occasion a speech full of biting irony. Ah, what virile eloquence and what accents of indignation this placid phi-

losopher could find! He was in the real world
this time and he followed his idea to the bitter
end; he forced it upon his hearers, he hammered
it in. Those Massachusetts vessels should have
been as sacred as temples! Of what use was the
government? The governor of Massachusetts was
incompetent; the State House was only a joke of
a capitol; the magistracy a body without honor.
Where then were the descendants of the great-
hearted Puritans? Before all, save the Union!
they cried. What remains of the Union when the
most sacred liberties are attacked? He lashed
these men without convictions, the hypocrites. No
civilization is possible so long as one race is oppressed by another. . . .

In 1845 the senator from Massachusetts, Samuel Hoar, was brutally expelled from South Caro-
lina where he had gone to defend the rights of
colored citizens. Sarcasms again bloomed on the
lips of Emerson. Oh, you who are leaving for
the Carolinas, forget not to carry a pistol in your
pocket; be careful to make your will and to leave
your pocketbook at home. . . . The attack was
only one incident of many; one leaf of the tree.

It is not Samuel Hoar we must avenge; we must cut down the tree. . . .

But events were rushing on: the annexation of Texas, the declaration of war on Mexico in violation of treaties. Emerson denounced this crime against civilization. The United States are annexing Mexico and Mexico will poison them. In 1850 was voted the Fugitive Slave Law. From then on every runaway slave must be returned to his master and the citizens were enjoined to aid the authorities. Here were Americans transformed into slave hunters. Fugitives were arrested in the heart of Boston, and Daniel Webster, senator from Massachusetts, was the promoter of the measure. Emerson could hold himself in no longer. America, its government, its civilization, the State of Massachusetts, the Church, the courts—with what brio, with what verve does he lash them. There was infamy in the air. Slavery was no longer clandestine; they ate it, drank it, breathed it, carried it on them like clothes, like a Nessus's cloak, gangrene, a corrosive, a poison. All was infected and soiled—the earth, the house one lived in, the very light. A father knew not how to answer his children conceived in dishonor; neighbors no longer dared look one another in the face. The Union! the Union! they cried. What mattered the Union when one had lost one's self-respect? Liberty was no longer anything but an empty word; it were better to hiss the flag. All the citizens participated in the legal crime which had been committed. As for those who voted the law, one would soil his hand to touch them. Morality, religion, speak no more of them. Religion is good only for dead dogs; morality is but pudding. America voted a rascally law, the most detestable of all laws.

Emerson appealed to the Universe. Above the laws of the State, there are those of Nature. If the State, the Church, the magistrature dishonors itself, it is the duty of man by himself to take up the defense of the right. The Union! the Union! people were crying. As soon as an immoral law is in force, the Union dissolves. There are two nations, two civilizations, face to face, the North and the South, freedom on one side, on the other, cannibals, pirates; two worlds separated not only by slavery, but by climate and temperament. Slavery is a canker, cholera, typhus. Extirpate it. Better an amputation than a cancer.

If one can buy the slaves, buy them. Let us sell our lands, our houses, our carriages, the wines in our cellars. Let the churches melt their sacred vessels; let children put in their pennies; let workmen and workwomen contribute. Meanwhile, if the law is not repealed, disobey it. . . .

Upon which Emerson finishes his portrait of Webster, the Olympian, once like Jupiter in look and mouth, but now stricken from the list of men of honor. This heartless jurist knows nothing of the eternal laws. Freedom on his lips is but a word. His United States is so much real estate, property to be exploited, a large farm. All the drops of his blood have eyes that look downward. The hope, the guide, the darling of America has sold his soul to the slave traders. Webster is dead; there remains only the Ichabod whom Whittier branded with a hot iron in a famous satire. What did the conscienceless statesman say? He assured the President of the United States that all the North was for his law. Had he consulted the millions of human beings who are born every day in the image of the universe? To make one accept his infamous law, it would be necessary to suppress all newspapers, books, the English language itself, and to strike out of the dictionary the word "honor." It would be necessary to abolish the Decalogue. . . . Above human laws there are divine and eternal laws which nothing can constrain a man to violate. Webster's law is impossible to obey or apply without transgression. But of what importance are Webster and his law? It is Fate which condemns slavery. The laws of Nature tend toward freedom. Above the Constitution of the United States is that of the universe. The moral laws are no more postponed than those of gravitation. Slowly but surely Nature takes her revenge, and punishment begins in the soul of the criminal. It is not the slave who is slave but his master; the enchained is not he who wears the chains but he who fastens them on. . . .

In 1854 the government of Washington had reported the bill which circumscribed slavery and had opened to it the new territories of Kansas and Nebraska. This time the muskets went off of their own accord. Slavery and anti-slavery men disputed the ground among them. The border ruffians and the settlers from the North had come to blows. They pillaged, killed, burned. Rescue societies were formed to deliver arms, provisions, and money to the immigrants. Emerson was again in the breach. This time no more doubt. The right is all on one side. How are such outrages possible and what is the government doing about it? Let the Capitol be hung in black; let the impotent politicians be deposed. Once more the reign of the individual man begins. I set the private man first! He denounced this representative government which did not represent, the big words of Liberty and Democracy which cover villainy, the Union which is now nothing more than the conspiracy of the South against the North. If that is the Law—well, run the plow over the foundations of the Capitol. If that is the government, down with it! There is now only one form of government possible: the pistol and the rope. Form committees of public safety; arrest at the frontier those Americans who are expatriating themselves lest on their return they find no further trace of liberty. It will then be time to go live in freedom elsewhere than in America. . . .

Then John Brown appeared, the private man, the man-empire—*l'Etat c'est moi*—the idealist who gave his life for his convictions. Emerson had found his hero. John Brown had appeared in Concord; Thoreau had introduced him; and he had passed an evening with the sage. Steady eyes of steel, gray hair brushed upright, streaming beard, haggard eye, John Brown for a speech had brought a knife and some chains, the chains which the dragoons of the United States had used to tie his son to the tails of their horses and which the poor wretch in delirium had rubbed together in his prison until they shone. Then Brown had brandished his enormous cutlass, crying, "The civilization of Missouri, here it is." And he had gone on to his fate: Harper's Ferry, the armed attack on the federal arsenal, the appeal to the slaves, the provisory government. John Brown was arrested, tried, hanged on a gibbet as glorious as the cross. . . . "Quick, drums and trumpets, strike up! Quick, judges and juries, silence him by sentence and execution of sentence, and hide in the ground this alarming fact. For, if everything comes to its right place, he goes up, and we down."

The second of December, 1859, at noon, under a sky heavy and threatening thunder, at the very

369

hour of his execution, the citizens of Concord united in prayer and Thoreau read "The Soul's Errand" by Sir Walter Raleigh. . . . Emerson helped one of the survivors of Harper's Ferry escape to Canada, and Concord gathered in the children of the martyr whose panegyric the philosopher pronounced. John Brown was not dead; the Union armies were soon moving forward in his name. His body lay moldering in the grave but his soul went marching on. . . .

CHAPTER IX

The Call to Arms

EIGHT million Southerners in rebellion; seven states, then eleven, in secession; the southern frontier of the United States, the Potomac; two presidents, two governments, two armies, the blues and the grays; a new flag with red and white bars with seven stars on a blue field; a monstrous war, four years of battle, of evasions, defeats, riots, victories, immense improvised armies, ill equipped, ill clothed, recruited painfully, pursuing each other in the void, snapping at each other, annihilating each other on the spot, wiping each other out; factions, intrigues in the Capitol, war in the suburbs of Washington, the threat of foreign intervention, the President at bay, the bombardment of Fort Sumter by the Southerners, all the boobies of Charleston rushing out to see where the bombs fell, the federal army tottering slowly across the Potomac, Bull Run, Manassas; confusion in a swarm of convoys, deserters, curiosity seekers, and reporters. Victories and defeats, the Southern army in Pennsylvania, Washington menaced, the North again beaten at Bull Run, at Chancellorsville, at Fredericksburg, the tragic struggle in the Wilderness; the *Merrimac* and the *Monitor*, then the dawn of victory; Gettysburg, Vicksburg, Chattanooga, Sherman's march to the sea, Atlanta in flames, the enemy driven back to the North, the fall of Petersburg, of Charleston, of Richmond; Jefferson Davis and the Confederacy stealing away without making a sound, Lee in his big musketeer's hat handing his sword to Grant at Appomattox, Booth's pistol-shot assassinating Lincoln in his box—*Sic semper tyrannis!* Ah, America was no longer flat.

Did the North really know—patriotism or philanthropy—why it was making war? Emerson at least had no doubts. The bombardment of Sumter had scattered his nightmare; the Americans had at last a country; at last they had a government, a conscience. He chanted a hymn to the war:

There was no need of trumpets,
There was no need of banners;
Every zephyr was a bugle,
Every woodthrush sang hosannas.
Sharp steel was his lieutenant
And powder was his men.
The land was all electric,
The mountain echoes roar,
Every crutch became a pike,
The woods and valleys shouted War,
Every valley shouted, "Strike!"

Those who might have had doubts about his declarations of spiritual independence and of the practical bearing of his meditations, saw clearly now. Self-reliance, Compensation, Fate, Power, Character, Courage, now all that flamed in red letters to the sound of cannon. He had said and resaid: American Civilization is a lie; Americans lack an ideal; they have lost from view the sublime realities. The war recalled them roughly to themselves. All is paid for; all is bought; liberty is not an empty word; the world lives by antagonism. No doubt the Universe is marching by itself toward its ends, but not without brave men giving it a hand. Man is an arsenal of force, a sheaf of thunderbolts. When an individual puts all his energies toward achieving the Right and looks toward the Ideal, all the Universe seconds him. War is a dynamometer, the test of character, a professor of reality, of sincerity; war is the mother of all things; force is always on the side of Right. War is Destiny armed. Who would be willing to forbid the use of the musket if by it he can assure himself freedom?

"When the cannon is aimed by ideas, when men with religious convictions are behind it, when men die for what they live for, and the mainspring that works daily urges them to hazard all, then the cannon articulates its explosions with the voice of a man, then the rifle seconds the cannon and the fowling piece the rifle, and the women make the cartridges, and all shoot at one mark; then gods join the combat; then poets are born, and the better code of laws at last records the victory." If to see shining upon the world the dawn of liberty means sacrificing an entire generation, who would not consent to die? Renan had said it and he cited him, "As soon as sacrifice becomes a duty and necessity to the man, I see no limit to the horizon which opens before me."

Emerson translated this into two famous verses of heroic conciseness:

> When Duty whispers low, Thou must,
> The youth replies, I can.

There was practical Emerson dispensing his energies, doubling his efforts, visiting arsenals, encouraging recruiting, saluting the departure of the volunteers, inspecting the Military Academy at West Point, celebrating the civilization built on powder, wishing to send all the young people to the front, thinking himself of taking a rifle. Poor, cramped—no more lectures, no more coupons to clip—during the long uncertain war, not an instant did he lose courage or doubt of victory. He was hissed, booed, prevented from speaking; he remained stoical. The eternal forces are leagued with those of conscience. He gave long speeches; he prophesied through the firing the coming of a greater and better America, the spiritual mission of the American people. One would have thought him alone in understanding the transcendental import of events. The Union, slavery—little did they matter; it was the right, conscience, which the blue armies were defend-

EMERSON

ing. His war was indeed a war for the Union,
but in a sense unknown to the politicians. The
Union he had in view was ideal, transcendental,
a union of conscience and of hearts. Meanwhile
his puritanism did not capitulate. Secession! The
South and the North were antinomical, two
worlds separated by an abyss. No treaty, no constitution could draw together the two sides of the
crater. Bull Run, Manassas, Chancellorsville,
Fredericksburg, no defeat astonished him; immanent justice would repair them; the cause of
the Right would inevitably triumph. Slavery was
a crime against nature and the Universe is always
the same and faithful to itself. The longer the
war would last, the better the Americans would
recover themselves.

He had gone to Washington, had been witness
of the effervescence and the evasions of the Capitol. He had seen the enormous war machinery in
motion and had been introduced to the President.
Lincoln had given him a broad smile and had
discharged at him one of his homely jokes, hu-
morist in his spare time. This tall, forbearing,
imperturbable Lincoln whom he accused of slow-

ness, whom he found it difficult to admire until
he saw in him a man, the man of destiny, the
representative of the new America, of democracy in shirt sleeves swarming on the banks of
the Mississippi, a man from another world, without pedigree, without blue blood, without culture,
without manners, and who had read neither
Plato, nor Plotinus, nor the Bhagavat Gita, a
man simple and taciturn, lanky, his body swaying
in his too wide clothes, immense, interminable on
his pedestal of enormous shoes, little weasel eyes,
a huge mouth, a horseshoe beard, a frock coat and
a ridiculous tall hat, ugly, grotesque, the look of
a jumping-jack—but good faith, silence, conscience incarnate, a man *à la* Carlyle, the typical
American, *homo americanus.* Booth's pistol completely won him over to the martyred president.

He impatiently awaited the emancipation of
the slaves. Lincoln tergiversated, took counsel,
wanted to strike a sure blow. Finally on the
twenty-second of September, 1862, all the bells
in the North began to ring in unison. All the
slaves in the states in rebellion were declared free.
Emerson exulted. The soldiers of the Right had

not died in vain. Here were defeats changed to victories,

> Whoever fights, whoever falls,
> Justice conquers evermore. . . .

The stain was washed out, the nightmare ended; America could look other nations in the face. War in arms had killed the unhearing war in the soul. Keep back the dying from death that they may carry with them the good news. . . . For the first time Emerson bent over the blacks, he the Boston gentleman, the man with the white hands. He greeted these eternally oppressed whose bronze bodies had been carved out by subjection, whose pitiful soul sought freedom in melancholy songs. Welcome them now as brothers and pay their ransoms richly.

> Pay ransom to the owner
> And fill the bag to the brim.
> Who is the owner? The slave is the owner,
> And ever was. Pay him.

Ever heroic Concord had been among the first to send volunteers to the armies. Cannon shot, tocsin, prayers, speeches and weeping at the station. They had gone, forty-seven strong, a little troop

soon accrued who had formed a company. The
Massachusetts regiments had been among the first
to fight, the Fifth, the Forty-seventh, the Forty-
ninth, and above all that heroic Thirty-second,
under Colonel Prescott. Emerson stirred himself,
distributed aid and consolation to their families,
welcomed the survivors, encouraged the recruits,
but especially collected the letters which formed
the golden book of his village. Concord's volunteers were in the thick of it, judging from
these letters from the front. Ten days in the mud
up to their knees during the retreat from the
Peninsula, without other rations than blackberries and tea. At Gettysburg the Thirty-second
remained seventy-two hours in the line. In the
interminable struggles in the Wilderness, seventeen days and seventeen nights without budging
(40,000 dead). At Petersburg came the great
holocaust. The Thirty-second was thrown upon
the ten-yard embankments swept by Southern
shot. The regiment lost almost its entire strength
and the heroic Prescott fell on the battlefield. The
regiment had its reward: it presented arms at
Lee's surrender at Appomattox.

Finally peace, freedom, the Union. There was

now a great map of America above all the mantelpieces. A new America was born, of states united, an America worn out by war whose future remained uncertain, but the American peacock had completely turned into an eagle.

CHAPTER X

Westward Ho!

I'LL bet you fifty dollars a day for three weeks that you will not leave your library, and wade, and freeze, and ride, and run, and suffer all manner of indignities, and stand up for an hour each night reading in a hall.—Emerson had won the bet. It was hard and he would have preferred to stay in his chimney corner. Was it not cruel to drag out of his home in the middle of winter an old gentleman to take his chances with trains and hotels? But he had to earn his daily bread and increase the little income of six per cent on his modest capital of twenty-two thousand dollars, the dividends of which had suffered their ups and downs during the war. The times were not safe. Peace had come; he had therefore taken up his trips again. Up till then he had scarcely left New England and the Atlantic

381

Coast, Boston, New York, Philadelphia, Baltimore, Washington; now he must venture farther and farther into the West.

During twenty years each winter he pushed on to the Mississippi and beyond. At the age of seventy he was still traveling, intrepid pedlar of the ideal. In the time of the diligences it took a good twenty-four hours to go from Concord to New York and thirty to go on to Philadelphia. Then the railroads had come to facilitate his trips. But the railroads of that time were not *trains de luxe.* Emerson set out in the depths of winter at Siberian temperatures, for days and nights of travel in primitive cars hooked on to a locomotive heated as well as possible with a wood fire, whistling, spitting, howling, shaken, and tossed, come what might. The landscape of the great western plains was without charm and the trains were not in a hurry. The traveler had time to count the pickets of the fences, the snow banks, the clumps of trees, or to listen to the wind crying like a child, complaining like a saw-mill, whistling like a fife, mowing like an idiot, roaring like the sea, yelling like a devil. On arriving—hotels which smelled rancid, smelled of melted butter and distilled beefsteaks, sticky corridors and the promiscuity of drummers and other itinerants. Signs on the walls announced to the guests: "No gentleman permitted to seat at the table without his coat. No gambling permitted in the house." The people of the West were shameless and great lovers of poker. Emerson, who like all good New Englanders was very fond of pie, heard the diners boldly claim the best quarter-section of it. . . .

At twenty or thirty degrees below zero he thus covered Illinois, Iowa, Ohio, Michigan, Indiana, every winter, arriving often at break of day in a bad tavern after two nights of railroad or forty hours of carriage travel, frozen, downcast, starved, to set off again immediately to lecture elsewhere, dragged at the tail of a speech which he had to repeat to the point of satiety. Sometimes the inn caught fire and Emerson left, dragging his trunk through the corridors. The railroads did not often take one to his destination and one had to take the boat, sleep on the floor of a small craft with the legs of his fellow voyagers across his body. Or else long sleigh rides in blizzards, the torture of the snow, behind those great trot-

383

ting horses whose stoicism so like his own he admired, happy if he did not sink into the fat mud of the prairie up to his shoulders. Twenty years of this life, three times across the Mississippi on the ice while the Father of Waters was frozen from its source to Natchez, or perhaps in a rowboat. . . .

His troubles were by no means over, once arrived. He had to appear before audiences who were often illiterate, to whom he had been announced as "the Celebrated Essayist and Poet," "the Illustrious Metaphysician." People came half-heartedly; there were some who left before the hour was over. These rough fellows cared little about the Over-Soul; they preferred the itinerant humorists, the Petroleum Vesuvius Nasbys, the John Phoenixes, the Artemus Wards. They asked to be made to laugh a hearty laugh and they wanted their money's worth. The benign and conscientious Emerson did not lack humor, and he spiced his lectures with anecdotes and jokes which were not retained in his Greekgowned essays. He adapted himself to his audiences and consoled himself by thinking that if Franklin, Æsop, or Shakespeare had been in his place they would have done as much. His beautiful deep barytone voice rose and fell, his eyes shot flames, his humor spurted forth without a break. Emerson had won his fifty dollars.

A new experience for the sage. Climate and people, all was new to him. A rough trial for an idealist. It was no longer the refined audience of Boston. These primitive people scarce wanted finesse and they said so. They took pleasure in the beautiful lecture of "the Boston Essayist," but they found him a bit too tall, a bit too thin, "physically the least remarkable man who had appeared on the stage." As always, naturally, "in the lectures of our Yankee brethren," there was a good deal "of sensible and well-applied physiology" (it is a doctor speaking); it was very poetic, very beautiful, but "a bit mystifying." It was as good as the kaleidoscope—we should say "the movies" today. In short, "it was a rattler!"

A great lover of sincerity, these rough people after all did not displease him. They were chatterers, braggarts, bluffers, but good as gold, openhearted, and had not the shadow of pedantry about them. . . . To beguile the monotony of the trip and to remain in contact with the civilized universe, he used to carry along some of his favorite books in a valise, Dante, Horace, Æschylus, Goethe, Beaumarchais, or simply a French novel to pass the time in the train. While the covered wagon was taking the road to the Far West, the old-style traveler Emerson was discovering America, book in hand.

He saw a new world growing up about him, saw new villages sprouting whose founders were presented to him, rough brave souls, democracy in shirt sleeves, the America of tomorrow. Carlyle was much amused to read the recital of his friend's discovery of the West. Corn, paddies, and pigs! But the pigs ate the rattlesnakes and Jonathan followed with his plow to eat the pigs. Carlyle made merry over this raw and still unformed world, which astonished and amazed him in spite of himself, immense, amorphous, enormous, but grandiose as an epic, as a myth, so grand, so vast, pumping out men, millions of men, a hundred millions in fifty years who would read the English Bible and Shakespeare. It was providential and divine, this Jonathanization of John Bull. It was too much for the imagination to grasp. Here was "the great American opportunity," America

in formation, naked, raw, still far from complete,
coarse, but, like the bronze of Corinth, the amalgam of the races would produce a new metal, a
new people.

Emerson rubbed against people, he questioned,
he investigated, he conferred with business men,
prospectors, real estate agents, politicians; he visited the mines, talked real estate and railroads.
One felt him to be drunk on this practical optimism which was conquering the West, which
is somewhat that of the world-discoverers, of the
conquistadors. He was taking a bath of reality,
a bath of hope. He loved the West, he felt
its force, its promise, its sublime geography. He
had a bit too far forgotten America for humanity, but his youthful enthusiasms were recap-
turing him; the epoch when he dedicated his
"Wide Worlds" "to the Spirit of America,"
when he naïvely but fervently announced that
growing America would relegate into oblivion
the history of those nations who have disappeared
—Rome, Greece, England.

He had never doubted the destiny and the
providential mission of his country and he found
them in these immense virgin lands which were

giving to American life a new aspect and rhythm, and where already in his notes at a half century's distance modern America is recognizable trait for trait.

Where have we seen them—in the novels of Mark Twain or Sinclair Lewis?—these Americans who march with a careless swagger to the height of power, without worrying much about their own liberty or that of other people, who pooh-pooh the acquisitions of history, and barter all for sordid gain; that America of parvenus where every one once home is sure to find a shelter from the rain, coal to set his stove roaring, ham and cornbread; those people who die of boredom when they have no work to do, honest people, conscious of their rights and defending them to the teeth, ambitious to assure for their children a better education than they received themselves, wrapped up in politics, progress, reform, inventive, hungry for novelty, for pseudo-science, tolerant of all religions, on their knees before public opinion and numbers, members of the Ku Klux Klan and adepts of the lynching rope? Has luck equal to theirs ever been seen in geography and history?

"Here in America are all the wealth of soil, of timber, of mines, and of the sea, put into the possession of a people who wield also these wonderful machines, have the secret of steam, of electricity; and have the power and habit of invention in their brain. We Americans have got suppled into the state of melioration. Life is always rapid here, but what acceleration to its pulse in ten years! We have seen the railroad and telegraph subdue our enormous geography; we have seen the snowy deserts on the northeast, seats of Esquimaux, become land of promise. When our population, swarming west, had reached the boundary of arable land—as if to stimulate our energy, on the face of the sterile waste beyond, the land was suddenly in parts found covered with gold and silver, floored with coal. . . . Resources of America! why, one thinks of St. Simon's saying, 'The Golden Age is not behind, but before you!' Here is man in the Garden of Eden; here the Genesis and the Exodus. . . . America is such a garden of plenty, such a magazine of power, that at her shores all the common rules of political economy utterly fail. Here are bread, and wealth, and power, and education for every man who has the heart to use his opportunity. The creation of power never had any parallel." . . .

Who made this little speech enameled with reassuring hyperbole—Emerson or George Babbitt, the realtor of Zenith? But Emerson did not forget the reverse of the medal. He distrusted as much as he admired this democracy, savage, incomplete, "the riot of mediocrities and dishonesties and fudges—the age of the omnibus, of the third person plural, of Tammany Hall." Beauty must not be confused with abundance. Let America be a nation and not a horde. The flower of civilization is not the bluff but the gentleman, not bustle but dignity and repose. Emerson was not an imperialist. He denounced those men prompt to throw themselves upon their prey and to grab the first piece of a continent that fell under their fingers. His America was pre-Rooseveltian and pre-protection, America before Americanization: equal opportunity for all, equality of civic rights, of education, of power, of riches, the open door, freedom of trade with the whole world, no customs houses, America accessible to all peoples without exception of race or color, the white, yellow, red, black, success to the stronger, and the soil had bread for all. How many points on this program failed to find disciples!

The star on the horizon shone always brightly to guide the wagon. Emerson's patriotism was that of an idealist. Above America was humanity. America was the gift which God made to the world. She should publish mankind's bill of rights, or Royal Proclamation of the Intellect ascending the throne. "The soul of God is poured into the world through the thoughts of men. The world stands on ideas, and not on iron or cotton; and the iron of iron, the fire of fire, the ether and source of all the elements is moral force. As cloud on cloud, as snow on snow, as the bird on the air, and the planet on space in its flight, so do nations of men and their institutions rest on thoughts." Hitch your wagon to a star.

In a letter of 1856 to Carlyle Emerson announced the publication and forwarding of a strange book, "a nondescript monster which yet had terrible eyes and buffalo strength, . . . and was indisputably American . . . but wanting good morals. . . . It is called *Leaves of Grass*—was written and printed by a journeyman printer in

Brooklyn, New York, named Walter Whitman; and after you have looked into it, if you think, as you may, that it is only an auctioneer's inventory of a warehouse, you can light your pipe with it."

Treacherous Emerson thus to abandon to the ire of Teufelsdroeckh him whom some time before he had saluted at the beginning of a glorious career, the singer of the Universal, of the America of Comrades, the big-hearted poet who soldered together in his all-embracing chants the body and soul electric of his country. However, he had prophesied this poet whose Word flowed out like Nature, whose tyrannical eye annexed the incomparable resources of a continent, whose mythical imagination resuscitated the Homeric gods in Barbary, in the heights of modern materialism. Verses in full liberty, hard as a horse's gallop, sonorous as the drone of a cathedral, irresistible as a cannon ball, verses which, from the womb of Chaos and ancient Night, threw a bridge across oceans of space and cried out to the sons of the morning that the Creation was beginning; these verses Walt Whitman had composed. Rivers, forests, mountains, the American

oceans, the commerce of the North, the planta-
tions of the South, the clearings of the West,
Oregon, Texas, the negroes, the Indians; yes,
America was a poem; her geographical amplitude
dazzled the imagination, and she was awaiting
her Homer, and Walt Whitman had come, called,
announced by Emerson, and his songs had lit not
the calumet of Carlyle but a gigantic fire whose
gleam the world still wonders at, and it was he
and not God who made a gift of America to the
world.

CHAPTER XI

The Search for Unity

Philosophers are lined with eyes within,
And, being so, the sage unmakes the man.

FATE and Illusion, the life of Emerson, like
his book *The Conduct of Life*, held all
between these two terms. The Devil's Advocate
who might have turned the pages of his *Journal*
when Emerson was about sixty could have wondered with reason whether this apostle of faith
was not about to fall into doubt.

There were two men within him; his consciousness was double. He shot off fireworks, he
excited others, he excited himself, pen in hand
before an audience; but *in petto*, alone by himself,
he ill succeeded in harmonizing himself, in unify-
ing himself, and his doubts became chronic. He
felt himself pinched in a world which was escaping him; he felt himself alone. He did not waver

on his principles but he sometimes doubted their utility. His dreams were on one side, the world on the other. An élite followed him, admired him, but men remained deaf to his voice. The awakening to this was painful. He felt that America was escaping him, was going beyond him; he doubted his "old saws." Dualism, antinomy, bipolarity, he perceived the unity without being able to attain it. He saw the two points where the ends and the beginnings joined but his geometry could not span the extreme points. No bridge between him and the abyss.

On the one hand he affirmed melioration, progress, on the other the eternal self-equality of Nature. He proclaimed the sacred character of the individual, the strict duty of self-confidence, but cities and phalansteries had their advantages. He maintained that man was a god, but without playing the Tartuffe, how deny his debt to bread, coffee and coal? How resolve the antinomy between the absolute and the conditional, the One and the Many? As much as to say that the compensations, keystone of his whole system, no longer worked. His life was a drama of solitude. He would have liked to live a hundred lives, to be the universal and innumerable man whom he celebrated in his Superman. Alas! all greatness has a pitiful end. All terminates in the routine of domestic and bourgeois life. He passed his days among unfit companions.

It seemed that he had in his life a fault line, a break. Consciousness is double. There was the public man and the private man, both in conflict, freedom within, fate without, the double consciousness. He wrote without transition that "the end of life is that the man should take up the universal unto himself," but "experience gives me no ground to believe that I can rashly realize my aspirations, and with these hands and feet and head obey the poetic rule." Optimism no longer seemed as natural to him; in any event it was less spontaneous. He adored solitude, he fled men but could not do without them. He believed sometimes that his forces were failing him, that his organs were playing him false. But no, the world soul was there, the opulent soul which through his feeble eyes had read so many books, so many poets. . . . He scolds himself, checks himself. "Look, look, old mole! there, straight up before you, is the magnificent Sun. If only for the instant you see it"—the sun which refines and warms each particle and makes every creature a channel of light through which beatific life rolls in directions always new and infinite. Self-disparagement is human but our failings have no effect upon the eternal laws, those old laws, which spring up like the arch of the sky, like sunlight which all the winds of the world cannot blow away, "high old laws, round, unremovable, self-executing." See them at least, compute their curve! "Dwarves may see the rainbow, as well as giants."

At another time he meditates upon the uselessness of scholars, of men of thought whom society has reduced to inaction, who are isolated, who for opium court the Muses and the philosophers, lacking better, useless, and resigned dreamers. There is no doubt that he is speaking of himself when he laments upon the fate of the neglected dreamer, who in a more favorable environment would have become an Archimedes or a Newton. It is the power of Fate which crushes him, the tragic "oppression of the submind." He was tired of scraps. He did not wish to be a literary ragman. "Away with this Jew's rag-bag of ends and tuft of brocade, velvet and cloth-of-gold." Let him spin some yards or miles of helpful twine, "a clew to lead to one kingly truth, a cord to bind wholesome and belonging facts." Alas, he could not realize his dream. . . . His dear compensations, his decisive weapon, the keystone of his thought —he became less sure of them. What good of compensation if to look at an object we turn away from every other object in the universe?

He had lost the taste for writing. He preferred rather to read than to write. His natural leaning was toward reading. If there had been true writers, natural writers, he would never have written. In 1859 he interrupted his *Journal* which he had faithfully kept every day for forty years. One would have thought him drained dry. He saw few people and the people he saw disappointed him. He complained of having no new thoughts. It seemed to him that his life was finished and he gave us the key to his solitude. You ask him why he hides in his library and skulks in the woods. It is because the old magnetism which flows in others has gone from his bones. He needs to be charged with electricity, to rub against people like an electric eel. Lacking people who inspire him he remained alone, and there he who could

have shone like a sun lay inert like a flint. As for
his influence, he was not less sceptical. After the
passage of thirty years, he had not a single disciple. Why, moreover, should he have any? So
much the better if he repel people. What would
they do if they came to him? They would bother
him, encumber him. No disciples? So much the
better. He was proud of it. How impure his intuitions if instead of freeing, they attached.
Reality rules Destiny. . . .

Faithful to his favorite tactics, he renounced,
stripped himself, belittled himself before Destiny. Illusions, Maya, the sole true wisdom is that
of the Hindus: peel oneself of matter, affections,
emotions, persons, actions, escape transmigrations
and rebirths to offer oneself naked to Brahma and
thus arrive at the contemplation of Life, of the
Cause of Causes. Of isolation, of ataraxy, he
made himself a philosophy and an art. The pure
intellect is sceptical. The pure renounce power,
Being suffices them. Health exists and unfolds in
the rose, in the sea, in circular and endless astronomy. The magnet in his drawer has lost none
of his power, the electric fluid conserves its energy without being discharged. Perhaps individu-

399

ality is only an illusion, perhaps bodily existence
is a fall, the result of sin. The pure live in God,
radiant and flowing. . . .

He brought about the abdication of his will.
There is no will except abandonment to the eternal Necessity. Nirvana, absorption, to be absorbed
into God as a phial of water broken in the ocean.
He would be the fakir of the intelligence, would
fast and pray, renounce himself. Pallor, sterility,
celibacy, poverty, humility, insignificance, what
matter? He would wear the livery of his master,
honest infirmities, honorable scars. . . . Renunciation, purification, thus would he assure himself the conquest of principles, thus forever would
he mount and ride on the back of his thoughts,
steeds which course the ethereal plains. Time is
nothing, there is no hurry, thought ripens slowly.
Summers of contemplation for a handful of sen-
tences, few but resplendent as the sun which saw
them come to life. The depth of science does
not depend on the length of life. . . . Memory,
Imagination, Perception, Inspiration, Intellect,
those are the oracles and the masters. "Abandon
yourself," he said, "to the leading, when the
Leader comes; this was the sum of wisdom and

duty. Shake off from your shoes the dust of
Europe and Asia, the rotten religions and per-
sonalities of nations. Act from your heart, where
the wise temperate guidance is instantly born."

One problem beset him from then on, the
problem of the Spirit. He had begun by the exploration of Nature; he ended by that of the
powers of the Soul, the two ways joining together at the very heart of the thinking subject.
This problem he attacked in two ways, by the
exploration of the sciences and by intuition. There
were two classes of spirits, two mediums, two
methods; the way of analysis, that of the great
mathematicians and geometers of the intellect:
Heraclitus, Parmenides, Plato, Spinoza, Hume,
Kant, Schelling, and Hegel, winged spirits who
in the thin air have scaled the dizzy pinnacle of
the World of Thought. Then there were the ab-
normal spirits, the seers, the soothsayers: William
Blake, Swedenborg, Behmen, Blake particularly
who instead of perceiving objects saw through
them, the sibyline, the oracular men, the Tris-
megistes, revealing to us the secret of Mind.

Fascinated by the parallelism of Spirit-Nature,
Emerson dreamed of composing a calendar, an

almanac of the mind by way of metaphysics. The
equation, thought-nature, was true beyond doubt;
the laws of the physical universe were those of
the spirit itself; vegetation, nutrition, parturi-
tion, gravitation, polarity. Identity, identity! It
is in vain that one would conserve the barriers of
species and genera: the pedant becomes a poet in
spite of himself. Cuvier must join Geoffroy Saint-
Hilaire. Here appear those implacable monists,
the Okens and the Goethes. Unity, unity! There
is that wicked Spirit, that tyrannical Spirit with
its currents irresistible as the falls of Niagara.
The Spirit must think by the mediation of Matter and of Nature which give it words for its
expression. The world is a school, a university
from which one graduates to the heaven of
thought. Perception, Memory, Imagination,
Metamorphosis, emanation, flux, amelioration,
ascent. The steps of the Intellect are organic;
the powers of the Soul are gods.

How great is the mind! If only we knew how
to use it. Let us abandon ourselves to spontaneous
thought which comes like the breath of the morning, like our daily bread, to those who love and
obey it, thought which attends us at our waking

and which rewards health, temperance, and good
will. The Spirit does not lie; intellectual power
is the presence of the divine within us.

Emerson celebrated the Intellect and its beati-
tudes. Thinking—how refuse oneself to this inspiration, this joy, this transport which snatches
the philosopher from his chair and makes him
stride up and down his chamber like a tiger in
his cage, too far beyond himself to be able to fix
in writing what he glimpses, what he feels, secret thoughts, ineffable exaltation? The Spirit
moves from within without. The Intellect is an
ethereal sea, ebb and flow, which rises and pushes
its water here and there, which bears all its
strength into the inlets and coves it bathes. Being—there is the insoluble miracle, inner being,
outer being, Spirit, Nature. Emerson was on the
banks of a river whose infinite current sweeps
away objects of all shapes and colors, which one
must pursue to grasp. Whence do they come and
whither do they go? The mystic river has made
its valley, its banks, and perhaps even the spectator who looks on. . . .

Who has ever found the limits of the human
mind; who has drawn up the map of its course;

who has explored the sources of this wonderful Nile, of this river whence all reality emanates, of this supreme Intellect which overhangs consciousness like a sky within a sky, degree above degree? Identity! Unity! There is within the spirit a tyrannical instinct which makes it reduce all to a few laws, to a single law. There are no more solitary thoughts than solitary flowers. All is linked together, all holds together, all is balanced. The Universe is reeled off from any idea like a ball of yarn. And this is our hope: the infinity of the world which reappears in the least of its parts. There is a remedy for every wrong and every wall is a gate.

All which is intellectual is moral. All perception uncovers and consents to an order; ethics and science are but one, duty and thought are equivalent, the order of nature corresponds to the order of mind. All is moral. The unity of thought and of ethics runs through all animated nature. From the humblest insects to man, there is no difference of quality. All mounts higher and higher. The world is composed of moral forces of which none is isolated. From the gorilla to the gentleman, to Plato, Newton, or Shakespeare, the road is long

but sure. Confidence and abandon! A beneficent
and eternal Necessity never ceases to conduct all
to the good. Man's excellence consists in the com-
pleteness with which "the lower system is taken
up into the higher." There are monsters and evils,
but also always fawns bounding in the forest and
lilies with graceful springing stems.

Analogies, affinities, correspondences, coinci-
dences, presentiments, dreams, secret movements
of the soul, mysteries of the Imagination, of the
Perception, of the Memory, sharp leaps, spontaneous spurts of thought, inspiration, instinct,
states of mind, what he sketched thus in the *Natural History of Intellect* and the essay on "Poetry
and Imagination," was a philosophy of the
Unconscious, a vast animated symbolism in
perpetual evolution, a philosophy all in *nuances*,
where music and the dance served as interpreters
and of which poetry was the summit. He was ill
equipped; he could not and would not be system-
atic; but intuitions and lyric flights took the
place of logic. By an astonishing return to youth,
as he grew older the poet awoke in him and he
more and more reduced the problem of the spirit
to that of poetry. He returned to the views of

Tnamurya, Alcott, and Samson Reed, the Swedenborgian apothecary. The world exists for thought. It is from the soul that matter is born. Let us abandon ourselves to the circulations, the universal currents. The necessity of the mind is poetic. Poetry is the only verity. All is poetic. The poet takes the world and transposes it in his verses by a sort of transubstantiation. Poetry is the joyful wisdom, liberation, freedom. The critic destroys, the poet affirms. Poetry is true science, the poet the true logician. Poetry is creation; it repeats the rhythms of nature. Poetry is organic and rhythm is equally so. All is rhyme and rhythm in nature, expansion, concentration, compensation, ebb and flow. The great poets transport us in their rhythms as in a whirlwind, a cyclone. They put words into the same great order as the planets, the seasons, the winds.

Prose, poetry, what does it matter? There are thoughts naturally poetic; the best thoughts seek the best words. There is a height of thought when it becomes necessarily poetry. Watches are not enclosed in wooden cases but in crystal; rhyme is the transparent frame which allows almost the pure architecture of thought to become visible to the mental eye. Poetry is an end in itself. It is a supervoluntary end attained by supervoluntary means. In true poetry thought and rhythm are inseparable. Philosophers are poets who have failed. True poetry is Handel, Beethoven; it is the "thorough-base of the sea-shore," vast as astronomy, deep as the heart. . . . Poetry is power, the supreme power of man; it is, in the retreats of the spirit, the explosive energy which sets the world in motion. . . . Poetry is the piety of the intellect. Zoroaster, Plato, Saint John, Menu, they are the poets. "The Muse shall be the counterpart of Nature, and equally rich." It will rise above itself and invite us to rise still higher. The dance, music, abandon yourself to Bacchus. . . .

Leave him his fair abstractions. Do not tease him about the uncertainty of his aphorisms. Do not ask him the name of the river, its source and its confluence. Do not cavil with him over that force which is only abandon, that knowledge ignorant of its origin, that wave which detaches him whom it is carrying along from the object he is about to grasp, that intellect which is but instinct. . . . Pardon him for so many new intuitions, prophecies, anticipations, and that respect for the mystery of mysteries. Modern philosophers, you will shoot many a ball on the private and underground preserves of Emerson.

CHAPTER XII

Threads of Destiny

THE Fates and the statue of Isis are still above the mantelpiece. Guido's "Aurora" still drives her chariot by the sleeping Endymion. The portraits of Montaigne, Shakespeare, and Swedenborg still look out from their frames under the gruff eye of Teufelsdroeckh. The books are still on the shelves. The Æolian harp still weeps on the roof. The tree Yggdrasil still blossoms in the garden. The shadow of the pines has thickened and the sun still shines on the universe forever young.

> The world rolls round—mistrust it not—
> Befalls again what once befell;
> All things return, both sphere and mote,
> And I shall hear my bluebird's note,
> And dream the dream of Auburn dell. . . .

Emerson is still by the fire in his wadded robe,

rocking himself in his rocking chair. . . . Winter has come, the winter of life as well as the other. Time, the little gray man who pulls illusions from his pocket, has presented Emerson with a pair of spectacles. It is old age. It is time to call an indignation meeting and to compose his *de Senectute*. Emerson worries little about old age. He believes in it no more than in sickness and death. The world is an eternal Present. Each day is a new morning.

Old age rests and detaches one, and when it comes it brings among other consolations the hope of an early deliverance. One's work is done; one is no longer preoccupied with success. . . . Old age is a joke of nature who amuses herself confiding to shoulders still young an exhausted heart and by conserving a young heart under eighty winters. . . . Old age is the escape from time, that poison, the entrance into the harbor. The ship's insurance lapses in sight of land.

> It is time to be old,
> To take in sail ——
>
> As the bird trims her to the gale,
> I trim myself to the storm of time,
> I man the rudder, reef the sail,

Obey the voice at eve obeyed at prime:
"Lowly faithful, banish fear,
Right onward drive unharmed;
The port, well worth the cruise, is near,
And every wave is charmed."

Emerson has not aged. At seventy he still feels
his mind free and lucid. He had never paid much
attention to his infirmities. Once youth was
passed, he had scarcely been ill. At the slightest
tumor on his shoulder his wife was afraid of cancer and that amused him. Illness—fiddlesticks!
All sick men are rascals. Are you ill? Your doctor is water, open air, heat, especially heat. Wrap
yourself up in your room, heat your stove red
hot, bathe your lungs, your liver, your head and
feet in caloric, heat on heat. It is delightful to
be ill. For the first time one notices the design on
the rugs and the color of the walls. . . . Within
he had not a wrinkle, no wear on the heart; his
sole infirmity was unsatiated youth, unspent
youth, a word of regret which says much and on
which one could write a long epilogue. Unspent
youth, famine of friendship, famine of love, puritan childhood, cloistration, decorum, apathy,
coldness. Unspent youth! A tragic confidence

which Emerson does not make with a light heart.
"I live too much alone." Ellen, Margaret, Hermione, Una, listen to this regret from the depth
of your tombs or from the ethereal sphere where
you have been relegated by an ardent imagination
but a heart too timid. . . . Too late, too late.
Let him console himself with his eternal
ideas. . . .

Emerson is still by his fireside. . . . He muses.
. . . He dreams. . . . He listens to his voices.
. . . Sixty, seventy years have flown by, forty
years of solitude. . . . The wide worlds are finished, exploration is over. . . . The traveler is
stopped in sight of the mysterious isles. . . .
Silence! Secrets! Arcana! Mystery! . . . He
has believed; he has seen; he has delivered his
message. His works are there on the shelves,
Nature, the *Essays*, *Representative Men*, *The
Conduct of Life*, his *Poems* . . . and he sees
that all is well . . . London, Paris, the revolutions, the Civil War, parents, friends, the Social
Circle of Concord, the conversations by the fire,
the walks, the philosophic reveries, Walden, the
woods, the slow river under the great plumed
elms. . . . Good Alcott is still there, still there

faithful Channing. . . . Every last Saturday in
the month Emerson dines in Boston, at the Saturday Club, among gentlemen. There are Longfellow, Oliver Wendell Holmes, James Russell
Lowell, Hawthorne, jovial Agassiz, learned naturalist and gay companion, great hunter of turtles,
fish, and lizards. From time to time picnics in
the country, camping in the Adirondacks, throwing to the trout harmless bait or playing at hunting with that transcendental gun "which threw
shot from one end and ball from the other." . . .
The America of that day was not yet the country
of the business man's quick lunch. The art of
conversation had not been killed by the telephone.
These gentlemen read each other their essays and
poems; they talked. The Saturday Club was the
last of the symposiums, of the academic banquets.
Emerson listened more than he spoke. He roamed
round the tables to find a man; he engraved in
his memory witticisms, *mots*, his neck stretched
out, his eye fixed like an eagle's, gathering crumbs
from the feasts of the gods. . . .

The living and the dead. . . . In life's theater many actors had left the stage: Ellen, the
child Waldo, Charles Chauncy, Edward Bliss,

413

his beloved brothers, his mother, and Tnamurya,
the Sybil whose magical charms he heard until
the end (Ralph, aim high! Ralph, despise trifles!
Excelsior! Excelsior! The images, the sweet immortal images within the heart.) Thoreau died
on a cold caught flirting with a tree in the snow,
died as a stoic, as a pantheist, a thrifty pantheist
(One world at a time!). He left Emerson his
oriental library, which he put to good use.
Nirvana, Brahma! the ninety incarnations of
Vishnu, the beatitude of the Eight Gods. . . .
And this Ophelia floating toward him on the
misty water, she who spread the perfume of
amber about her, the insatiable Margaret who
wanted to swallow the world ("like an egg, like
an oyster," said Carlyle), and who cast her challenge to the fates. . . . And John Sterling, the
friend of a day, philosopher, humanist, drama-
turge, free-thinker, whom Carlyle had brought
to him, through a communion with Montaigne,
and with whom he exchanged beautiful letters
in the antique manner. . . . Shadows, a parade
of shadows, and the rest is silence. . . . Carlyle
over there, more and more somber and scowling,
who cursed more and more "this world of mud,"

"this kennel of a world," "this rain of frogs," but whose rough heart grew tenderer as he aged and who clung to him as to the sole being who had understood him, like a poor devil . . . *Nux erketai*, the Night is coming . . . March on and quickly, for the sun is setting. . . .

Life, death. . . . Life is a series of surprises. Dream delivers us to dream. Our life does not belong to us; it is we who belong to it. Eternal necessity, eternal compensation, unfathomable potency, inviolate silence, peace, purity, absolute abandon, perpetual observation, perpetual ac-quiescence, perpetual recognition. . . . These great flashes with which he excited others, he took them back now for himself. His aphorisms, his "old saws," formed now a concert, an inte-rior monologue which the still small voice sang to him. Fate, illusion, transition, metamorphosis, passage, and the supreme Soul which floats above us. Emerson listened to his inner voice, his de-mon in the calm of his study. . . .

"Where do we find ourselves? In a series of which we do not know the extremes, and believe that it has none. We wake and find ourselves on a stairs; there are stairs below us, which we seem to have ascended; there are stairs above us, many a one, which go upward and out of sight. . . . Sleep lingers all our lifetime about our eyes, as night hovers all day in the boughs of the fir tree. All things swim and glitter. . . . Life is a train of moods like a string of beads, and as we pass through them they prove to be many colored lenses which paint the world their own hue, and each shows only what lies in the focus. . . . Life itself is a bubble and a scepticism, and a sleep within a sleep. . . . Do you see that kitten chasing so prettily her own tail? If you could look with her eyes, you might see her surrounded with hundreds of figures performing complex dramas, with tragic and comic issues, long conversations, many characters, many ups and downs of fate— and meantime it is only puss and her tail. . . . Illusion, Temperament, Succession, Surface, Surprise, Reality, Subjectiveness—these are the threads on the loom of time, these are the lords of life. . . . Are we tickled trout, and fools of nature? . . . To the intelligent nature converts itself into a vast promise, and will not be rashly explained. Her secret is untold.

> Flow, flow, the waves hated, accursed, adored,
> The waves of mutation . . .

"Nothing is fixed, all pushes, bustles; the world is fluid and volatile. All seems at rest and permanent so long as we do not know its secret, but all escapes us. Every ultimate fact is only the first of a new series, every general law is but the particular fact of a law more general. . . . The world is a system of self-evolving circles rushing on all sides to infinity. . . . We skate on surfaces which glide under us. . . . No sleep, no rest. . . . In Nature each instant is new, the past is forgotten, change alone is sacred, nothing is certain but life, transition, expansion, the spirit in full energy. . . . Let us live onward! . . .

"How doubt and how fear? It must be that when God speaketh he should communicate not one thing, but all things; should fill the world with his voice; should scatter forth light, nature, time, souls, from the center of the present thought; and new date and new create the whole. Creation is perpetual; time is an illu-

sion. . . . O my brothers, God exists. There is
a soul at the center of nature and over the will of
every man, so that none of us can wrong the universe. . . . The whole course of things goes to
teach us faith. We need only to obey. . . . Place
yourself in the middle of the stream of power
and wisdom which animates all whom it floats,
and you are without effort impelled to truth, to
right and a perfect contentment . . .

"We live in succession, in division, in parts, in
particles. Meantime within man is the soul of
the whole; the wise silence, the universal beauty,
to which every part and particle is equally related; the eternal ONE. . . . Ineffable is the
union of man and God in every act of the soul.
The simplest person who in his integrity worships God, becomes God . . . The feeling of
the divine presence is the doubling of the heart
itself, nay, the infinite enlargement of the heart
with a power of growth to a new infinity on every
side. . . . Let man then learn the revelation of
all nature and all thought to his heart; this,
namely: that the Highest dwells with him; that
the sources of nature are in his own mind, if the

sentiment of duty is there . . . The soul's beauty is immense and the world is a perennial miracle which the soul produces. Let us build altars to the Blessed Unity which holds Nature and souls in perfect solution and compels every atom to serve an universal end. Necessity plants the rose of beauty on the brow of chaos and reveals to us the central purpose of Nature, which is harmony and joy. . . .

"Let us build altars to the Beautiful Necessity which assures us that Law reigns throughout existence. . . .

"The ways of life are wonderful. The way of life is by abandonment. The rich spirit lies in the sun and sleeps; he is Nature. These roses under my window make no references to former roses or to better ones; they are for what they are; they exist with God today. There is no time to them. There is simply the rose; it is perfect in every moment of its existence. Before a leaf-bud has burst, its whole life acts; in the full-blown flower there is no more; in the leafless root there is no less. . . . But man postpones or remembers. To be happy and strong, one must live *hic et nunc* with Nature, above time. . . . To finish the moment, to find the journey's end in every step of the road, to live the greatest possible number of good hours, that is wisdom. . . . Five minutes of today are worth as much to us as five minutes in the next millennium. . . . Each instant of our life is so astonishing that it eclipses all novels. Our life rests in sounds which we do not hear, in odors which we do not smell, and impressions so delicate that we do not discover them unless our attention is called to them. . . .

"Underneath the inharmonious and trivial particulars, is a musical perfection; the Ideal journeying always with us, the heaven without rent or seam . . ." All is illusion, but somewhere above us opens an eternal region with inland mountains with tranquil eternal meadows where flocks graze and shepherds dance to the sound of pipes. Clap your hands like children before this august magnificence, young with the life of life, the sunbright Mecca of the desert. . . . Fortune, Minerva, the Muse, the Holy Ghost, let us kneel before the ineffable Cause for which philosophers and sages have sought in vain a name.

420

Let the divine spread through us and we shall have peace, the morning peace. Onward and onward! . . .

"The consciousness that we are traversing the whole scale of being, from the center to the poles of Nature, and that we have some stake in every possibility, lends a sublime lustre to death.

And through man and woman and sea and star
Saw the dance of Nature forward and far,
Through worlds and races and terms and times,
Saw musical order and pairing rhymes. . . .
How all things sparkle,
The dust is alive,
To the birth they arrive:
I snuff the breath of my morning afar,
I see the pale lustres condense to a star;
The fading colors fix,
The vanishing are seen,
And the world that shall be
Twins the world that has been. . . .
My heart at the heart of things
Heeds no longer lapse of time,
Rushing ages moult their wings,
Bathing in the day sublime.
The sun set but set not his hope:
Stars rose, his faith was earlier up. . . .

"The longest life is but a morning, but where is the day?"

CHAPTER XIII

The Eternal Now

No, HE had not aged, the poet who at sixty-four published "May Day." Nature, Eternity—perpetual rejuvenation of the world. He had had a dream. His friends awaited him at the door of his house to see the procession of Spring pass by. Spring, floods of love, the hymen of plants, birds, beasts, and men. The warm south wind softens the earth; the ice explodes in joyful cannonades on the river and the ponds; the sap is rising; the wine ferments in the cellars; the animals leave their dens; the birds begin to migrate. Crowned with new buds, Spring goes forth, escorted by the Nights, the Days, and the troop of the gods in garlands. Sun, rainbow, birdsong, and the distant note of the horn in the valley. The hot mist sways and floats on the wings of the south wind.

Soft on the south-wind sleeps the haze:
So on thy broad mystic van
Lie the opal colored days,
And waft the miracle to man. . . .
Speaking by the tongues of flowers,
By the ten-tongued laurel speaking,
Singing by the oriole songs,
Heart of bird the man's heart seeking;
Whispering hints of treasure hid
Under Morn's unlifted lid,
Islands looming just beyond
The dim horizon's utmost bound. . . .

May days, May nights, renewal, eternal recur-
rence, the push of life, ascension of beings,

A subtle chain of countless rings
The next unto the farthest brings,
And striving to be man, the worm
Mounts through all the spires of form. . . .

Emerson celebrates the perpetual miracles, the
metamorphoses and the affinities of the Universe.

No ray is dimmed, no atom worn,
My oldest force is good as new,
And the fresh rose on yonder thorn
Gives back the bending heaven in dew. . . .

He sings the mystic River which goes from Time
to Eternity:

The stream I love unbounded goes,
Through flood and sea and firmament;
Through light, through life, it forward flows. . . .

He sings the Sea:

Behold the Sea;
The opaline, the plentiful and strong,
Yet beautiful as is the rose in June,
Fresh as the trickling rainbow of July. . . .

Says the Sea:

Illusion dwells forever with the wave.
I know what spells are laid. Leave me to deal
With credulous and imaginative man;
For, though he scoop my water in his palm,
A few rods off he deems it gems and clouds.
Planting strange fruits and sunshine on the shore;
I make some coast alluring, some lone isle,
To distant men, who must go there, or die.

He makes his prayer to the Stars:

O birds of ether without wings!
O heavenly ships without a sail!
O mariners who never fail!
Sail swiftly through your amber vault,
An animated law, a presence to exalt. . . .
The stars are glowing wheels,
Giddy with motion Nature reels,
Sun, moon, man, undulate and stream,

The mountains flow, the solids seem,
Change acts, reacts; back, forward hurled.
And pause were palsy to the world. . . .

Spring, peace, and solitude, music, and light:

Let me go where'er I will
I hear a sky-born music still . . .
There alway, alway something sings. . . .

Hope, confidence:

Still on the seeds of all he made,
The rose of beauty burns;
Through times that wear and forms that fade,
Immortal youth returns. . . .

To plunge himself into the Universe of matter
or to elevate himself to a dream divine, such is
the poet's desire:

In the deep heart of man a poet dwells
Who all the day of life his summer story tells. . . .

Spring still makes spring in the mind,
When sixty years are told;
Love wakes anew this throbbing heart,
And we are never old.
Over the winter glaciers
I see the summer glow,
And through the wild-piled snow-drift,
The warm rosebuds below. . . .

Roses upon roses, Emerson sees the world rose-colored, not the roses of Epicurus, but roses of ice, mystic roses, puritan roses, edelweiss dipped in the mirage of Saadi and Hafiz, tinged with the joyful wisdom and unchangeable youth.

It was indeed the honey of his thought that he gave us in *Society and Solitude*, a restful book, a book charming in its intimate and familiar note. *The Conduct of Life* was the gospel of action; *Society and Solitude* is the breviary of the inner life. "A calm insight, piercing to the very center; a beautiful sympathy, a beautiful *epic* humor; a soul peaceably irrefragable in this loud jangling world, of which it sees the ugliness, but *notices* only the huge new *opulences*, still so anarchic. . . . Such brevity, simplicity, softness, homely grace; with such a penetrating meaning, *soft* enough, but irresistible, going down to the depths and up to the heights, as *silent electricity* goes." Thus spoke Carlyle painting *in extremis* the man as well as the book. Receipts, advice, portraits, *genre* pictures, muted lyricism, and above all a contagious and universal repose. Domestic life, farming, books, art, old age, a little of everything, this ledger takes up the gospel of the homely and sublime. It opens upon a portrait of the author by himself. For years he had disguised himself under the traits of Osman, Saadi, in Turkish or in Persian costume, camouflaging his *mea culpa's* in an oriental *laissez-aller*.

Osman is the affable man whose only vice is solitude and who is afflicted with a sort of paralysis of the will, evasive, timid in speech as a young girl. If he buys a house, quick, Osman plants trees around it. Here a hedge, there an oak, trees behind trees, especially evergreens which will keep a secret all year round. The greatest pleasure you can give Osman is not to recognize him if you meet him on the street. Always clothed in the same color as the walls, he is the first to suffer from his awkwardness and he flees to the country to get rid of his nervous twitchings and shruggings of shoulders in company. He would have given his soul for the ring of Gyges. Emerson, it is true, pleaded extenuating circumstances for his misanthrope. Few substances are found pure in nature. To bear the rough dealing of the world, one needs, he tells us, a common dough, iron, salt, air, water. Certain metals, like potassium and sodium, to be kept pure, must be preserved under naphtha. One is compelled to remain on his tripod to save his electricity. And he cited, envying them, those angels whom Swedenborg billeted in the middle of the sky, each in a house of his own, and whom he called the best of the angels.

Society, solitude. . . . Nature puts us at the bottom of the wall, but the sage takes a diagonal, keeping his head on one side and his hands on the other, keeping his independence without alienating his sympathies. Come to the end of life, Emerson was still pleading his own cause and felt the need of excusing his timidity and coldness. *Society and Solitude* was an *apologia pro vita sua*, and was a new recantation. In *The Conduct of Life* he exalted modern genius, science, machines, inventions. In *Society and Solitude*, half enthusiast, half satirist, he burned what he had adored. He drew up the list of inventions, from the steam engine to dental surgery, vaccination, anæsthesia, blood transfusion, "a Parisian invention which enables a man to change his blood as often as his linen," gutta percha, tunnels, the great maritime canals, the transatlantic cable. Here are balloons, and "the next war will be fought in the air." Who knows if we shall not find "a rose water that will wash the negro white"? Always faster, better, farther. And then? Emerson opened wide parentheses and multiplied his question marks.

Steam, photography, balloons, astronomical discoveries—will they help us find salvation? Machinery is aggressive. The weaver becomes a loom; the machinist a machine. If you do not use your tools, it is they who will use you. Man is the slave of his works. Is it certain that machines have lightened our labor? The machine unmakes the man and when it is perfect, the engineer counts no more. With all its inventions, the world is not better; it is worse. What have all these new arts done to ameliorate character; what are they worth to humanity? Are men better? We have made a bad investment. Works and days are offered us and we have sacrificed the days to the works. And yet, Day—Dyaus, Deus, Zeus, Zeupater, Jupiter—is a divine Power, a divine manifestation, the name found by the ancients to denote the supreme Power. He alone is rich who owns the day. Days are ever divine, as they were for the first Aryans. Ah, the charm, the color, the numberless attractions of the days, their richness! Nature heaps up and mobilizes her treasures for us, marvels of sky and earth, marvels of our senses, abyss within an abyss.

An everlasting Now reigns in Nature; Nature affixes the same roses on our bushes as those which charmed the Romans and the Chaldeans in their hanging gardens. Write it in your hearts: every day is the best of days, each day is Doomsday. It is in her least and humblest that Nature is truly and fully herself. You ask a long life, but it is a deep life, grand moments which count. Let Time's measure be spiritual and not mechanical. All life is longer than is needed. Moments of insight, of fine personal relations, a smile, a glance, there is life. He alone makes me rich who can recommend to me the space between sun and sun. It is the measure of man, his apprehension of a day. Life is good only as it is magic and musical, a chord, a perfect timing and concert. Do not dissect it; do not analyze it. Treat the days respectfully, be a day ourselves. Come, let the morning be. . . . Life's duration! It is its depth which matters; time is only its fugitive surface; the least acceleration of thought, the least increase of spiritual energy, renders life vast. The value of life is its inner quality, the art of knowing how to enjoy our faculties.

Everything in the world is wonderful. We live among gods whom we create ourselves. Life is not all knowledge; it is love. Cultivate sympathy; enrich sensibility. It is not by discovering new objects that we shall make the world vaster, but by discovering new affinities and potencies in the objects which we hold in our hands. "For truly, the heart at the center of the universe with every throb hurls the flood of happiness into every artery, vein, and veinlet, so that the whole system is inundated with the tides of joy. The plenty of the poorest place is too great; the harvest cannot be gathered. Every sound ends in music. The edge of every surface is tinged with prismatic rays."

Let us affirm; let us embrace the affirmative. A man is a man only if he makes life and nature happier to us. Be optimistic. Let us not hang dismal pictures on our walls; in conversation let us not daub with sables and glooms. Let us not groan; let us not complain; let us omit all that is negative—roses, still more roses. The affirmation of affirmations is love. Whatever there is of love, there is of perception. It is good will which makes insight. There are two lives, the inner and the external; choose. True life is sage and calm perception. It sits at home and makes the present great. "Truth and goodness subsist for evermore. It is true that there is evil and good, night and day: but these are not equal. The day is great and final. The night is for the day, but the day is not for the night. What is this immortal demand for more, which belongs to our constitution? this enormous ideal? There is no such critic and beggar as this terrible soul."

*   *   *

Thus in its revolutions the planet presents itself to the sun from successive points of view, multiple and changing aspects, which cannot be contradictory, for light does not change. It is in this chapter on "Works and Days" in *Society and Solitude* that one sees, that one feels the shining aura, the true Emersonian light, phosphorescence and beams, light which is at the same time music and to which responds beyond space and time that which seems to be really immortal in us, music of pure duration, of the soul which listens to itself, of the soul which finds the Over-Soul, music, thought, the song of a spring in the evening.

Irresistible optimist, how doubt, hearing you after so many passionate affirmations? If the reason disputes you, the heart ceases to contradict you and gives in. Yes, all is good, all is beautiful; you have said it and resaid it so fervently that one must admit it. To deny is henceforward too easy; to affirm is alone heroic, and what is true if your dream is not? Spirit-Matter, Thought-World; suppressing all problems, you drown them in the sovereign flood which pulls us along despite ourselves. All the Mind's authority, all the joy of Nature connive with you. Yes, you have bound together the Good, the Beautiful, and the True in your spherical intuitions concentric with the All. If we ever doubt, it shall only be with you.

―――――――

CHAPTER XIV

Twilight

―――――――

L IFE'S evening, a great repose, a great silence.
The masqueraders withdraw with shouts of
laughter and the rattle of tambourines. At seventy years Emerson is still green, still young and
serene, still tall, still straight, his hair thick, his
complexion rosy, his eagle's profile illuminated
with a steadfast smile. All is beautiful, all is good.
Old age has brought him leisure. He takes up his
"Wide Worlds," he composes an index for them,
he rummages in his papers, arranges, groups. For
ten years he has not kept his *Journal*, but he has
his notebooks at hand: notebook IL (intellect),
PY (philosophy), LI (literature), TO (toler-
ance). He continues to put in a stitch here and
there, to explore, to hem in the riddle, always
optimistic, but with several grains of salt and
muted irony. These brief notes in undress give us

434

his intimate thought with all frankness. All has not been rosy in his life; he has paid the price of solitude. The sky of Intellect is solitary and deserted. Yet the best hours of his life are those which he has passed in this better world where he has tasted ineffable joys which the eye has not seen nor ear heard, and which have carried him to the seventh heaven.

No, the great enigma has not told him its last word; life remains mysterious. There are more things in the world than his philosophy. He admits it with a sublime triviality. "The most advanced man in his most advanced moment—contemplating himself and Nature—sees how rude an idiot he is, how utterly unknown is the Cause and the Necessity—its roots and its future all unknown—a gigantic dream." Certainly there is only reception, perception, receiving, perceiving, affirming the presence and the excellence of the Laws, testimony which is worth that of all the martyrs. The Spirit does not lie, but our thoughts are uncertain and fugitive. Transition, passage, metamorphosis, there is the organic destiny of the spirit, transition, amelioration, progress. . . . Our thoughts are the great universal currents made harmonious. "Every new thought which makes day in our souls has its long morning twilight to announce its coming. Add the aurora that precedes a beloved name." *Subjectiveness* itself is the question and Nature is the answer; the Universe is the blackboard on which we write. Philosophy is called the homesickness of the soul. Insatiable soul! With this eternal need of more than belongs to our modest condition, where shall we find help? The gods themselves cannot aid us. They are as embarrassed as we. "Perception has a destiny." We speak, but Heaven keeps silent. To deny the perfect order of the Universe is blasphemy, but in the evening of his life Emerson surrounded his optimism with reservations, nuances, and disguised it as the *gaie science*.

His creed, the creed of the scholar, of the man of thought, can be held in the hollow of one's hand.

"I believe that all men are born free and equal *quoad* the laws.

"That all men have a right to their life, *quoad* the laws.

"I believe in freedom of opinion religious and political.

"I believe in universal suffrage, in public schools, in free trade.

"I believe the soul makes the body.

"I believe that casualty is perfect."

A minimum of liberty, a minimum of dogma, prudence, prudence! A very summary creed, very simple, disconcertingly agnostic, but overflowing with a host of compensatory prophetic insights.

* * *

He was still a lecturer. He gave the Harvard students his course on the "Natural History of Intellect," a course ill knit, unsystematic, but one in which one saw the dawn of a new philosophy rising through the exploration and the sounding of the secret powers of the soul. He did not teach; he did better: he inspired. After thirty years the Phi Beta Kappa society had again chosen him for its orator. He was a member of the *Institut de France*, member of the Board of Overseers of Harvard College. From time to time he continued his walks; he showed himself in Boston where he stopped pensively on the spots where his childhood had been spent. In the spring of 1871 he made the trip to the Far West and California. In Salt Lake City he called on Brigham Young, Young who like him was an authentic product of Yankee mysticism.

In July, 1872, his house caught fire. His books were hastily rescued as well as his manuscripts, and he took refuge once more in the Old Manse, asylum of his youth where he had written *Nature*. In the disorder of his flight he was annoyed at having forgotten the chocolate bags in which he kept Fustel de Coulange's *Cité Antique* and Taine's *English Literature*. The shock was too much for an old man. Emerson had been suffering for some time from aphasia. He, the enchanter, the poet, could not find the words he wanted and had to have recourse to gestures to designate the simplest objects, a fork, an umbrella. He had forgotten the word "sun" and could not recall the names of his best friends. . . . His faithful companions were watching over him; American generosity is never at a loss. He was given a check for five thousand dollars and while waiting to regain his home, he started out for the Orient in company with his daughter Ellen. It was his third, his last voyage before the great parting.

Here he was back in London in the autumn of

1872 and here he was back with Carlyle, who was very sad, aged, broken, hoary, white, in despair, but always faithful. He opened his arms to him, looked at him gravely, and embraced him, saying, "I am happy to see you again once more in the flesh." In spite of their divergences of temperament and principle, they were pledged to the same ideal. The cornmeal mush, the recipe of which Emerson had given to Teufelsdroeckh to which he had added a barrel of Indian wheat, had not Americanized him. During the Civil War he had not spared the Northerners his sarcasms. But Emerson had pardoned. He had received the last volume of the complete works of his friend. Carlyle could bind about his forehead the crown at the great Pan-Saxon games. Poor Jane Carlyle was dead; Teufelsdroeckh was alone in his "imperial sorrow," "so completely and composedly wretched, one is equal to the very gods."

By way of Paris, Nice, Genoa, and Naples, Emerson had started toward Egypt, but the land of the dead was not made for him. Death did not interest him. He admired the colossal temples whose mass crushed all that the nineteenth century had done; but this desert of mud left

439

EMERSON

him cold. He missed trees—but he had seen the
sacred lotus. He had ridden a donkey, he had seen
a crocodile. He preferred to the landscape the natives draped like antique statues and he compared
them to old philosophers going to the School of
Athens. He wanted to see the tomb of "him who
sleeps at Phyle," and he went up the Nile on the
dahabeah, *Aurora.* He went to Assuan, to Thebes,
to Phyle. He missed his interview with the
Sphinx. "The Sphinxes scorn dunces," he noted,
but what a dialogue she might have had with
Emerson. He had sketched this dialogue in one
of his poems, in the rôle of an optimistic and none
too courteous Oedipus, who made light of the
Sphinx and denied the riddle.

"Dull Sphinx, Jove keep thy five wits;
    Thy sight is growing blear;
Rue, myrrh, and cummin for the Sphinx,
    Her muddy eyes to clear!"
The old Sphinx bit her thick lip ——
"Who taught thee me to name?"

The name of the Sphinx is Spirit; the answer to
the riddle is Nature. A riddle solved gives the
key to all the riddles.

"I am thy spirit, yoke-fellow!
  Of thine eye I am eyebeam.

"Thou art the unanswered question;
    Couldst see thy proper eye,
  Alway it asketh, asketh;
    And each answer is a lie.
  So take thy quest through nature,
    It through thousand natures ply,
  Ask on, thou clothed eternity ——
    Time is the false reply."

Uprose the merry Sphinx,
    And crouched no more in stone,
  She melted into purple cloud,
    She silvered in the moon,
  She spired into a yellow flame,
    She flowered in blossoms red,
  She flowed into a foaming wave,
    She stood Monadnoc's head.

Thorough a thousand voices
    Spoke the universal dame;
  "Who telleth one of my meanings,
    Is master of all I am."

Emerson was now less sure of the solution of the
riddle, to judge by the notebooks we were de-
ciphering just now, and, if he had gone over the
dialogue in the twilight of his life, no doubt he

EMERSON

would have been more polite to the Sphinx. There were still riddles . . .

Returning from Egypt he stopped in Paris where he met Renan, Taine, Elie de Beaumont, and Turgeniev. In London he saw Carlyle, Browning, John Stuart Mill, Gladstone. At Oxford he visited Max Müller. He went to a lecture of Ruskin's, whom he was to see at his home, but whose social pessimism repelled him. He made a last pilgrimage to Stratford and took the ship at Liverpool. On his return a great surprise was in store for him. All Concord was at the station. The school children made a double line and conducted him home to music under a triumphal arch and he found his house rebuilt. All was in place, his books, his manuscripts, the picture of the Fates, the statue of Isis, the portraits . . . Ten more years of life ahead of him . . .

Emerson classified his papers, published his last essays with the help of the faithful James Eliot Cabot, his memorialist, always happy, always in good humor, interesting himself more and more in the children. He announced his candidacy for the rectorship of the University of Glasgow. He received five hundred votes, but it was Disraeli,

442

"the *chiffonier*," the statue without a pedestal, who won. Emerson was to be rector only of the University of Concord, where a school of philosophy was founded under his auspices. He saw again with emotion Ellen's house in Concord, New Hampshire; he read Kant, Hegel; he extolled the new inventions, the steamboat, the railroads, the telegraph, photography, the spectroscope . . . and opened his arms to the new times. . . .

April 16, 1882, he took cold but refused to go to bed. He went out; he worked at his desk. With the exception of a few moments when he thought himself a stranger in his house, he kept all his lucidity. He was heard talking at night in his deep musical voice as if he were reading a lecture. He recognized the portrait of Carlyle on the wall. "Ah, yes, there is that man, my man." The eve of his death he insisted again on covering the fire in the fireplace and in preparing all for the night. He said good-by to his friends and family; he was seen to smile. Some one heard him cry out, "Oh, the beautiful boy!" as if the child Waldo were coming to meet him from the depths of the night. And he died gently Thursday, April 27, 1882, on the eve of his seventy-ninth birthday. Teufelsdroeckh—ay me!—had preceded him into the Infinite at eighty-five years, February 5, 1881.

On the thirtieth of April he was buried in Sleepy Hollow, the beautiful vale where he had dreamed and poetized in his youth, where he had transcendentally flirted with Margaret. His grave is at the foot of a great pine near Hawthorne (and his ghosts!), and Thoreau, the Pan of the woods. The inscription on the stone faithfully sums up his destiny.

> The passive Master lent his hand
> To the vast soul that o'er him planned.

THE END